Healing at the Borderland
of Medicine and Religion

DISCARD

STUDIES IN SOCIAL MEDICINE

Allan M. Brandt & Larry R. Churchill, editors

MICHAEL H. COHEN

Healing at the Borderland
of Medicine and Religion

The University of North Carolina Press

CHAPEL HILL

This book was published with the assistance of the Anniversary Endowment Fund of the University of North Carolina Press.

The paper in this book meets the guidelines for permanence and durability of the Committee on Production Guidelines for Book Longevity of the Council on Library Resources.

Library of Congress
Cataloging-in-Publication Data
Cohen, Michael H.
Healing at the borderland of medicine and religion / by Michael H. Cohen.
p. ; cm. — (Studies in social medicine)
Includes bibliographical references and index.
ISBN-13: 978-0-8078-3043-7 (cloth: alk. paper)
ISBN-10: 0-8078-3043-7 (cloth: alk. paper)
ISBN-13: 978-0-8078-5760-1 (pbk.: alk. paper)
ISBN-10: 0-8078-5760-2 (pbk.: alk. paper)
1. Alternative medicine—United States.
2. Integrative medicine—United States.
3. Medicine—Religious aspects. 4. Healing.
[DNLM: 1. Complementary Therapies—standards—United States. 2. Complementary Therapies—legislation & jurisprudence—United States. 3. Ethics, Professional—United States. 4. Health Knowledge, Attitudes, Practice—United States. 5. Religion and Medicine—United States. 6. Research—standards—United States. WB 890 C678h 2006]
I. Title. II. Series.
R733.C647 2006
610—dc22   2006005197

Portions of this book were previously published in somewhat different form: Chapter 1 as "Negotiating Integrative Medicine: A Framework for Provider-Patient Conversations," *Negotiation Journal* 30, no. 3 (2004): 409–33; Chapter 2 as "Of Rogues and Regulation: A Review of *Accommodating Pluralism: The Role of Complementary and Alternative Medicine*," *Vermont Law Review* 27, no. 3 (2003): 801–15; Chapter 3 as "Regulation, Religious Experience, and Epilepsy: A Lens on Complementary Therapies," *Epilepsy and Behavior* 4, no. 6 (December 2003): 602–6; Chapter 4 as "Regulating 'Healing': Notes on the Ecology of Awareness and the Awareness of Ecology," *St. John's Law Review* 78, no. 4 (2005): 1167–92; Chapter 5 as "Lateral Thinking: What Is the Matrix? A Radical Look at Medico-Legal Reform," *Alternative and Complementary Therapies* 5, no. 5 (October 1999): 319–21; Chapter 6 as "Healing at the Borderland between Medicine and Religion: Regulating Potential Abuse of Authority by Spiritual Healers," *Journal of Law and Religion* 18, no. 2 (2002–3): 373–426. All are reprinted here with permission.

CLOTH   10 09 08 07 06   5 4 3 2 1
PAPER   10 09 08 07 06   5 4 3 2 1

*For my family
and for all families everywhere*

May all beings be free from suffering
May I be the doctor and the medicine
Until all beings are healed.
—adaptation of a Buddhist prayer by Shantideva (8th century)

In the sufferer let me see only the human being. Illumine
my mind that it recognize what presents itself and that it may
comprehend what is absent or hidden. . . . For great and
sacred are the thoughtful deliberations required to preserve
the lives and health of Thy creatures.
—from Maimonides' prayer (12th century)

His feet, my feet, restore.
His limbs, my limbs, restore.
His body, my body, restore.
His mind, my mind, restore.
His voice, my voice, restore.
His plumes, my plumes, restore. . . .
It is finished in beauty. It is finished in beauty.
—from Navajo healing prayer

Thy Name is my healing, O my God, and remembrance
of Thee is my remedy.
Nearness to Thee is my hope, and love for Thee is my
companion.
—from Baha'i healing prayer

Be near me in my time of weakness and pain;
sustain me by your grace, that my strength and courage may
not fail;
heal me according to your will;
and help me always to believe that what happens to me
here is of
little account if you hold me in eternal life.
—from the Book of Common Prayer

O Allah remove the hardship, O Lord of mankind, grant cure
for You are the Healer. There is no cure but from You, a cure
which leaves no illness behind.
—from supplication of the Prophet Muhammad

CONTENTS

ACKNOWLEDGMENTS

This book has benefited from an extraordinarily thorough review by Sherman Cohn, professor of law at Georgetown University. His contribution to integrative medicine and the new health care is immense, encompassing (among many contributions) several decades of scholarship and professional service to the development of credentialing and accreditation standards for acupuncture and traditional oriental medicine.

Mary Ruggie, at Harvard University's Kennedy School of Government, has been a valued colleague and friend in innumerable conversations regarding the sociology of complementary therapies and made many valuable suggestions and contributions to the manuscript. Daniel L. Shapiro at Harvard Law School's Program on Negotiation (PON) provided critical input into my understanding of negotiation theory and practice. Susan Hackley and Professor Roger Fisher of the program also warmly invited me into the extended PON family. Larry Sullivan, former director at the Center for the Study of World Religions, Harvard Divinity School, was kind enough to welcome me to a one-year fellowship program during which a portion of this book was written. Midge Murphy and Alan Dumoff provided invaluable support in the practice of law relating to integrative medicine.

Frank Conroy was a mentor at the Iowa Writers' Workshop and supervised my thesis there. He helped me hone my writing skills and way of perceiving the world. Barry Bryant, a Buddhist who helped sponsor Tibetan monks to bring sand mandalas to the United States, became a friend who helped me see the world through different eyes. Calvin Eversley, Linda Davis, and Thaddeus McDonald have provided support through warm welcome to the faculty at the College of the Bahamas. I also thank attorney Verona Douglas-Sands and my island friends on Eleuthera and throughout the Bahamas.

Throughout my professional life there have been many teachers, and each contribution, great or small, is recognized with appreciation. I thank Rabbi Joseph Gelberman for creating the New Seminary. My friend Peter Faust has also been an incredible teacher on matters of complementary medicine and the intersection of spirituality with the mundane. Erik P. Jensen has been a steadfast friend and teacher too. I have also benefited from the incredible teachings of Castor, Pollux, and Ujayi and many other four-legged friends.

I thank the series editors, Allan Brandt and Larry Churchill, and my editor, Sian Hunter, at the University of North Carolina Press. In the Institute of Medicine committee on which I served as consultant, Lyla Hernandez provided the intellectual glue for the project. Over the years many pioneers in the field of complementary and integrative medicine also have been influential, notably Ted J. Kaptchuk, Wayne B. Jonas, Kathi J. Kemper, Brian M. Berman, and Fredi Kronenberg. I also thank David Studdert, Michelle Mello, and Troy Brennan for sponsoring my course in complementary medicine health law and policy through the Law and Public Health Program in the Department of Health, Policy, and Management at the Harvard School of Public Health.

Various agencies and foundations have provided support for a variety of projects over the years underpinning the material in this book. These have included the Greenwall Foundation, the Rudolph Steiner Foundation, the National Center for Complementary and Alternative Medicine, the National Library of Medicine, American Specialty Health, and the Medtronic Foundation. More recently, the Helen M. and Annetta E. Himmelfarb Foundation and the Frederick S. Upton Foundation have provided gracious startup support to the Institute for Integrative and Energy Medicine. David Upton's support is particularly appreciated, as are the efforts of Larry Mervine. I am grateful for all support I have received, although the views in this book are solely my own.

I thank my parents, Perry M. Cohen and Margo P. Cohen, for their wisdom and love of Judaism, the spiritual treasures of which ignited my spiritual path, and for their reverence for education, which sparked my interest in continually expanding my intellectual horizons.

I thank my wife, Elaine, as always for her editorial gifts and steadfast love.

ignited my spiritual path, and for their reverence for education, which sparked my interest in continually expanding my intellectual horizons.

I thank my wife, Elaine, as always for her editorial gifts and steadfast love.

Healing at the Borderland
of Medicine and Religion

Introduction

The Wheel of Time

At the First International Congress on Tibetan Medicine in Washington, D.C., the Dalai Lama reminded the audience that the *first, international* congress on Tibetan medicine was actually held in the seventh or eight century, not the twentieth. Furthermore, the congress was held in Tibet, not in the American capital, and finally, the historical conclave focused on the shared medical traditions of India, Nepal, China, Persia, and Tibet, traditions that already reflected an ethic of medical pluralism.[1] The Dalai Lama went on to point out that even at that meeting—long before the notion of "complementary therapies" had become popular in the United States— Tibetan medical culture already represented an amalgamation of influences from other traditions, and it already manifested deep respect for international collaboration and shared research efforts.

With gentle humor, in his keynote address the Dalai Lama reflected on the hubris and ethnocentrism often described as embedded in modern scientific efforts within the Western Hemisphere to understand indigenous and other medical traditions. The medical stance implicitly critiqued by the Dalai Lama has been described by some critics as one of "co-optation" and assimilation, rather than true collaboration between camps.[2] In other words, even when open to exploring other medical systems, clinicians and research scientists adhering too rigidly to the Western, scientific model—that is, without fully appreciating the asserted role of consciousness in mediating healing therapies—tend to imagine that the medical system adopted relatively recently in human history, in part of the globe, authoritatively can filter, understand, and synthesize other medical traditions.

The Dalai Lama's assertion that this approach may suffer from hubris does not deny the power and elegance of the scientific method to probe questions of safety, efficacy, and mechanism. No doubt scientific inquiry represents a powerful method for discerning truth in discovery. Scientific study to date has invalidated a number of would-be cures outside conventional medicine (such as laetrile for cancer) and validated others (such as acupuncture to control nausea following chemotherapy).

But science is not the whole of authority, and the Dalai Lama was not criticizing the power of medicine and science but, rather, the exclusive claim these disciplines hold on our epistemological framework—on what we hold to be true, real, and valid. Balanced against scientific method are other modes of inquiry, from other disciplines in the humanities and from within human experience.

The lineage within which the Dalai Lama sits represents one of the great contributions to human understanding of the realms of mind and spirit—a technology of consciousness, if you will. His implicit critique of biomedical ethnocentrism suggests a need to balance current scientific inquiry, on one hand, and tolerance and respect for foreign theories and systems of health care, on the other. His challenge is in essence about embracing pluralism: momentarily suspending categorical disbelief, and being willing to try to understand some of the methods in these nonbiomedical healing systems (such as the mysterious "pulse diagnosis" in Tibetan medicine) on their own terms. Those terms of reference may include framing healing as a transfer of consciousness, healing intention, or therapeutic information through the medium of "spiritual energy"—for lack of better terminology—that is, through as yet unknown mechanisms. Contrary to reductionistic attempts to boil all inner awakening down to biochemical processes (a posture William James termed "medical materialism"),[3] an opening to pluralism refuses to dismiss phenomena that may not yet be validated under generally accepted frameworks in one cultural frame of reference, as "implausible" and therefore invalid.[4]

In other words, the Dalai Lama's challenge—and the parallel objective of this book—is to navigate or negotiate the bridge between these seemingly opposite parts of the world of healing. Some parts are objective, while others are entirely subjective. Some are externalized; others, deeply within. Some are comprehensible according to commonly agreed standards, but others are incomprehensible or inaccessible to generally accepted rules of evidence. Some operate according to known rules, and others are touted by believers, on one hand, as authoritative and dismissed by skeptics, on the other, as irrational and hallucinatory.

This navigational task is freighted with contradictions. For example, the catchphrase "mind-body" (as in mind-body medicine, one of the terms bandied about in moving beyond conventional or "orthodox" medicine) itself embodies (so to speak) deep contradictions, a presumptive crossing of chasms that may be unbridgeable if rhetoric alone purports to mediate understanding. A subtle aspect of the challenge in bridging these disparate arenas is to include tools from both worlds (e.g., science and religion, physics and metaphysics, concrete and consciousness). Hence the emphasis in this book is on "negotiating" the new health care—a task of harmonizing where possible, integrating where appropriate, and synthesizing where beneficial. The negotiation at the borderland of healing and medicine is not only between M.D. and patient but also between M.D.'s, D.O.'s, allied health providers, and practitioners of complementary and alternative medicine (CAM). The negotiation between West and East, biomedicine and CAM—whatever metaphor one chooses—affects *all* health care professionals (and patients and those who study and those who regulate these dynamics), not only physicians. The multifaceted negotiation includes negotiating different worldviews, epistemologies, hermeneutics, and metaphors for health and healing.

During the Tibetan medicine conference, the contrast between Western, scientific medicine (or biomedicine) and Tibetan medicine was visually demonstrated in the difference between many of the speakers (in starched shirts, knotted ties, and expensive haircuts) and the monks (with their saffron robes and shaved heads); between the disposable conference brochures formatted on high-speed laser printers and the Kalachakra (Wheel of Time) mandala, with its pristine colors and precise figurines of deities, painted in colored sands according to ancient Tibetan prescription;[5] between the preoccupation with position, status, academic affiliation, or salary (or dependency on communication gadgets) and the ceremonial gesture of sweeping away the beautiful mandala at the conference's conclusion —a ritualistic meditation on impermanence.

The contrast reminded me of a meeting about five years earlier, when I was an associate at Davis Polk & Wardwell, a Wall Street law firm. The theme of negotiating bridges between worlds was present even then, metaphorically and literally. I was negotiating a copyright agreement between a Tibetan cultural foundation, our pro bono client, and a group of monks that the foundation had brought to the West to share knowledge of the Kalachakra sand painting.

My client and I met with the monks and their lawyer in a room about twenty feet behind the New York stage on which the Dalai Lama was giving a talk. I recall greeting the monks individually, meeting their steady gaze, and noticing the head-bows and the hands folded in *Namaste* or prayer position. While negotiating the agreement's terms with their representative, I had the sense that these monks were sending blessings our way: their silence was profoundly full. In a fleeting way—without being distracted from my role as a lawyer—I could almost feel the ghosts, deities, and subtle levels of consciousness that Tibetan teachings describe, as we sat, within the energy field of the Dalai Lama, unseen and yet present, trying to reach consensus.

At the Tibetan medicine conference, political and medical landscapes had shifted since that earlier negotiation. The monks and their mandala were not new to the West; the agreement had long been concluded, and many books about their spiritual healing traditions had been published. CAM therapies, such as (in order of most commonly licensed providers) chiropractic, acupuncture and traditional oriental medicine, massage therapy, and naturopathic medicine figured on biomedical, regulatory, and political maps. Some of the leading medical schools were offering courses on CAM therapies, while others had invited Tibetan physicians to participate in research studies. I had moved from Wall Street to legal academe to explore legal, regulatory, ethical, and policy questions at the intersection of conventional and complementary medicine.

At the conference, my role involved not a hardheaded, softhearted negotiation between client and monks but, instead, the task of leading a panel, composed of Tibetan medicine practitioners and representatives from various nations, on licensure, liability, and other legal considerations involved in bringing Tibetan medicine to the United States. The old dichotomies seemed to have melted into a world in which ancient and modern had to find mechanisms for peaceful coexistence and even mutual respect and accommodation.

During the conference, I had the opportunity to meet one of the senior physicians to the Dalai Lama and to experience his mind, consciousness, and knowledge of Tibetan medicine. My encounter with him was mysterious, sublime, and portending of things below the surface of conversation. Yet, by biomedical standards, this subjective impression might be dismissed as anecdotal, ungrounded, or—using the often applied label for a beneficial effect whose only basis is the "good medicine" of relationship—placebo. Again, the contrast between my felt sense of the encounter and how it might be analyzed from a contemporary biomedical perspective reminded me that, although the conference aimed to explore scientific analysis of the Tibetan arts, in many ways the two worlds remained apart, and polarities persisted. Scientists and religious leaders were engaged in dialogue and in the attempt to find common language, yet many "truths" the religious leaders took for granted could not possibly be tested or validated scientifically. The fundamental epistemological assumptions of each camp and the starting premises of each for inquiry were startlingly dissimilar.

This gap seemed particularly acute during a session on Tibetan understanding of death and dying and of the *bardo*, or transition states between death and rebirth; these were realms scientific inquiry could not touch. The Tibetan monks were presenting the unprovable as truth, and yet modern diagnostic and therapeutic tools were useless in these realms, where the only tools were found in the laboratory of human consciousness.

To quote "The Ballad of East and West" by Rudyard Kipling, it seemed once again that "East is East and West is West, and never the Twain shall Meet." Or, to quote a famous Zen statement,

Before enlightenment, mountains are mountains and rivers are rivers.
During enlightenment, mountains are no longer mountains and rivers are no longer rivers.
After enlightenment, mountains are once again mountains and rivers are once again rivers.

I found myself looking forward to the possibility of enlightenment or even the phase beyond that—the one where everything that had been shaking into a startlingly unfamiliar place begins once again to resume its ordinary status, even while something extraordinary has shifted within. I could not say that I had reached anything other than a momentary displacement of my usual frame of mental reference. But in the moment, the old, structured landscapes of mind and epistemological maps of yore seemed a bit less solid and reliable than before.

Material vs. Spiritual Worldviews

The Dalai Lama's gentle admonition highlighted the difference between understandings of medical reality based exclusively on materiality and on spirituality. Briefly, Tibetan medicine views medical knowledge as a gift of the Medicine Buddha, the aspect of transcendental consciousness that understands nature as an abundant repository of healing gifts for humankind; it acknowledges the healing potential of plants, animals, thunder, stones, trees, mineral substances—everything. If one truly wants to understand global medicine, the Dalai Lama's comment hinted, one must drop the pretension of trying to know/control/arrange/rearrange; one must balance the drive toward knowledge (expressed by this conference) against the wisdom of coming to terms with our planetary healing heritage as humans.

At a still deeper level, the Dalai Lama's comment suggested, understanding international collaboration involving medical traditions may mean a shift from the arrogance of assuming that scientific evidence, despite its apparent power in many arenas, could move the whole universe of knowledge, the full spectrum of levers. Scientific inquiry has a shadow aspect that manifests as dominance, exploitation, subjugation, and arrogant imposition of authority. The opposite involves a posture of humility and surrender in the face of what is unknown and what is given in stewardship.[6] In his keynote the Dalai Lama did not suggest either abdicating science for religion, on one hand, or abdicating religion for science, on the other; rather, he expressed his respect for science alongside religion, and he offered his hope that our age would find a union between scientific and religious perspectives in the search for knowledge of the healing traditions.[7]

The Dalai Lama's message as I understood it—a message of respectful attempts to reconcile biomedical and other (e.g., Tibetan) medical traditions while acknowledging their distinct approaches— became a touchstone in my effort, together with the efforts of colleagues in academic medicine, law, ethics, and other fields, to understand the growing phenomenon known as integrative medicine (or integrative health care). As an attorney representing clients developing integrative medicine clinics, in my role as a Harvard Medical School faculty member helping to devise models of integrative care and consensus documents for use across Harvard-affiliated hospitals, and as a speaker at many medical schools and other educational and clinical institutions, I have been mindful of tending the balance of which the Dalai Lama spoke. I have seen how conversations between, for example, neurologists, chiropractors, and acupuncturists about a shared patient involve transcultural as well as transdisciplinary communication, with differing emphases on material versus nonmaterial perspectives, on scientific evidence versus intuitive approaches, and on rational versus emotional or psychological modes of discourse.

The notion of integration is central to this multimodal conversation across clinical fields and training. Integration also is the central plank in the bridge between science and the humanities in the effort to understand health and healing.

The term "integrative medicine" is of relatively recent coinage. It describes the effort to integrate the best biomedical therapies and CAM therapies that have a reasonable level of evidence of safety and efficacy as published in the medical literature. Integrative medicine also emphasizes a partnership between patients and caregivers to find the safest and most effective therapeutic approach.[8] Integrative medicine is gaining increasing recognition in hospitals, academic medical centers, freestanding "integrative care" clinics, and individual physician practices across the United States and internationally.[9] Yet, as the Dalai Lama pointed out, the notion of integrating medical wisdom reflects a human tradition from more than a millennium ago, and there are many dimensions to the search for integration.

Efforts to create viable models of integrative care have clinical, legal, cultural, and political implications. While there are now an increasing number of books offering examples of clinical pathways to integrative care;[10] books for researchers of complementary therapies;[11] books for patients,[12] including *Alternative Medicine for Dummies*;[13] and even a book or two on professionalism and ethics,[14] few—if any—explicitly address the implications of this shift toward integrative models of care with a focus on legal and policy issues, in terms of what synthesis might actually mean for an expanded consciousness of healing. By this I refer to the implications of integrative health care for such disparate yet interwoven arenas as notions of medical pluralism, environmental concerns, and religious mystical experience. This book uniquely focuses on the larger social and psychospiritual ripples of integrative care, grounding such focus in the legal and regulatory shifts the change in medical culture augurs.

Western vs. Eastern Perspectives

A second touchstone for understanding integrative health care comes from *Zen Buddhism and Psychoanalysis*, by D. T. Suzuki, Erich Fromm, and Richard DeMartino.[15] In this book, Suzuki and colleagues grapple with the fundamental connections—and divides—between what they conceptualize as classically Eastern and Western ways of encountering the world. While the search for East-West synthesis and reconciliation has become increasingly familiar since the 1960s, and even (perhaps) clichéd, Suzuki, in the opening chapter titled "Lectures on Zen Buddhism," establishes some dichotomies that are still worth considering, because the archetypes they express still resonate with deep divides in global medical culture.

Suzuki begins by comparing and contrasting two poems—one a haiku by Basho (the great Japanese poet of the seventeenth century), and the other a poem by Tennyson—in which the poets appreciate a flower blooming by a hedge and by a "crannied wall," respectively.[16] Basho grasps the plant in its totality, achieving a rare and precious moment of enlightenment during which his consciousness merges in a state of united awareness with the beauty of the flower. Tennyson, equally appreciative of the beauty of nature, approaches its immense and ungraspable marvel by uprooting the flower and examining it in wonder; he detaches the rose from its environment and separates himself from the object of his analysis.

Suzuki comments that both poets probably had similar feelings, the difference being that Basho "does not pluck the flower. He just looks at it. . . . For he has no words to utter; his feeling is too full, too deep, and he has no desire to conceptualize it." Tennyson, however, is relentlessly "active and analytical" as he tears the flower "away from the crannied wall, 'root and all,' which means it must die."[17]

According to Suzuki, these two modes of operating exemplify the difference between "East" and "West" insofar as these terms represent archetypes of consciousness: "two basic characteristic approaches to reality"—the "intuitive" versus the "analytic."[18] Suzuki goes on to describe "East" as "synthetic, totalizing, integrative, nondiscriminative, deductive, nonsystematic, dogmatic, intuitive (rather, affective), nondiscursive, subjective, spiritually individualistic and socially group-minded," and "West" as "analytical, discriminatory, differential, inductive, individualistic, intellectual, objective, scientific, generalizing, conceptual, schematic, impersonal, legalistic, organizing, power-wielding, self-assertive, disposed to impose its will upon others."[19]

While Suzuki's conceptualization expresses generalizations, the comparison does echo holistic health care's critique of biomedicine as generally analytical rather than intuitive, impersonal rather than personal, and differential and objective rather than totalizing and close to the source. The dichotomy expresses a split between subjective and objective, between inductive and deductive. The notion of holistic health care resurfaced in the 1960s, in part, in reaction to biomedicine's reliance on two major historical influences: Cartesian dualism and Newtonian physics. These two intellectual currents exemplify the qualifies that Suzuki describes as "Western."[20]

Cartesian dualism refers to the separation of mind from body in the philosophic system that Descartes expressed in the phrase "I think, therefore I am."[21] Biomedicine has been criticized for failing to adequately incorporate (and synthesize) the connections between a patient's thoughts and feelings and physical symptoms and the physiological aspects of disease;[22] hence the emphasis on and demand for more "holistic" therapies connecting mental, physical, spiritual, and environmental aspects of disease and health.

In a fashion somewhat analogous to Cartesian dualism's separation of mind from body, Newtonian physics views the universe as a magnificent machine that can be deconstructed and rebuilt, and not as some unfathomable and mysterious unity to be grasped in totality only in a moment of enlightenment, serendipity, or grace. Critics have argued that biomedicine, influenced by Newtonian physics, expresses a mechanistic and reductionistic view of the disease process —again, viewing the body in mechanical terms and paying inadequate attention to the complex connections between physical, mental, emotional, and even spiritual factors.[23] Biomedicine's emphasis on cure, the argument proceeds, has resulted in inadequate attention to the larger and more ambiguous (but also important) notion of healing or personal wholeness.[24]

Integration as Negotiated Synthesis

While proponents of integrative medicine in the medical literature emphasize the importance of evidence-based integration, the process of synthesizing CAM and conventional therapies also has broader dimensions. Specifically, such integration can be said to represent an emerging synthesis of Suzuki's polarities of East and West, with consequences not only for the medical profession but also for the way our culture views health, healing, disease, and death, as well as our relationship with the cosmos.

To use Suzuki's metaphor of examining the rose, the pending integration of East and West might involve, for example, striving toward a unified grasp of the rose as a whole, in its natural environment, while simultaneously appreciating how the analytic process might contribute to an even richer and more complete account of the rose's existence—or analyzing the rose while respecting its totality and without tearing it apart. Such an approach might be simultaneously synthetic and analytical, nondiscriminative and discriminative, and intuitive and intellectual, incorporating both subjective and objective components. In other words, the millennial human who combines East and West would have both polarities active at once.

For instance, in clinical terms, a particular caregiver might be called to be fluent in multiple Western and Eastern modalities, from biomedicine to traditional oriental medicine, and to be able to shift effortlessly between the two in the best interest in the patient. In institutional terms, such integration or synthesis might mean the ability to provide a care team conversant in multiple clinical disciplines and languages that can interactively assess, respond, and refine, initially diagnosing and subsequently measuring the patient's progress through multiple channels (both conventional and CAM).

In educational terms, this might be conceptualized as accentuating inclusion of biomedical curricular components in the study of acupuncture, chiropractic, and other CAM professions, while increasing inclusion in medical school curricula of yin-yang and meridian theory and other aspects of theory, philosophy, and practice from various CAM modalities.[25] In psychological terms, the synthesis might involve being able to operate on two levels simultaneously, the intellectual and the emotional/spiritual; negotiating an agreement, for example, while also attending to spiritual insights and personal feelings arising in the negotiation process;[26] or listening outwardly to the patient's medical history with an ear for medically significant details while listening internally—intuitively—for the most appropriate therapeutic action. In spiritual terms, such a synthesis might be conceptualized as maintaining an interior, contemplative focus even while engaging in exterior activities "in the world." The polarities are honored both individually and together for the gestalt they could create when operating in tandem. Such integration represents a shift from prior duality, as questions concerning the regulation of CAM have come to the forefront of clinical practice and regulatory concern.[27]

The Office for Unconventional Medical Practices at the National Institutes of Health, for example, opened in 1992 with a small budget, but it has blossomed into the National Center for Complementary and Alternative Medicine with an annual budget of more than $100 million for research grants.[28] Passage of the federal Dietary Supplements Health Education Act has allowed consumers access to vitamins, minerals, herbal products, and other "dietary supplements" without prior manufacturer proof of safety and efficacy and without premarket approval by the Food and Drug Administration.[29] Recent legislation in states such as California, Minnesota, and Rhode Island allows nonlicensed providers of numerous CAM therapies to offer services to the public.[30]

In 2004 the Institute of Medicine (IOM) at the National Academy of Sciences created a two-year Committee on the Use of Complementary and Alternative Medicine. The committee was charged, among other things, with evaluating the "impact of current regulation/legislation on CAM research and integration" and providing a report to the public, to industry, to the medical community, and to

Congress.[31] The creation of this committee followed creation of (and report to the U.S. president by) the White House Commission on Complementary and Alternative Medicine Policy. Together, the reports by the IOM and the White House commission established credible voices within the mainstream medical and regulatory communities for negotiating integration of CAM therapies into the conventional health care model.

Both reports emphasized the need to bridge the worlds of conventional medicine and CAM in terms of clinical research, education, and policy. Both, for example, recommended that medical education include information about current scientific evidence concerning CAM therapies and that education of CAM clinicians include more of the basic sciences as well as scientific research skills. Both reports also emphasized the need to increase federal research dollars available for study of CAM therapies and the need for institutional and government policy to acknowledge growing consumer and clinician interest in integrative models of health care. In addition, numerous states have created similar committees with reports to governors and legislatures on complementary medicine policy.[32]

Negotiating Interdisciplinary Connections

In short, despite continued resistance, skepticism, and rhetoric from different camps, the Berlin Wall between different systems of medical practice has begun to come down. A more fluid situation now exists in which shared notions of health care pluralism garner ever greater respect. This book aims to contribute to that interdisciplinary scholarly conversation concerning the desired parameters of a pluralistic health care environment.

The book's chapters are intentionally eclectic in focus and style in order to mirror the broad range of CAM therapies, from those more comprehensible to current scientific theories to those ranging toward the spiritual (and hence "subjective") realms. For example, while Chapter 1 proceeds with a straightforward, analytical presentation of legal, ethical, and negotiation frameworks regarding complementary therapies, Chapter 2 is in the form of a book review, a provocative way of examining how influential portions of the bio-medical community currently understand the integration of complementary therapies into conventional medical settings.

Chapter 3 then turns to epilepsy, a condition at the borderland of medicine and religion, in an effort to jump-start the discussion of the extent to which subjective, mystical experience—consciousness—matters. Are epileptic experiences biological or transpersonal? This question echoes the issue as to whether acupuncture occurs through a biological mechanism that is not yet understood or through the transmission of this mysterious phenomenon that traditional oriental medicine calls chi. If a therapy is "not biologically plausible" but nonetheless effective, how do we assimilate it—if at all—into the new health care? That is the koan offered by negotiating a new health care that includes complementary therapies.

Chapter 4 continues this inquiry into the contrast between the biological and the transpersonal by opening the question of negotiation and integration in an entirely novel area: ecological concerns. Will deeper integration of complementary therapies in conventional medical settings in the new health care affect our view of and connection to nature more generally? Or will enhanced attention to ecological issues influence the integration of CAM therapies? Chapter 4 explores this issue by comparing and contrasting two visionary books with shared goals—examining healing in the broadest sense—yet opposing perspectives on the influence of science on such healing. Chapter 5 deepens the investigation, shape-shifting form again to draw parallels between a film, an ancient Indian scripture, and the question of medicolegal reform. Closing the circle, Chapter 6 addresses the legal implications of introducing spiritually based therapies within a secular context.

In short, form mirrors content. The synthetic approach of this book deliberately mirrors the many dimensions of synthesizing knowledge, embodies the notion that expanded consciousness can be bold yet at the same time acknowledge its limitations; and suggests that integrative health care may have implications for such diverse arenas as negotiation theory, ecology, and spirituality. Like previous works, this book moves from the most grounded and concrete theoretical models (e.g., from negotiation theory and analysis) to the most subjective and challenging aspects of integrative care (e.g., clinical, regulatory, and professional responses to modalities involving religious and spiritual experience).

Negotiating Medical Pluralism

This book builds on three earlier works. *Complementary and Alternative Medicine: Legal Boundaries and Regulatory Perspectives* (1998) focuses on issues such as licensure and scope of practice, malpractice, professional discipline, food and drug law, and third-party reimbursement as they pertain to regulation of CAM therapies. *Beyond Complementary Medicine: Legal and Ethical Perspectives on Health Care and Human Evolution* (2000) expands the discussion to institutional credentialing, liability, and policy and then explores ethical and even bioethical issues raised by inclusion of CAM therapies in conventional medical settings. *Future Medicine: Ethical Dilemmas, Regulatory Challenges, and Therapeutic Pathways to Health and Healing in Human Transformation* (2003) explores the potential impact of energy healing on health care as well its regulation. *Future Medicine* also draws an analogy between Abraham Maslow's hierarchy of needs and regulatory values, exploring how regulatory goals can move from addressing the most pathological side of human nature (attempting to control fraud) to the most transcendent (encouraging self-actualization and transformation).

These three books offer a framework for law, regulation, ethics, and policy to build on the structure originally created as biomedicine assumed dominance in the late nineteenth century, to grow into a health care system that can incorporate selected CAM therapies. For example, liability issues dominate the landscape as hospitals, clinics, and other health care delivery institutions are called to respond to patients' requests concerning inclusion of CAM therapies, grapple with issues such as the need to set policy concerning dietary supplements, and address credentialing issues as providers such as chiropractors and acupuncturists seek entry into inpatient and outpatient settings.

In the present volume, the concept of negotiating the new health care serves as an overarching theme: health care professionals, patients, institutions, and regulators are negotiating, with or without appropriate tools, this new territory in which conventional and CAM therapies increasingly are interwoven. The leitmotif of "negotiation" has a double meaning, referring not only to the process of interest-based negotiation as a means for reaching agreement in dispute resolution but also to the process of navigating the new territory. Negotiation of the new health care is not only about financial or insurance reform or even about access to medical treatment. It deals with the borderland between medicine and religion, between the scientific and the mystical, between knowledge that is considered objective and publicly accessible and knowledge that is considered subjective and privately accessible, and between outer and inner, material and spiritual, overt and covert, and quantifiable and perhaps immeasurable. This borderland lacks clear rules, in both a clinical and a legal sense; it requires an integration of emerging understandings of consciousness and an appreciation of conceptualizations in other medical traditions of innate forces, such as acupuncture's chi. It evokes tolerance and health care pluralism and, therefore, controversy.

Historically, although the American colonies began with pluralistic notions of health care, the poor state of the science, paltry qualifications of many would-be physicians, general lack of medical standards, and cornucopia of true charlatans eventually led to state regulation of healers—largely through mechanisms of licensure—and thereby to the triumph of biomedicine over competing communities of healers such as naturopathic and homeopathic physicians. Legally, state statutes made the unlawful practice of medicine a crime and defined medicine in broad terms, encompassing any activity that potentially could be construed as diagnosis and treatment of disease.[33]

New constructs have been slow to emerge. Further, as the international community becomes increasingly aware of the political interdependence of all peoples, ideas, and cultures—both through efforts to combat the escalation of international terrorism and the concomitant, attenuated awareness of our shared vulnerability—international health care, too, finds itself in the midst of a transition from a stratification of health care traditions toward a more unified understanding of what Wayne Jonas, former director of the Office of Alternative Medicine at the National Institutes of Health, has called "global medicine."

Different medical traditions have existed in many forms at many times within history, from the Ayurvedic medical tradition of ancient India to acupuncture and traditional oriental medicine in China, Japan, and other Asian nations to Native American herbalism to Latin American folk medicine. Yet on each continent the same debate recurs: Should Chinese hospitals, for example, use biomedicine or traditional Chinese medicine as the line of first care for the patient? Should herbs continue to be included in the acupuncturist's scope of practice, if proven by 5,000 years of China's medical tradition but unproven by Western science? Should complementary therapies be used for cure as well as adjunctive treatment? How can ancient therapies be used in modern medical settings without losing their traditional flavor, philosophy, and potency?

Health care is changing of its own accord, driven as much by consumer demand and legislation as by clinical trials and evidence. The purpose of my scholarly work thus far has been to facilitate the development of institutional and regulatory policy that matches these shifts in health care and satisfactorily accommodates often conflicting variables, and then to build much-needed bridges between CAM clinical research and education and religious studies and other disciplines in the humanities. That purpose remains, in expanded form, in the present book.

CHAPTER ONE

Negotiating the New Health Care

Beyond Uns and Nons

The inclusion of complementary and alternative medicine (CAM) therapies such as chiropractic, acupuncture and traditional oriental medicine, massage therapy, and herbal medicine into conventional medical therapies is creating an escalating series of unresolved, and perhaps largely unrecognized, negotiation challenges among the various players in the U.S. health care system, most notably between doctor and patient. Such negotiation challenges, while perhaps historically endemic to the emergence of the various health care professions in this country, also present new puzzles and possibilities.

The practice of medicine within the United States began as competition among rival sects, each advancing different theories and services in an unregulated environment.[1] By the late nineteenth century, with innovations in surgery and anesthesia and increased political and economic consolidation of groups of professionals, scientifically based medical practice had begun to triumph over competitors such as homeopathy and herbal medicine. Through the enactment of medical licensing laws, which controlled whether providers with specified training could be given a state license to practice medicine, this "scientific" (or "regular"; later "conventional" or "orthodox") medicine assumed a position of legally sanctioned dominance in health care and ultimately evolved into the mainstream medical care we know today.[2]

Such conventional care has become the standard in hospitals and other modern health care facilities. It tends to regard its resurgent competitors as "un" or "non"—unscientific, nonscientific, unorthodox, unconventional, nonorthodox, nonconventional, and nonconforming.

As suggested in the Introduction, philosophically such conventional care (or biomedicine) is rooted in Cartesian dualism—the notion that the outer world of the body is objective and amenable to rigorous scientific inquiry, while the inner world of the mind is subjective and only marginally accessible—and in Newtonian physics, with its understanding of the body (and heavenly bodies) as objectively analyzable in terms of mechanical parts and laws.[3] Care patterns in the United States follow this Cartesian split. The patient typically visits a licensed medical doctor first (that is, before an "alternative" provider) for conventional diagnosis and treatment. Medical diagnosis follows scientific principles by classifying diseases into standard categories, and medical treatment, accordingly, typically relies on technologically validated mechanisms, such as prescription pharmaceuticals and surgery, to cure the diagnosed disease.[4]

Such prevailing care models can be said to result in reductionism, that is, the reduction of a complex individual to a standardized disease category, and mechanism, or the reduction of complex interactions of emotions, physiological processes, environmental influences, and even, perhaps, spiritual forces to engineering changes among a series of parts.[5] At the same time, conventional care typically excels in treating acute and emergency conditions, but it is less successful with chronic diseases and with diseases that have multifaceted causes and symptoms.[6]

Diseases such as AIDS, chronic fatigue, and cancer have challenged the dominance of conventional care and the medical model of diagnosis and treatment.[7] So has the advent of intractable problems in medical ethics such as decision making surrounding dying, issues in genetic engineering and cloning, and various reproductive technologies.[8] As a result, movements have arisen both within and outside conventional medicine to try to improve on these perceived limitations and thereby move beyond the reductionism and mechanism that have been the twin legacies of Cartesian dualism and Newtonian physics in biomedical care.[9] In other words, both West and East have tried to address the imbalance or unidimensionality perceived as Western medicine's trademark—the strength that also furnishes its weakness.

A Tale of Two Camps

In the 1960s, health care consumers expressed renewed interest in the notion of holistic health care, with a stated aim to treat the "whole" person, as one effort to overcome some of the perceived limitations of conventional care. The notion of holism came from earlier work by Jan Smuts, who argued in 1926 that all organisms, including human beings, have "whole-making" tendencies and that the drive toward such wholeness is a creative, evolutionary force in health and human development.[10] The notion of holistic care thus implied an effort to address, in addition to physiological conditions, the environmental, psychological, social and cultural, and even spiritual aspects of illness.[11]

The clash between conventional medical care and the holistic model led to entrenchment of positions, acceleration of rhetoric, and accusations from both camps. For example, in the 1950s the Code of Ethics of the American Medical Association (AMA) forbade physicians from referring patients to "cult" practitioners such as chiropractors[12] and declared such associations to be unethical. Epithets raged on both sides and found legal expression in, among other things, prosecution of various healers for the unlicensed practice of medicine.[13] By the 1980s, chiropractors were licensed in most states, and in *Wilk v. AMA* the chiropractic profession successfully sued the AMA for anticompetitive practices, with the Seventh Circuit finding that the AMA had engaged in a "nationwide conspiracy" to eliminate the chiropractic profession.[14]

The war of epithets continued, however, with the AMA's Council on Scientific Affairs declaring, as recently as 1996, that "some of the interest in alternative medicine . . . [is due to] New Age interest in 'channeling' and astrology, modern 'witch trials' concerning Satanic child abuse rituals, and alleged capture by space aliens."[15] In 1998 the editors of the *Journal of the American Medical Association* declared that there "is no alternative medicine" but "only scientifically proven, evidence-based medicine supported by solid data or unproven medicine."[16] A century of hostility and rivalry thus found renewed support in efforts to suppress "alternative" medicine's drive toward legitimacy.

One medical researcher has attempted to explain this rivalry as follows: "Because one's concept of health is entwined with one's fundamental assumptions about reality, an attack on someone's belief in unorthodox healing becomes a threat to his or her entire metaphysical outlook."[17] Countering this position, however, another author pointed out that hostility is mutual; thus, if one "simply substitutes 'orthodox' for 'unorthodox' in this above quote, one has a reasonable explanation for the biased and largely non-evidence based tone and approach" taken.[18]

Such opposing positions have created a variety of legal and social barriers to integration of CAM therapies within conventional care. Such barriers have included institutional obstacles such as those surrounding the process of credentialing CAM providers like chiropractors, acupuncturists, and massage therapists to work in hospitals.[19] Given the contentious history between conventional and CAM care, it may not be surprising to suggest here that the analysis of principled negotiation analysis might provide a useful framework for reconciliation between these two camps.

This chapter describes and frames the negotiation problems within the effort to integrate CAM therapies into conventional care. It explores unresolved legal and ethical issues, discusses several levels of negotiation challenges and lessons these unresolved issues tend to create, describes problem solving frameworks taken from a liability analysis and an ethical analysis, and surmises ways in which theory and analysis of principled negotiation might contribute to future health care in new systems that effectively integrate CAM therapies.

Complementary and Alternative vs. Integrative

The "hunkering down" into oppositional positions begins, as suggested earlier, with language. The decade of the uns and nons has yielded new terminology. Today, in the medical literature, the term "CAM therapies" has been used to describe therapies that historically were not been widely taught in U.S. medical schools or generally available in most U.S. hospitals.[20] Such therapies thus generally have been delivered outside conventional medical models and settings. According to surveys published in the medical literature, the most commonly used CAM therapies among patients include herbal remedies, massage therapy, megavitamins, self-help groups, folk remedies, energy healing, and homeopathy.[21] These findings bear some rough correlation to the political map for CAM providers: the most commonly licensed CAM therapies include chiropractic, acupuncture and traditional oriental medicine, massage therapy, and naturopathic medicine.[22]

Prevalence of CAM therapies is increasing. While in 1993 a *New England Journal of Medicine* article revealed that at least one in three Americans was using these therapies,[23] the 1998 follow-up study, published in the *Journal of the American Medical Association*, found a 47 percent increase in total visits to CAM practitioners, from 427 million in 1990 to 629 million in 1997, with total 1997 out-of-pocket expenditures relating to alternative therapies estimated at $27 billion.[24] Following this study, a 2000–2001 survey of 5,810 hospitals by the American Hospital Association reported that 15 percent of the respondents offered CAM therapies.[25]

As a result of these and other epidemiological studies, some medical professional and regulatory organizations have begun to shift from a stance hostile to CAM therapies toward recognition that clinicians must learn the medical evidence concerning individual CAM therapies, because this is the only pragmatic way to address patient interest in including such therapies in conventional (biomedical) care.[26] Thus, for example, the position of the AMA has evolved since the *Wilk* case to its present recommendation that physicians "routinely inquire" concerning use of CAM therapies by their patients and "educate themselves and their patients about the state of scientific knowledge" regarding the CAM therapy that may be "used or contemplated."[27] In similar fashion, the American Academy of Family Physicians now "advocates the evaluation" of CAM therapies "through various means including evidence-based outcomes as to their efficacy." The academy's position paper asserts that the organization "believes that physicians can best serve their patients by recognizing and acknowledging the availability of such alternatives and by educating themselves" concerning their risks and benefits.[28]

Alongside increased support among medical professional organizations for initiating conversations with patients concerning use of CAM therapies, the National Institutes of Health has recognized the need for research into the safety, efficacy, and mechanism of CAM therapies by establishing the National Center for Complementary and Alternative Medicine (NCCAM), with its own grant-making authority. The NCCAM research budget has grown exponentially since the initial $2 million grant to well over $100 million in 2006. Further, NCCAM has moved beyond the original language of "CAM therapies" toward a notion of "integrative medicine." By this term, NCCAM denotes health care that "combines mainstream medical therapies and CAM therapies for which there is some high-quality scientific evidence of safety and effectiveness."[29] While slightly different from the definition offered earlier, NCCAM's perspective acknowledges that there must be "some high-quality" medical evidence behind the CAM therapy to be offered but does not set an evidence threshold.

These developments suggest an evolving worldview within the medical profession toward increased recognition of integrative medicine. For example, there now are numerous independent clinics as well as hospital-based centers pioneering efforts to deliver integrative health care across the United States and internationally.[30] Such developments do not yet fully allow conventional and CAM providers to easily refer patients to one another or fully communicate to one another the possibilities, as well as limitations, of therapies within each domain.[31]

Institutional change is slow and beset by a variety of forces, including limited perspectives and inadequate understanding of the potential ethical challenges in balancing patient desires against institutional mandates.[32] From the other side, many CAM providers fear being "co-opted" by the forces of conventional care[33] or share a concern that integration and accompanying regulation will deprive them of the individuality that makes CAM therapies unique.[34] Negotiation analysis offers a tool to focus on how to achieve integration and what integration might, on a very practical level, mean for patients, clinicians, and institutions.

Unresolved Legal and Ethical Dilemmas

Liability questions and other legal, regulatory, ethical, and policy issues remain undecided, creating indeterminacy for clinicians who are asked to counsel their patients concerning use or avoidance of CAM therapies[35] and for institutions called to advise their clinicians. Although professional organizations such as the AMA have, as noted, advised physicians to inquire about patient use of CAM therapies, such steps fail to provide concrete and specific guidance for clinicians about which therapies to recommend, accept, or discourage and exactly how to discuss patient requests (reasonable or otherwise) regarding such therapies. Further, professional organizations have failed to address liability concerns or to offer specific advice where clinicians disagree with patient perspectives and choices.[36] Nor have health care institutions necessarily filled the gap by addressing specific clinical scenarios clinicians and patients might face, including use of specific CAM therapies for serious conditions, possible contraindications, and interactions between pharmaceutical drugs and herbal remedies. Some institutions have even refused to draft policies to help guide clinicians through matters such as handling patient interest in dietary supplements.[37]

The present inadequacy of guidance among institutions and associations creates a tension for those wishing to advise patients responsibly yet limit their potential liability risk. Clinicians are caught between the Scylla of denial and evasion (professing ignorance regarding CAM therapies and/or refusing to offer the patient any meaningful recommendation) and the Charybdis of recommending therapies that may, despite best intentions, result in patient harm, thus heightening liability risks as well as potentially endangering the clinician's professional reputation and licensure. This can create a Hobson's choice: to be rejected by your patient if you "don't ask and don't tell"[38] about CAM therapies and sued if you do ask but fail to adequately describe potential risks and benefits.[39]

The problem is exacerbated by generalized warnings by some major medical leaders about the risks of "untested and unregulated" CAM therapies[40] and by case reports and other literature documenting safety issues and adverse effects of herbal remedies.[41] The "doctor's dilemma" regarding CAM therapies is heightened further by the paucity of relevant judicial opinions in the liability arena and by some difficult language in one of the few cases on point.

In *Charell v. Gonzales*, a New York court found a physician negligent for recommending nutritional care for cancer. The court concluded, "No practitioner of alternative medicine would prevail . . . as . . . the term 'non-conventional' may well necessitate a finding that the doctor who practices such medicine deviated from accepted medical standards."[42] Such language, though not necessarily binding on courts outside New York, is suggestive of malpractice per se—of automatic liability once a clinician embraces a therapeutic recommendation involving CAM therapies.[43] Added to this conundrum are the unresolved ethical issues around advising patients when the clinician disagrees with the patient's choice of CAM therapies. For example, when a patient decides to forgo a conventional therapy in favor of CAM therapies that may have some (but in the clinician's opinion probably not enough) evidence of safety and efficacy, the clinician may feel caught between the ethical poles of nonmaleficence (refusing to sanction a dangerous medical choice) and beneficence (allowing the patient to try therapies of possible benefit).[44]

From a liability perspective, the clinician in this same situation may be caught between articulating his or her opinion and thereby abandoning the patient (or being abandoned and rejected by the patient) and remaining clinically involved yet risking a lawsuit by the patient or the patient's family if therapy fails. Liability dilemmas in health care often track ethical dilemmas but find resolution in different sets of factors or considerations.

Negotiation Challenges and Lessons

MULTIPLE COMMUNICATION FAILURES

While clinicians and health care institutions can no longer ignore CAM therapies, they face a quandary about what to tell patients. The current state of legal, regulatory, ethical, and institutional chaos, combined with inadequate guidance from professional organizations, seems to pose an often unsolvable, and certainly legally and ethically perplexing, set of dilemmas to clinicians and institutions.[45] Thus, to the extent that the increasing attention to CAM therapies creates "difficult [but not insurmountable] conversations"[46] for clinicians, institutions, and their patients (and patients' families), these different stakeholders face dilemmas both in what is spoken and in the unspoken. To date, neither professional organizations nor legislators nor consumer advocacy groups have creatively met the challenge with consensus policies and procedures to help guide such conversations. This failure leaves the parties frozen in no-win positions.

In *Getting to Yes: Negotiating Agreement without Giving In*, Roger Fisher, William Ury, and Bruce Patton describe "principled negotiation" as a means to move beyond frozen positions toward mutually acceptable solutions. The authors discourage the black-and-white, either/or scenario in which parties "tend to lock themselves into positions" and "defend . . . against attack," making it "less and less likely" that any conversation will "wisely reconcile" their mutual interests.[47] Once the patient and the clinician each take a position on use of CAM therapies, it becomes difficult to reach agreement on the best therapeutic course of action. Consider, for example, the following two cases:[48]

(A)   *The Patient Who Wants to Use* CAM *instead of Conventional Therapies*

The patient has a premalignant condition that can be completely cured through surgery but, if left untreated, can progress to invasive cancer. The patient tells her physician that she plans to pursue meditation, colonics, and yoga and to work with her Reiki master rather than have surgery.

(B)   *The Patient Who Seeks Advice Regarding Inclusion of* CAM *Therapies*

The patient, a woman with recurrent metastatic ovarian adenocarcinoma, asks her oncologist to provide her with conventional treatment but to be open to evaluating and guiding her regarding available CAM therapies. The patient's insurance plan requires that she be seen by a particular oncologist.

The differing positions of patient and physician are illustrated for each case in Table 1.1.

This digging in to adverse positions, combined with the physician's refusal (or inability) to engage in shared decision making, leaves the patient without the necessary information to make a meaningful clinical decision. Further, it leaves the patient isolated from the very clinician the patient is counting on to save his or her life. At the very least, this situation potentially damages the therapeutic relationship; as *Getting to Yes* points out, "Positional bargaining becomes a contest of wills" that "sometimes shatters the relationship between the parties."[49] Since the relationship involves health and also may have a therapeutic or healing dimension—particularly in light of the so-called placebo effect, in which relationship itself may have health-enhancing effects—such disruption is unfortunate and may have severe though unintended consequences.

At the same time, this situation leaves the physician with few perceived options, none of which are attractive. In both cases, the most obvious choices are (1) to insist that the patient receive conventional care; (2) to acquiesce to the patient without helping or attempting to set limits when therapies are considered that may be unsafe or lack efficacy; and (3) neither to insist on the physician's

TABLE 1.1. Sinking into Positions: Patient vs. Physician

CASE A

Patient's Position	Physician's Position
I believe in the body's ability to heal itself and in the importance of the relationship between illness and mental, emotional, and spiritual health. Even if you told me I would die next month without surgery, I still wouldn't have it.	If you delay treatment by trying some of these other methods, none of which have been shown to be effective in treating your condition, you may end up with cancer, which will be much more difficult, if not impossible, to cure.

CASE B

Patient's Position	Physician's Position
I would like you to help me evaluate complementary and alternative medical approaches so that I can include them in my treatment.	I refuse to recommend CAM treatments because they have not been subjected to scientific scrutiny. You risk your health in seeking these types of care.

position (refuse to provide CAM care or information) nor to bow to the patient's position (provide CAM care or information that the physician does not believe is effective), but instead to withdraw from the situation and stop caring for this particular patient. Each choice has consequences, as illustrated in Table 1.2.[50]

In the face of such unattractive options, physicians might try to opt out of the dilemma by providing the patient with a choice that seems to respect the patient's autonomy but effectively disempowers the patient and renders the notion of a choice absurd. Roger Fisher, the principal author of *Getting to Yes*, relates a version of this conversation: "The patient says: 'I'd rather not have surgery. Tell me what you think I should do.' The physician replies: 'I think you should have surgery—but it's your decision.' "[51] In this scenario, the physician is giving mixed signals: letting the patient know that the patient must take responsibility for the decision and, at the same time, signaling that the decision *not* to have surgery is wrong. The potential damage to the therapeutic relationship is implicit in this

TABLE 1.2. Choices and Consequences of Paring Down Options

Choices	Consequences
1. Insist that this patient receive conventional care	Patient may refuse to comply, leading to a potential rupture in the relationship as well as to patient injury; in addition, the combination of these factors can be a precursor to lawsuit.
2. Acquiesce to the patient's insistence on receiving CAM therapies, without setting limits	If the patient uses an unsafe CAM therapy and is injured or dies, the physician conceivably could be liable for negligence (failure to provide standard treatment). Acquiescence in such a case also may contravene the physician's belief in evidence-based medicine and the ethical and professional obligation to "do no harm."
3. Withdraw from caring for this particular patient (without referring the patient to an appropriate caregiver)	If the patient dies and the family sues, the physician could be liable for patient abandonment. In addition, by withdrawing from care without referring the patient to an appropriate caregiver, the physician may violate the obligation to "do no harm."

"difficult conversation" gone wrong: the patient may see the physician's statement as demonstrating "how little" the physician may care about the relationship. Further, in choosing either of the first two options, the physician may be either trading the relationship for the position or trading the position for the relationship.[52]

These three scenarios admittedly represent what some might consider extreme responses, and there are shades of gray in between. The point, however, is that clinicians who lack negotiation skills and knowledge can feel pushed into the extremes. In addition, one often finds these extremes represented in the literature, with rhetoric substituting for evidence (on both sides) and negative case reports sometimes constituting the basis for clinical practice or institutional policy in zones of the unknown, such as intake of dietary supplements. But before I discuss what negotiation theory might offer, it is worthwhile to describe the many different levels involved in negotiating integrative health care and to mention existing approaches to solving these dilemmas from liability and ethical perspectives.

MULTIPLE LEVELS OF REQUIRED NEGOTIATION

The negotiation challenges are broader than those between physician and patient. They involve several additional groups of constituents, each with different interests. The groups include CAM providers (such as chiropractors and acupuncturists); allied health providers (such as nurses and psychologists); policymakers and regulators; consumer groups; industry (e.g., manufacturers of dietary supplements and of other CAM substances and devices); research scientists; and insurers.[53] The range of interests is listed Table 1.3; the list is illustrative and representative, not exhaustive.

The chart could be critiqued as oversimplifying the various interests. One could also argue that the different interests are, in fact, overlapping rather than exclusive. For example, both patients and regulators would like access to CAM therapies to be characterized by the absence of fraudulent conduct. The chart focuses on the hypothesized primary interest in order to show the potential conflicts between the main interests of various groups. In the above example, while both patients and regulators may be concerned with potential fraud, patients are more likely to have cure as their primary interest; regulators will have fraud control as the primary interest, and consumer groups will emphasize access to CAM therapies.[54]

Take, for example, the patient who seeks access to a therapy that has not been approved as safe and effective by the Food and Drug Administration (FDA). The patient is likely to emphasize the need to obtain such a product for cure, while the FDA is likely to emphasize the need to protect patients from their own gullibility, vulnerability, and desperation.[55] Such a clash of primary interests often plays out in ethical terms, as a conflict between medical paternalism

TABLE 1.3. Multiple Levels of Required Negotiation

Group	Hypothesized Primary Interest
Patients and their families	Cure of identified disease
Physicians	Success of proposed intervention(s) while "doing no harm"
Allied health providers	Facilitation of effectiveness of medical intervention
CAM providers	Facilitation of healing
Policymakers and regulators	Prevention of fraud
Consumer groups	Access to pluralistic treatment modalities
Industry	Profit on approved drugs and devices
Research scientists	Safety and efficacy of proposed therapeutic interventions
Insurers	Cost-effectiveness

(the desire and sometimes perceived obligation to protect patients from their own foolish choices) and respect for patient autonomy (the wish to protect knowing, voluntary, and intelligent choices).[56]

In addition to the various communities and multiple stakeholders within each community, each of which may have overlapping and conflicting positions and interests, the shift from conventional toward integrative health care may involve negotiation in multiple domains, including the following: legal and ethical, business and economic, professional and regulatory, political, institutional, and social and cultural. Some of the key issues to be negotiated within each domain are listed in Table 1.4. These include offering CAM therapies and practicing innovatively without getting sued;[57] discussing therapeutic options involving CAM therapies with patients;[58] determining which CAM schools should be professionally accredited and accepted;[59] deciding who gets licensed;[60] specifying what a licensed provider can do or not do;[61] helping hospitals validate

TABLE 1.4. Key Issues to Be Negotiated within Each Domain

Domain	Key Issues
Legal	• How can physicians offer CAM therapies and practice innovatively without getting sued? • How can physicians discuss therapeutic options involving CAM therapies with patients?
Business and economic	• How can the expense of integrative care teams (e.g., of providing care by teams of physicians, nurses, acupuncturists, chiropractors, nutritionists, and others) be addressed? • How can the problem of relative lack of reimbursement for CAM care (including billing and coding issues) be addressed?
Professional and regulatory	• What modalities should be accepted as valid or proscribed? • Which CAM schools should be professionally accredited and accepted as valid?
Political	• Who gets licensed? • What can a licensed provider do or not do? • Should nonlicensed providers be allowed to practice? • When should licensed providers offering CAM be subject to professional discipline?
Institutional	• How will hospitals credential CAM providers? • How will hospitals handle dietary supplements?
Social and cultural	• What should clinicians (and the law) do when patients demand therapies that are deemed unsafe or are not FDA-approved? • How should clinicians, institutions, and regulators handle inclusion of spirituality within medicine and potential abuses of spiritual authority?

credentials of CAM providers;[62] determining when licensed providers offering CAM should be subject to professional discipline;[63] establishing how hospitals will handle dietary supplements;[64] determining what clinicians (and the law) should do when patients demand therapies that are either deemed unsafe or are not FDA-approved;[65] and resolving how clinicians, institutions, and regulators should handle inclusion of spirituality within medicine and potential abuses of spiritual authority.[66]

Legal issues have been analyzed extensively elsewhere and include such areas of the law as (1) licensure and credentialing, (2) scope of practice, (3) professional discipline, (4) malpractice liability, (5) the right of access to treatments, (6) third-party reimbursement, and (7) health care fraud.[67] Of these seven legal issues, the fear of malpractice liability seems to be one of the greatest challenges to use of principled negotiation in conversations between clinicians and patients around use (or avoidance) of CAM therapies.[68] Thus, before turning to possible ways that negotiation theory and analysis might help break the logjams identified above, it may be helpful to review the analysis based on liability concerns and the analysis of negotiation issues based on related ethical concerns.

Applying Liability and Ethical Analyses to Clinical Decision Making

THE LIABILITY ANALYSIS

The liability analysis starts with the observation that liability for malpractice (negligence) involving CAM therapies invokes the same definition that is used for medical malpractice generally: clinical care below applicable professional standards, causing the patient injury.[69] Generally, in assessing whether clinical care has met or fallen below applicable professional standards, experts are likely to testify regarding the accepted safety and efficacy of the therapeutic modality used. Accordingly, clinicians seeking to assess their potential malpractice liability risk in counseling patients concerning CAM therapies should evaluate whether the medical evidence (A) supports both safety and efficacy; (B) supports safety, but evidence regarding efficacy is inconclusive; (C) supports efficacy, but evidence regarding safety is inconclusive; or (D) indicates either serious risk or inefficacy.[70]

Under this framework, if (A) the medical evidence supports both safety and efficacy, liability is unlikely, and clinicians should recommend the CAM therapy. On the other hand, if (D) the medical evidence indicates either serious risk or inefficacy, liability is probable, and clinicians should avoid and actively discourage the patient from using the CAM therapy. If the medical evidence (B) supports safety, but evidence regarding efficacy is inconclusive, or (C) supports efficacy, but evidence regarding safety is inconclusive, then clinicians should caution the patient and, while accepting the patient's choice to try the CAM therapy, continue to monitor efficacy and safety, respectively. In either case B or case C, liability is conceivable but probably unlikely, particularly in case B, where the product is presumably safe.

This risk assessment framework is summarized in Table 1.5, which includes clinical examples. This framework is offered with the caveat that as medical evidence regarding safety and efficacy for any given therapy changes—as it does from time to time—a given therapy may shift from one portion of the grid to another. Thus, a therapy of dubious efficacy today may be proven effective and thereby easily recommended tomorrow, while new evidence may suggest that a therapy previously considered safe and effective for a given condition may in fact be of dubious efficacy and even unsafe. Further, the safety or efficacy of a given therapy may depend on its administration and whether it produces an adverse reaction in combination with other CAM therapies or in combination with specified conventional therapies (e.g., effect of ginkgo biloba on postsurgical bleeding).

Even if there is good evidence supporting safety and efficacy, the therapy may not necessarily benefit a given patient. Conversely, some therapies with poor evidence of efficacy may prove beneficial. Even a therapy adjudged safe can cause harm if inappropriately administered. Thus there are shades of gray within each region, and the reality may be more dynamic if the patient is interested in multiple therapies with cross-interactions. Further, the responsibility to

TABLE 1.5. Relation of Evidence to Therapeutic Posture and Liability Risk

B	A
Evidence supports safety, but evidence regarding efficacy is inconclusive.	*Evidence supports both safety and efficacy.*
THERAPEUTIC POSTURE: Tolerate, provide caution, and closely monitor effectiveness.	THERAPEUTIC POSTURE: Recommend and continue to monitor.
CLINICAL EXAMPLES: Acupuncture for chronic pain; homeopathy for seasonal rhinitis; dietar fat reduction for certain cancers; mind-body techniques for metastatic cancer; massage therapy for low back pain; self-hypnosis for the pain of metastatic cancer.	CLINICAL EXAMPLES: Chiropractic for acute low back pain; acupuncture for chemo-therapy-induced nausea and dental pain; mind-body techniques for chronic pain and insomnia.
POTENTIAL LIABILITY RISK: Conceivably liable, but probably acceptable.	POTENTIAL LIABILITY RISK: Probably not liable.

EFFICACY →

D	C
Evidence indicates either serious risk or inefficacy.	*Evidence supports efficacy, but evidence regarding safety is inconclusive.*
THERAPEUTIC POSTURE: Avoid and actively discourage.	THERAPEUTIC POSTURE: Consider tolerating, provide caution, and closely monitor safety.
CLINICAL EXAMPLES: Injections of unapproved substances; use of toxic herbs or substances; dangerous delay or replacement of curative conventional treatments; inattention to known herb-drug interactions (e.g., St. John's Wort and indinavir or cyclosporin).	CLINICAL EXAMPLES: St. John's Wort for depression; saw palmetto for benign prostatic hyperplasia; chondroitin sulfate for osteoarthritis; ginkgo biloba for cognitive function in dementia; acupuncture for breech presentation.
POTENTIAL LIABILITY RISK: Probably liable.	POTENTIAL LIABILITY RISK: Conceivably liable, but more than likely acceptable.

SAFETY

Source: Cohen and Eisenberg, "Potential Physician Malpractice," 597. Reprinted courtesy of *Annals of Internal Medicine*.

monitor safety and efficacy applies whether a therapy is labeled conventional or complementary, although the framework places particular emphasis on monitoring in grids B and C, where many CAM therapies will lie, and the evidence regarding safety or efficacy, respectively, may be less than satisfactory.

With the above caveats, this model offers a framework for assessing potential liability risk based on the existing medical evidence. The model admittedly is too static; it merely gives clinicians three options: recommend, avoid and discourage, or tolerate/accept while monitoring. In fact, medical risks change over time according to many factors, including disease progression and prognosis and the impact of combinations of the various therapies. In actuality, clinician and patient may be required to have not one but a series of conversations over time, as the patient uses some combination of conventional and CAM therapies with varying effects.[71] Further, integrative care presumes a model of shared decision making[72] rather than a hierarchical decision by the clinician to accept/avoid/tolerate; clinicians and patients ideally are equal partners in a joint process regarding care. This is why negotiation analysis is a necessary complement to the existing framework.

THE ETHICAL ANALYSIS

The ethical analysis also offers a useful but perhaps limited framework for clinicians contemplating whether and how to advise patients who inquire concerning use (or avoidance) of CAM therapies. Like the liability analysis, the ethical analysis expands the historic characterization of CAM therapies in terms of dichotomous dualities—for example, ethical/unethical. That characterization followed rhetoric between the two camps—for example, the notion of *un*conventional, *un*orthodox, and *alternative* medicine.

The ethical analysis expands the language of clinician choices by including multiple factors in decision making. Some of these factors are closer to the physician's education, training, and predisposition, and others are closer to the patient's. These factors can be applied to the decision to discourage the CAM therapy, on one hand, or recommend its use, on the other, as suggested in Table 1.6.

TABLE 1.6. Applying Ethical Factors to Recommendations of CAM Therapy

Ethical Factor	Discourages CAM Therapy	Encourages or Allows CAM Therapy
Severity and acuteness of illness	Yes	No
Curability with conventional treatment	Yes	No
Invasiveness, toxicities, and side effects of conventional treatment	No	Yes
Quality of evidence of safety and efficacy of the CAM treatment	No	Yes
Degree of understanding of the risks and benefits of conventional and CAM treatments	No	Yes
Knowing and voluntary acceptance of those risks by the patient	No	Yes
Persistence of patient's intention to utilize CAM treatment	No	Yes

Source: Adams et al., "Ethical Considerations," 661.

Thus, in case A, while the patient's illness might eventually be cured with conventional treatment, the treatment (surgery) is invasive; although the evidence for CAM is low, the patient understands and accepts the risks and insists on trying CAM therapies. Rather than allow medical paternalism to trump the patient's autonomous wishes, the physician ethically may accept the patient trying a regimen of CAM therapies, so long as the clinician continues to monitor and stands ready to intervene conventionally when medically necessary.[73] If the risk of cancer increases past a tolerable threshold, the physician should intensify attempts to persuade the patient that it is time to return to conventional methods of treatment.[74]

In case B, many adjunctive CAM therapies for cancer care have support in medical evidence and are not dangerous.[75] The clinician should be aware of pertinent evidence and be willing to consider any intervention (CAM or allopathic) that has an acceptable risk-benefit balance. The clinician's ethical obligation thus is to apprise the patient of acceptable options and make a recommendation that respects the patient's value system.[76]

The ethical analysis, while useful in expanding the range of factors to consider, has limitations. It does not offer clinicians a strategy for appropriately balancing the various factors and negotiating conversations accordingly with patients. The analysis also leaves the clinicians with a narrow range of options equivalent to accept/avoid and discourage/tolerate. Further, clinicians and patients still may be tempted to dig in to conflicting positions, or at least places of emphasis, within the analysis of these factors. For example, clinicians are likely to overemphasize (relative to patients) the fourth factor: the quality of evidence of safety and efficacy of the CAM treatment. Patients, however, may be very sensitive (as in the first case) to the invasiveness, toxicities, and side effects of the conventional treatment (third factor). They might underestimate the risks and benefits of conventional and CAM treatments (fifth factor) and persist in their intention to use the CAM therapy (seventh factor). Thus, the ethical analysis, once made, still requires a negotiated exchange between clinicians and patients and some clear basis for a principled negotiation.

Applying a Negotiation Analysis to Clinical Decision Making

A USEFUL FRAMEWORK

Negotiation theory and analysis provides useful tools for clinical decision making regarding use (or avoidance) of CAM therapies. The two-party encounter between clinician and patient offers a way to understand the application of principled negotiation to perhaps the most fundamental and charged place within the health care system within which the introduction of CAM therapies could disrupt relationships and produce conflict. The analysis below focuses on suggestions for clinicians who are called to guide patients in the borderland between medical evidence and personal belief systems.

As a starting proposition, principled negotiation aims to "produce a wise agreement," be "efficient," and "improve or at least not damage the relationship between the parties." The suggestion seems especially relevant to considerations involving CAM therapies. As suggested, the relationship between clinician and patient has a unique feature in that it is a *healing* relationship, wherein the quality of the therapeutic relationship itself may have an effect on health. Principled negotiation offers a well-accepted framework for negotiating in general and has utility in this situation. There are four major techniques within the framework: separate the people from the problem; focus on interests, not positions; invent options for mutual gain; and insist on using objective criteria.[77]

Separating the people from the problem suggests tackling the problem neutrally rather than making the problem about the people. Focusing on interests, not positions, means trying to find what each party is motivated to accomplish and where there might be common ground, rather than simply identifying where each has dug in. Inventing options for mutual gain suggests brainstorming about a variety of possible creative solutions before evaluating which one will succeed, while jointly developing objective criteria can help the parties determine how well any given option satisfies mutual interests. Another important technique in addition to these four is to know one's BATNA (best alternative to a negotiated agreement), or what will happen if the negotiation fails to produce a result. Principled negotiation is highly relational and suggests using empathy and communication skills to find solutions in the common ground, rather than focusing on what divides.

Beginning with the first technique—the need to address the substantive issues separately from the personalities involved—patients may have preconceptions about their caregivers' openness to CAM therapies and/or evidence-based medicine;[78] physicians may have preconceptions about patients' interest in such therapies.[79] "People tend to see what they want to see . . . to pick out and focus on those facts that confirm their prior perception and to disregard or misinterpret those that call their perceptions into question."[80] In case B, the physician may misperceive the patient as naive, gullible, or uninformed, while the patient may misperceive the physician as overly rigid, unyielding, and inflexibly tied to preconceptions about the evidence.

Principled negotiation emphasizes communication and empathy: putting oneself in the other party's shoes.[81] As a group of CAM researchers observes, "Only by letting go of previously held beliefs can new learning and discovery ever take place."[82] One of the gaps clinician and patient must bridge concerning CAM therapies is the relative role of medical evidence and personal experience, intuition, or trust in evaluating the potential safety and efficacy of any given therapy. For instance, in case A, the clinician and patient may have different views about the potential efficacy of the CAM therapies the patient has selected; yet there is always room in medicine for the unexpected, and it would be a mistake for the physician to completely (or even overly) discount the patient's value system and persistence. It would be an equal mistake for the patient to completely (or overly) discount the physician's value system, with its concomitant commitment to scientific method. One way to separate the person from the problem is to imagine a role reversal: each must sit in the shoes of the other in a negotiated exchange that respects the value of the way the other sees the world.

Active listening is an important component to this approach. The clinician, for example, would be called on to hear (if not invite) expression by the patient of any vulnerability and frustration with conventional care received. It might also be helpful to invite discussion of any information the patient may have received regarding CAM therapeutic approaches and the source of this information. This would help the clinician understand the reasons for the patient's proposed choices. The clinician then could present an evidence-based perspective in a respectful and nonjudgmental way, acknowledging any limitations of the available evidence and of reliance on the evidence compiled to date. Not surprisingly, such an approach is likely to reduce liability risk, since effective physician-patient communication tends to reduce malpractice exposure. A sensible negotiation strategy involving separating the people from the problem thus is essential for clinicians seeking to reduce such risk when advising regarding integration of CAM therapies.

Turning to the second element of principled negotiation, in moving from positions to interests, the two parties share a common objective to restore the patient to health as quickly and fully as possible. While they may differ in emphasis and sense of responsibility (and some clinicians may be more or less paternalistic than others), the shared interest in promoting health addresses one of the patient's most basic needs—"those bedrock concerns which motivate all people." Negotiations are unlikely to progress if one party believes that basic needs are being threatened by the other.[83] Therefore, in both case A and case B, the clinician is advised to move from a position that negates and threatens the patient's self-perception of what is necessary and appropriate for restoration of health to an emphasis on the shared interest.

Differing interests that are complementary also can lead to a deal. Thus, if the physician is interested in cure (as soon as possible and without delay) and the patient is interested in cure (without unnecessary invasion or trauma) and healing (that promotes wholeness on all levels as well as physical health), the two may be able to work out an arrangement in which the patient tries the desired CAM therapy for a defined period of time and, if such therapy fails to reach a prespecified benchmark of health within a certain period, the patient agrees to return to the conventional care advised by the physician. Such a "wise agreement" respects both interests and values their complementary approaches.[84] It also engages shared decision making: a process of conversation and dialogue rather than the bureaucratic and authoritarian model that traditionally has accompanied informed consent.[85]

The third suggestion involves inventing options for mutual gain. Clinicians and patients can move beyond the either/or, yes/no dilemmas presented in cases A and B. The liability assessment framework suggests several strategies that provide a range of options. For example, clinician and patient can agree to try CAM care for a period of time while continuing conventional monitoring so that the clinician can intervene (and the patient is open to such intervention) with conventional medical care when necessary. In such an agreement, the clinician and patient are more likely to become partners rather than ideological adversaries. By working together and continuing conventional monitoring (and treatment where necessary), they ideally can invent options that satisfy the patient's interest in pursuing CAM therapies yet fulfill the clinician's obligation to do no harm and practice in an evidence-based manner.

Roger and Elliott Fisher have argued that in the end, the quality of a medical decision should be judged not only by outcome but also by the quality of the decision-making process. This includes "not only the care with which the decision is reached but also how satisfied the patient, physician, and other affected parties are with both the decision-making process and the substance of the final decision." A good decision requires effective communication between clinician and patient, including consideration of a "well-considered alternative to agreement with the physician's final proposal."[86] Inventing options for mutual gain that incorporate both conventional and CAM therapies may offer a decision-making process that respects the values and emphases of both sides.

The final plank in principled negotiation involves insisting on objective criteria to settle differences. This frees the negotiating parties from reliance on subjective standards that may fail to satisfy general criteria. A salient question here is whether the legal and ethical frameworks presented earlier in fact provide objective criteria for negotiation. Certainly, the quality of medical evidence concerning safety and efficacy provides one yardstick for assessing known potential risks and benefits of a given CAM therapy. Even if the patient does not value the medical evidence to the same extent or in the same way as the clinician, attention to the evidence can help guide a foundational discussion between the two. Similarly, the medical evidence might offer a series of endpoints, which if reached by the patient, could suggest a mutually agreed-upon decision to either renew or continue to forgo conventional care in favor of CAM options for a prescribed period.

The liability framework focuses on worst-case scenarios and asks, "Under what circumstances am I (the clinician or institution, as the case may be) most likely to be sued?" The answer, according to the grid, is to avoid region D, be safe in region A, and use caution in regions B and C (where either safety or efficacy is disputed). The ethical framework balances considerations of interest to the patient and to the clinician; it offers a multifactorial analysis in which the combination of various circumstances may tip the scales one way or another.

Principled negotiation distills the puzzle into interests, options, and criteria. Returning to the two cases discussed earlier, case A (in which the patient wants to use CAM therapies instead of conventional care) and case B (in which the patient merely seeks the physician's advice concerning CAM therapies of potential utility), principled negotiation adds a process rather than an endpoint. The very questions it asks aim to refocus the parties on how to work together toward a win-win solution. This is in contrast to the legal and ethical frameworks that, while useful, could focus the parties on either avoiding worst-case scenarios or wrestling with multifactorial balancing.

The solutions that principled negotiation gives also tend to move the parties away from entrenched positions and expand the range of potential outcomes, as suggested in Table 1.8.

While principled negotiation clearly adds to the liability and ethical frameworks, its methods may not entirely solve this new and complex shift in U.S. health care. One consideration involves the significant amount of emotion the patient may have invested in making autonomous choices regarding CAM therapies and/or in rejecting certain CAM therapies, such as, for example, the recommended chemotherapy in case A. Since emotions lie behind positions, the fact that principled negotiation encourages the effort to

TABLE 1.7. Main Question Each Framework Asks

Liability Framework	Ethical Framework	Principled Negotiation
How can I best avoid an unnecessary and burdensome lawsuit?	What combination of ethical factors best balances patient autonomy and professional medical concerns?	What interests, options, and objective criteria will produce a wise agreement that is fair to both sides and preserves the therapeutic relationship?

"make emotions explicit and acknowledge them as legitimate" may be helpful.[87] At the same time, illness brings up intense emotions, since it engages what may be our greatest shared vulnerability as humans, the fragility of the body; our greatest collective fear, our eventual bodily deterioration and death; and our greatest arena of shared speculation, what (if anything) lies beyond the dissolution of the body.[88] All this suggests a heightened need for a frank discussion between clinician and client in which mutual fears, vulnerabilities, and perceptions around power (or lack thereof) are explicitly acknowledged.[89]

The traditional therapeutic distance between clinician and healer suggests a need by clinicians, perhaps in self-protection, to detach or move away from explicit acknowledgment of emotions. As suggested, the notion of integrative medicine critiques this therapeutic distance as unnecessary and unhelpful. As case B (patient seeks physician's advice concerning CAM therapies) suggests, when the clinician has preexisting biases and perspectives regarding particular therapies, such perspectives may increase rather than decrease any preexisting therapeutic distance. Clinicians who are prone to emphasize therapeutic distance cannot simply be "warmed" by references to stated principles of integrative care.

Principled negotiation's emphasis on using objective criteria offers one approach to structure conversations (i.e., around diagnosis and treatment) that can bring up intense emotions. In fact, the notion of objective criteria resonates with the legal and ethical obligation of

TABLE 1.8. Solutions/Approaches Each Framework Proposes to Cases

Liability Framework	Ethical Framework	Principled Negotiation
• Encourage therapies of proven safety and efficacy. • Discourage therapies of proven danger and inefficacy. • Cautiously tolerate and monitor therapies of unknown safety or efficacy.	• Discourage therapies if the illness is severe and acute; curable conventionally without undue invasiveness, toxicities, or side effects; therapy lacks sufficient evidence; and patient poorly understands and marginally accepts risks and does not persist in using CAM therapies. • Allow in the reverse case.	• Find that ultimate combination of CAM therapies and conventional care (while continuing to monitor conventionally) that optimizes respect for the shared interest in the patient's well-being and optimally accounts for the potential risks and benefits of the various tools from all the healing traditions (conventional and CAM) available to clinician and patient.

informed consent. This obligation essentially mandates disclosure and discussion of all risks and benefits material to a treatment decision. As regards inclusion of CAM therapies, this means that clinicians may be obligated to offer the patient full disclosure about the risks and benefits of the conventional therapy, the CAM therapy, and delaying or deferring one therapy for the other. This disclosure should include an honest discussion of preconceptions and biases.[90] The discussion of risks and benefits can use objective information from evidence-based medicine as one set of criteria by which clinicians and patients can assess whether and how to proceed.

Naturally, there may be constraints on the clinician's ability to learn about a range of CAM therapies and to communicate such information within the time allotted for a patient visit. Further, some conventional clinicians may view recommendations regarding

CAM therapies or referrals to CAM providers as threatening to their sense of identity within a certain range of medical theories and practices. Since emotions can bypass the logical circuitry of objective criteria, there is the danger that clinician and patient may use such criteria to lapse into positional bargaining over the legitimacy of such criteria. (Such dangers also are inherent in negotiations over medication, surgery, and conventional medicine, although they may be exacerbated where clinicians and patients differ regarding their philosophical orientation toward [or against] a given medical system, such as Ayurveda or traditional oriental medicine.)

By drawing parallels between existing liability and ethical frameworks and the principled negotiation outlined by Fisher, Ury, and Patton, this analysis aims to fill some of the blanks between these diverging perspectives. Using principled negotiation should help improve the ability of clinicians to counsel patients regarding inclusion of CAM therapies in ways that respect both parties' value systems, underlying beliefs, and shared as well as diverse yet complementary interests.

An Ongoing Shift

This chapter has described the ongoing shift from conventional care alone to a medical system in which CAM therapies are integrated with prescription pharmaceuticals, surgery, and high-technology medicine. The chapter has suggested ways in which liability and ethical analysis may be useful in helping clinicians discuss use or avoidance of CAM therapies with patients, and it has suggested the limitations of these approaches that offer a creative contribution for negotiation theory. The chapter also has provided a preliminary outline of how negotiation theory and analysis might enhance the earlier frameworks by contributing methods for clinicians and patients to discuss the various therapeutic options that integrate the different kinds of care.

As integrative medicine continues to emerge, it is likely to engender more conflicts at various levels of the health care system: from the one-on-one conversation between doctor and patient to the broader conversation between departments within a health care institution about whether, how, or how fast to integrate CAM therapies (for example, should an acupuncturist be ensconced in the anesthesia department or a chiropractor work alongside the orthopedic surgeon?). Much more theoretical and empirical work needs to be done to help bridge these divergent worlds and multiple levels of potential conflict. The approach suggested by principled negotiation provides a useful start. It assumes, however, that the parties are willing to negotiate and have incentives to do so.

CHAPTER TWO

Regulating Health Care Rogues

A Question of Pluralism

Implementing strategies for negotiating complementary and alternative medicine (CAM) therapies may lead to more rational discussion or inclusion of such therapies in conventional medical delivery. But as suggested, negotiation theory offers a tool for integration only if parties are willing to negotiate. And willingness to negotiate may not be present if one party does not acknowledge the other's legitimacy—that is, if one perceives the other to be a rogue that must be dismissed, regulated out of existence, or governed more tightly than one's own peer group.[1] This chapter addresses the acknowledgment of legitimacy that is a prerequisite to such willingness to negotiate, arguing that some acceptance of medical pluralism underlies the very possibility of negotiated conversations.

Medical pluralism as it pertains to CAM therapies implicates questions such as which tradition will dominate, which will be co-opted or assimilated, and how much respect will be accorded to medical traditions that seek understanding and implementation on their own (and not foreign) terms.[2] In other words, it may be difficult to discuss a movement toward greater medical pluralism without exploring how biomedical and legal communities incorporate, assimilate, or otherwise regulate what they consider to be health care rogues. Satisfactory inquiry into the process of accommodating pluralism requires sensitive attention to the nuances of language and posture that accompany the stated ideal of including in conventional care those CAM therapies "for which there is some high-quality scientific evidence of safety and effectiveness."[3]

This chapter explores one attempt to establish a scholarly basis for medical pluralism with regard to integration of conventional and CAM therapies in the new health care: a volume of essays titled *The Role of Complementary and Alternative Medicine: Accommodating Pluralism*, edited by Daniel Callahan, a distinguished philosopher, bioethicist, and founder of the Hastings Institute.[4] The chapter also explores one oppositional response that appeared in the pages of the *Journal of the American Medical Association*.[5]

The stated aim of *Accommodating Pluralism*, as suggested by the subtitle, was to break barriers and encourage negotiation (or at the least conversation) between the two polarities in medicine that Suzuki and colleagues had identified as West and East. The book's introduction suggested that biomedicine was in part "hostile" to CAM, while the review also responded by labeling the book's editor and authors as "advocates" of CAM therapies. By focusing on this illustrative clash, this chapter hopes to illuminate an emerging clash in worldviews about the new health care, a deadlock sometimes expressed in epithets rather than analysis.

In the process of separating rhetoric from clear thinking, the chapter will offer ways to frame the debate surrounding clinical recommendations involving CAM therapies; thoughts about the conflux of social and cultural, political, ideological, legal, and medical forces shaping this debate; and some possibilities for transformational perspectives concerning health, illness, and healing.[6] The chapter briefly describes the content of Callahan's book; analyzes the journal's critique and points out some flaws and distortions in that critique; and then offers some emerging potentialities for regulatory contemplation.

Conceptualizing Pluralism

Once defined as therapies not commonly used in U.S. hospitals or taught in U.S. medical schools,[7] CAM therapies now include modalities that sometimes are used adjunctively to biomedicine (for example, in-hospital massage for stress reduction and relief from depression, or acupuncture to help relieve nausea following chemotherapy) and sometimes are used for a specified time to see if a condition can be ameliorated less invasively or toxically than through conventional care. One widely accepted definition of CAM therapies that appears in *Accommodating Pluralism* is "a broad domain of healing resources that accompanies all health care systems, modalities, and practices and their accompanying theories and beliefs other than those intrinsic to the politically dominant health care of a particular society or culture in a given period."[8]

This definition differs from those offered earlier in emphasizing the politically volatile nature of CAM therapies: such modalities are predominantly defined by their exclusion from politically dominant channels. Though some CAM therapies have been shown to be safe and effective and others have been declared unsafe and/or ineffective in various clinical trials,[9] the definition emphasizes the primacy of political control rather than medical evidence.

In his introduction, Callahan articulates his vision for the book as "putting together a research group . . . with good critical faculties, aware of the arguments about, and objections to" CAM therapies "but able to make their own judgments . . . take it seriously, and yet . . . [be] quite willing to subject it to criticism." According to Callahan, the book attempts to address four basic problems: Is there only one acceptable method of scientific evaluation? How tolerant should medicine be of different methodologies and standards of evaluation? What does it mean to say that a therapy works or does not work? What is a suitable research agenda for alternative and complementary medicine?[10]

These are not legal, regulatory, or ethical questions but questions directed to the current rubric for measuring acceptance of CAM therapies. The questions challenge biomedical orthodoxy by explicitly asking whether the tools and conventions of biomedicine themselves are sufficient to explore CAM therapies with adequate rigor yet openness. Callahan suggests that examining the meaning of public interest in CAM therapies is "no less important" than examining efficacy; in fact, he argues, such examination transcends the current focus of the research agenda established by the National Institutes of Health for CAM therapies.[11]

The first chapter, "Assessments of Efficacy in Biomedicine: The Turn toward Biomedical Pluralism," strikingly presents the attempt to accommodate pluralism in an intellectually honest fashion. In his material on assessments of efficacy, author Schaffner questions the "unity of method for science practitioners" and argues that there is "no common method!" Rather, according to Schaffner, developments in the philosophy of science by Thomas Kuhn and Paul Feyerabend, among others, have "lent support to what have been termed variously relativist, instrumentalist, or constructivist analyses of scientific theories." Schaffner explains: "Relativists view scientific evidence as relative to an accepted paradigm. Instrumentalists view theories and hypotheses as tools, and not as purportedly true descriptors of the world. Constructivists . . . conceive of many biomedical entities . . . as being 'constructed' rather than 'discovered.' " Schaffner comments that while such positions are "attractive and even exciting to some," they are "distressing and outrageous to others." Further, these ultimately suggest a "methodological pluralism" in which science is seen as progressing by a "disunity" of methodologies. On this point, Schaffner concludes, "These disunity views open up the possibility that all methodologies may be local, and that complementary and alternative medicine may be pointing toward methods that diverge legitimately from traditional science. But appeals for a common unified (at least at a general level) methodology have their strong defenders in contemporary medicine."[12]

Having suggested a disunity of scientific methodology and discovery, Schaffner goes on to discuss the different kinds of study design typically used to answer different clinical questions; the differences between "efficacy" (an intervention shown to be superior to placebo in randomized controlled trials), "effectiveness" (that the treatment still works when used by the average clinician with the average patient), and "efficiency" (the level of resources required to produce benefit); and the different types of validation question dependent on the sense or type of scientific "evidence."[13] After laying this groundwork, Schaffner provocatively questions whether evidence is "*para-*

digm dependent," in the sense that "standard diagnostic categories, permissible measurement outcomes, and experimental design criteria represent an imperialistic 'Western' mode of thinking that obscures important health results only *evident* from a non-Western perspective." Schaffner admits that this may be an "overly strident" way of putting things, but he goes on to suggest that "just as . . . the notion of 'evidence' become[s] more complex on analysis, the notion of [what therapy] 'works' also has some subtle nuances."[14]

While Schaffner proceeds to spin out different variations of understanding what works, he ultimately subverts the argument for methodological pluralism and disunity by suggesting that although CAM may or may not have "different evidentiary standards," the best way to gather medical evidence may be to use the "tried and true methodologies" and "to have agreed-upon measures of abnormal physiology." Yet, Schaffner asserts in closing, "something *has* changed: CAM can help make us realize both that the influence of belief systems may have powerful effects on health and disease and that discerning these effects may require a relaxation of the most Procrustean standards." The dialogue, he claims, has "only begun."[15]

Whether or not Schaffner succeeds in unseating medical orthodoxy as the arbiter of scientific truth and thereby the sole determinant of validity for CAM therapies,[16] he raises enough provocative questions to stimulate the reader's thinking about pluralism in health care. He does so in a way that respects contemporary evidence-based, medical standards as an important—though not exclusive—method for determining what works. Weaning the reader from certainty to questioning, from absolutism to relativism, and from the despotism of declaration to the freedom of openness, Schaffner attempts to create a corresponding increase in ambiguity around the validity and meaning of CAM therapies. His work accords with Callahan's stated purpose, which is to handle pluralism with sensitivity, judgment, and respect for its bridging function.

A Critique of Pluralism

The review of *Accommodating Pluralism* critiques the book by asserting that the "vast majority" of chapters are nothing more than "defenses of CAM," and that each defense is fallacious. According to the review, the book's authors "attempt to discredit critics of CAM, they offer support for the view that CAM has worth and should be used to rectify some of mainstream medicine's shortcomings, and construct a very general, nonmedical justification for the study and/or practice of CAM."[17]

The review's logical fallacies illuminate medical pluralism's possibilities, perils, and challenges to current thinking. To begin, the review mischaracterizes the book as unabashed endorsement of CAM therapies. As Callahan notes in his introduction, the book's major aim is to move beyond the rhetoric of "hostility" by finding contributors that are sympathetic to CAM therapies yet have sufficient distance to be intellectually rigorous. In Schaffner's own chapter, for example, the objective is not to discredit critics but, on the contrary, to welcome them, yet in so doing to question methodological orthodoxy by asserting the plausibility of methodological pluralism. Similarly, in the chapter titled "Evidence, Ethics, and the Evaluation of Global Medicine," Wayne Jonas outlines a model for research strategies "that attempts to be true to the core scientific advances of the past century and yet allows for a more balanced role for research methods often considered secondary to experimental approaches."[18] Likewise, Loretta Kopelman, in her chapter on the role of science in assessing CAM therapies, argues that "even if we agree that science should play an essential role in testing conventional medicine and CAM, its role is limited . . . in some frames of reference."[19] Yet, "despite such limitations," Kopelman writes, "science has an essential role to play in all frames of reference that make causal claims about how to promote health or avoid illness."[20] These are hardly knee-jerk defenses of CAM.

The review also appears to dismiss the book's inclusion of disciplines such as philosophy, anthropology/ethnography, behavioral science and psychiatry, and sociology by labeling these "a very gen-

eral, nonmedical justification for the study and/or practice of CAM."
It perhaps would be more fitting to consider these disciplines from
the humanities as different sets of lenses through which to view
interest in CAM therapies. By including such new perspectives, the
book challenges biomedicine's historical tendency to regard itself as
ultimate arbiter of therapeutic meaning as well as value.

The second sentence of the review observes that "eight contributors hold the MD degree, six do not."[21] This observation is somewhat
ironic given that the reviewer is listed as having a Ph.D. but not an
M.D. The distinction between the M.D. and all other professionals in
the healing arts has a history, too: there was a time when biomedicine labeled CAM providers as "cult" practitioners;[22] used the ethical
code of physicians to forbid consultations with such providers;[23] and
engaged in anticompetitive practices such as those exposed in *Wilk v.
American Medical Association* (AMA), in which the Seventh Circuit
found a "nationwide conspiracy" by the American Medical Association's Committee on Quackery to "eliminate a licensed profession"
(namely, chiropractic).[24] This very history of hegemonic biomedical
authority over social definitions of illness and health[25] makes multiple scholarly lenses both useful and necessary.

Although the reviewer is critical of the interpretations and analyses in *Accommodating Pluralism* of controlled clinical trials, he is on
shaky ground in offering as a key reason for consumer use of CAM
that "it holds out promise of easy cure or because of advertising."
Dispensing with methodological rigor to prove a point, the reviewer
cites as evidence for this hypothesis his own sample of advertising
"in a single day on cable TV and radio that targeted a 'mature'
audience."[26] In lending personal testimony to this hypothesis, the
review overlooks or neglects law relevant to deception and fraudulent claims[27] and law relevant to false claims in advertising.[28] The
review also violates the scientific maxim that the plural of anecdote
is not evidence; at the least it sets up a double standard in relying on
the reviewer's experiences in a single day while dismissing the experiences of patients over time.

The review concludes that the "justifications" for CAM therapies
offered by *Accommodating Pluralism*, which include "cultural diver-

sity, pluralism, folk beliefs and psychology, spiritual values, and the instability of communal standards for objectivity," are all "logically and causally irrelevant to establishing the efficacy of any medical treatments."[29] But, as noted, neither Callahan nor his contributors affirms interest in pushing any of these notions as ways to establish medical efficacy. Rather, the editor and authors attempt to amplify policy discussions with considerations additional to conventional notions of medical efficacy. In other words, the book both questions monolithic notions of efficacy, effectiveness, and efficiency and addresses other policy considerations that might bear on patient access to a variety of therapies.

For example, the chapter written by Jonas suggests using research strategies that also respect the information preferences of audiences other than scientists and clinical researchers—including preferences of patients, practitioners, and policymakers. Jonas calls these new research strategies "a balanced pluralism." He does not repudiate existing strategies or the need to find accurate ways to measure medical efficacy. The point is that other values, perspectives, and considerations might bear on the debate as to the appropriateness of inclusion of such therapies in health care.[30]

Finally, the review argues that it would be a "waste of resources" to spend research funds on study of CAM therapies, since "my reading of the text under review convinces me that advocates of CAM" would simply dismiss negative study results by claiming that conventional study methods "cannot properly be used to test CAM."[31] The review's objectivity is compromised in a summary conclusion that the authors of chapters in *Accommodating Pluralism* necessarily ignore scientific evidence.

The review concludes that it may be "virtually impossible" to be both "sympathetic" to CAM therapies yet able to evaluate them objectively. This may be true, although Heisenberg's uncertainty principle also suggests that it might be impossible to evaluate just about anything objectively without subjectivity interfering. The review is far more generous in its concluding lines, which suggest an alternative, possible world of "caveat emptor," in which absent significant harm (reportable by law to a government agency), consumers can access CAM therapies at will, provided they are informed, in writing, that the therapy has no government-recognized evidence of effectiveness and that the treatment might produce harm. But this could be criticized as abandonment of evidence-based medical decision making and utter deference to consumer autonomy and choice, a kind of black-and-white thinking that does not represent the approach of "balanced pluralism" that Jonas and other contributors have urged.[32]

From Rogues to Negotiation Partners

As noted, *Accommodating Pluralism* offers a counterpoint to the historic rhetoric and rivalries between biomedical and CAM practitioners and infuses the debate with perspectives from disciplines such as philosophy, sociology, and anthropology. In so doing, the book seeks to substitute creative thinking for old dogmas. By squarely facing the question of medical pluralism and the need to move conversation via multidisciplinary dialogue, including an examination of the epistemological assumptions underlying contemporary biomedical critique of CAM systems, *Accommodating Pluralism* creates the possibility for negotiation between these differing perspectives, rather than outright dismissal. The book thus moves the present scenario from rivalry among rogues to the possibility of exchange between partners.

Arguably, both medical and regulatory perspectives on CAM therapies will benefit from a fresh look at how medicine and public policy have viewed the debate to date. Biomedicine emerged the victor in the sectarian rivalries of the late nineteenth century, with developments including the elimination of homeopaths as the major competitors to the "regular" physicians, the rise of faith in the power of scientific discovery, the growing power of the AMA as the most powerful voice in U.S. medicine, and the issuance by the Carnegie Foundation for the Advancement in Teaching of the *Flexner Report*, which advocated denying philanthropic funds to homeopathic and other medical schools outside a growing biomedical orthodoxy.[33] Medical licensing laws helped enforce biomedical dominance,[34] as did cases broadly interpreting the statutory proscription in different states against the unlicensed practice of medicine.[35] In large part, since the late nineteenth century, the legal paradigm has mirrored "biomedicine's historical view of holistic practice as deviant, suspect, or 'on the fringe.'"[36]

In similar fashion, ethical analysis of CAM therapies has reflected biomedical dominance and continues to echo stale notions of conventional versus CAM, the black-and-white, either/or, dualistic approach by which one system typically judges the other. Such analysis

> often rests on and builds in the assumptions, premises, and judgments of biomedicine. These include, for example, the following: an inherent skepticism or antipathy toward therapies outside the paradigm of biomedicine . . . ; the assumption that prevailing scientific models are the ultimate arbiter of evidence relating to health; the notion that regulation of complementary and alternative medical providers by and large is nonexistent or is less rigorous than regulation of comparable allied health professionals . . . ; the reliance on the material and physically demonstrable and the concomitant decision to decline to integrate the nonphysical . . . ; and the tendency, criticized even within biomedicine, to view medical events in isolation from sociological, psychological, and religious ones.[37]

Future Medicine argued that one way to move past these limitations might involve regarding CAM policy (and related ethical problem solving) as occupying a potential range of regulatory values, of which interest in controlling deviance by preventing fraud is only a first rung. Policy goals additional to fraud control would include quality assurance, health care freedom, functional integration, and human transformation. "Fraud control" refers to preventing dangerous and deceptive practices by CAM practitioners or by physicians and allied health providers delivering CAM modalities. "Quality assurance" means promoting professional standards so that products and therapies are relatively safe for public use and consumption. "Health care freedom" refers to safeguarding the flow of information so that consumers can feel they belong to a system in which they are allowed to make intelligent, autonomous health care choices. "Functional integration" means advancing the safe, effective, and appropriate clinical integration of all world systems of knowledge about healing. "Transformation" involves promoting healing of mind-body-spirit, igniting individuation, advancing human wholeness, and moving toward individual and collective enlightenment on the scale of planetary evolution.[38] This pyramid accounts for an expanded regulatory framework that takes account of a more robust range of human motivations and needs.

As suggested, such a hierarchy of regulatory values is analogous to the hierarchy of human needs hypothesized by psychologist Abraham Maslow.[39] Each regulatory need or value is important, yet each succeeding value can only emerge once the preceding ones have been fulfilled. Further, each regulatory value can be viewed as corresponding to one of the basic human needs identified by Maslow, with fraud control representing Maslow's "physiological needs," and transformation corresponding to Maslow's notion of "self-actualization."[40]

According to Maslow, a healthy society is one in which human beings are able to satisfy all five sets of needs; by analogy, health care regulation facilitates a healthy society when it incorporates the full range of values. On the other hand, focusing entirely on fraud control skews regulation and delivery of health care services in a way that protects biomedical dominance and prevents innovation: "That . . . [CAM] regulation to date has focused on the neurotic, the sick, and the despotic, rather than on the positive potential for human transformation, reflects, in Maslow's terms, the psychological predisposition and collective consciousness of those creating the regulatory structure. . . . As intellectual hostilities soften, a healthier, more positive dialogue may emerge."[41]

Such a positive dialogue between regulators, providers, and philosophers of biomedicine and CAM therapies may lead to a contemplation of the extent to which the process of seeking health—a word that is etymologically related to "wholeness" and "holiness"—involves a search for transcendence and growth beyond the cure of the body, whether the tools used are biomedical or CAM therapies, and whether the provider is a physician, allied health professional, or CAM professional.

Transforming Health Care Delivery

The acknowledgment of and search for transcendence alongside fraud control would transform delivery of health care, because integration ultimately requires tolerance, if not mutual respect, and an acknowledgment that pluralism has value. In conceptualizing those it regulates as rogues, policy cuts off the possibility of negotiation between differing perspectives and devalues patient interest in choice. On the other hand, in embracing the possibility of a broader framework for health, regulation can transform the spectrum of options, from allowing only the most material and biologically tangible to potentially including and even integrating those from foreign cultures and systems of thought.

The *Report on Complementary and Alternative Medicine* issued by the Institute of Medicine (IOM) at the National Academy of Sciences listed pluralism as a fourth value, together with the more traditional ethical values of nonmaleficence, beneficence, and autonomy. The report defined pluralism to include "a moral commitment of openness to diverse interpretations of health and healing," including "suspending any categorical disbelief in CAM therapies." Notions of pluralism were even inherent in the report's interpretation of nonmaleficence, embracing the values of "respecting divergent cultural beliefs; creating an emotionally safe environment for the discussion of CAM; and appreciating how CAM may fit into a patient's larger social, familial, or spiritual life." The report further added a fifth value—accountability—to include "consideration of the vast array of perspectives that constitute the national (and even international) heritage of healing traditions."[42]

By explicitly including pluralism as a value, the IOM report echoes Callahan's thesis that the biomedical community needs to embrace a more open attitude to a variety of healing traditions (and patients' choices regarding such traditions), even while maintaining the standards of good science and the ethical imperatives of nonmaleficence and beneficence. This approach accords with the liability, ethical, and negotiation frameworks presented earlier, in shifting from the either/ or, dualistic language of ethical/unethical, validated/implausible (and hence invalidated), and conventional (or orthodox)/unconventional (or unorthodox) to the more robust and inclusive language of medical pluralism. As suggested earlier, this translates into clinical practice as offering the patient full disclosure about the risks and benefits not only of applicable conventional therapies but also of potentially beneficial CAM therapies, likely interactions between conventional and CAM therapies, and possible dangers of delaying or deferring one therapy for the other. The other translation involves considering the ethical stance of accepting patient choices involving CAM, if supported by some level of safety and efficacy—even if below what the clinician personally finds acceptable—while continuing to closely monitor and standing ready to intervene conventionally.

In terms of Callahan's core questions, "Is there only one acceptable method of scientific evaluation?" and "How tolerant should medicine be of different methodologies and standards of evaluation," the IOM report clarifies that "the same principles and standards of evidence should apply regardless of a treatment's origin." The report notes that its "core message" is that "the same principles and standards of evidence of treatment effectiveness apply to all treatments, whether currently labeled as conventional medicine or CAM. Implementing this recommendation requires that investigators use and develop as necessary common methods, measures, and standards for the generation and interpretation of evidence necessary for making decisions about the use of CAM and conventional therapies."[43]

At the same time, the report not only discusses and describes innovative research methods to determine the safety and efficacy of various CAM therapies but also recognizes that

> the significance of a given therapeutic intervention may be less about efficacy on the physiological level and more about emotional health, coping, psychological growth, transformation, and self-actualization. Likewise, therapeutic efficacy may involve such

arguably vague but no less powerful spiritual themes as reconciliation with the divine or other formulations of "at-one-ment"
and wholeness, or simply, perhaps, a renewed or more expanded
sense of self. Stated in these terms, providers offering (and clients
availing themselves of) some of these therapies may focus less on
the kind of physiological results validated by evidence in medicine and public health and more on intangible, yet nonetheless
compelling, personal benefits. Such services may have less kinship with technologically oriented, biomedical interventions and
greater kinship with therapies at the borderland of psychological
and spiritual care that are offered in professions such as pastoral
counseling and hospice.[44]

The report's range from scientific research methods to the psychological and spiritual landscape of patient care is as enormous and
diverse as the ethical value of pluralism the report acknowledges.
Ultimately, the patient's spiritual quest and journey—with all its
nonscientific subjectivity, individuality, and lack of amenability to
the certainty and precision of conventional methodologies—may
become a critical and valued part of the discussion of clinical practice and of policy. So would the psychospiritual process of those
administering and regulating delivery of health care services. The
legal and ethical obligation of informed consent would subsume the
duty to discuss openly the possibility of cam therapies—such as yoga
and guided imagery—that may have some evidentiary backing in the
scientific literature but also touch on the patient's inner life as well as
objectively measurable biochemical reality.[45]

In such a world, medical efficacy and quality assurance fill in part
of the diagnostic and therapeutic picture, and disciplines such as
psychology, sociology, anthropology, and the rest of the humanities
would enrich the conversation concerning the patient's trajectory of
health and healing. Entirely new frontiers of bioethics might yield
new insights when opened to worldviews of selected cam therapies.[46] This would be a health care environment different from the
current one in which conventional and cam providers often find
themselves in adversarial political positions.

As suggested, integration has multiple domains for which the clinical sits at the base of the pyramid. It may be impossible to fashion integrative practice and policy without enriching current methods with new models of inquiry. One effort to broaden and deepen the dialogue involves examining the potential range of regulatory activity, focusing on how this might reflect not only health but consciousness itself.

Just as the summit at Abraham Maslow's hierarchy of basic human needs requires ever-expanding investigation, in similar fashion the summit of regulatory values remains largely unexplored, since most health care regulation governing CAM therapies is aimed at preventing fraud.[47] Maslow defined "self-actualization" as the summit of human experience, a state characterized by " 'ego-transcendence and obliteration, of leaving behind self-consciousness . . . [and] of fusion with the world and identification with it.' "[48] Certainly many CAM therapies speak to such states of being rather than only the eradication of physiological pathology; notions of balance, wholeness, and healing permeate the expressed philosophy of therapies such as acupuncture, chiropractic, and various somatic modalities, suggesting that—concerns for charlatanry notwithstanding—regulation ought to account for the need to safeguard clinicians' ability to evoke, nurture, and even guide such states during the healing journey.

If health care policy begins to consciously address the possibility of achieving these states, then institutions, regulators, and providers and their patients may find themselves reevaluating the current focus on fraud control and assessing the convergence of CAM and biomedical therapies in a softer, more humanistic light.[49] Here the Dalai Lama's challenge—which Suzuki has echoed—resonates in slightly different form: to transcend the world of constriction, of limiting beliefs, while remaining appropriately grounded in present methods and values.

CHAPTER THREE

Regulation, Religious Experience, and Epilepsy

Pluralism at the Frontier

As Chapters 1 and 2 have suggested, analytical frameworks from negotiation theory and practice as well as an ethical orientation toward accommodating pluralism can help relevant actors (such as governmental agencies, professional organizations, health care educational institutions, clinicians, attorneys, and patients and their families) navigate the borderland between the old and the new health care—between a care system based on science alone and one incorporating spirituality and insights from a variety of healing traditions. Yet, difficulty remains in integrating this transition into clinical care, a process that moves beyond the pages of academic debate between pluralism enthusiasts and opponents and into practical efforts to grapple with disease conditions (as well as therapies) that draw on the uncomfortable borderland between medicine and religion. Here lies one region where negotiations tend to cease, where dialogue rarely begins, and where the unknown frequently calls researchers and those who proselytize alike to stake a position.

Assume, for a moment, that using the framework in Chapter 1, regulators, institutions, and health care providers in the integrative care setting move from an either/or, black-and-white, yes/no approach to patient requests (and medical decisions) regarding use of complementary and alternative medicine (CAM) therapies to a negotiated exchange in which some minimal level of medical pluralism can be acknowledged. Assume further that, per Chapter 2, they are able to refrain from regarding each other as rogues and can engage in dialogue at a sufficiently respectful and sustained level as to move up the hierarchy of regulatory needs and recognize the patient's (and their own) interest in transcendence.

At this point new issues arise: the fact that the various CAM therapies themselves claim to occupy the full pyramid and address the entire range of needs that Maslow identified, from physiological needs to security needs to love and self-esteem needs to self-actualization. In other words, some CAM therapies purport to address the body or body and mind together (e.g., massage therapy for relaxation or St. John's Wort for depression), while others purport to operate on spiritual levels that aim to translate into physiological benefits (e.g., traditional oriental medicine to reduce "dampness," which may translate into faster healing from a bronchial condition or perhaps alleviation of grief). There are numerous typologies of CAM therapies;[1] some emphasize distinctions between biologically based modalities and modalities based on a "vital energy" (see Chapter 4).[2] The latter especially challenge biomedical dominance.

For our purposes, if we blend Maslow's pyramid of needs into Suzuki's broad categories of West and East, then CAM therapies can be categorized broadly into therapies that are more familiar to biomedical practice and scientific methods (such as the application of pressure to muscles for relaxation in massage therapy) and those more on the frontier, having to do with claims about transfer of healing intention and consciousness (such as spiritual healing).[3] But sometimes conditions and therapies on the frontier overlap with those in the more conventional realm. This chapter offers some preliminary suggestions for clinicians facing overlap and conflict between spiritual definitions of states of consciousness and medical definitions of associated disease states. The paradigmatic example is epilepsy.

Spiritual Healing and Frontier Science

One of the biggest controversies involving clinical consideration of CAM therapies arises when a given therapy lacks a satisfactory evidentiary basis for safety and efficacy yet offers hope and possibility to patients whose belief systems encompass spiritual forms of healing.[4] Though spiritual healing historically has been connected with religious movements, more recently the phenomenon has entered secular, clinical contexts such as nursing practice.[5] Indeed, there may be significant overlap between CAM therapies such as massage therapy and healing practices involving touch that suggest spiritual practice.

For example, chiropractic, one of the most commonly accessed CAM therapies, partly originated in its founder's interest in so-called magnetic healing (referring to the notion that a fluid "magnetism" exists between individuals) and shares ground with spiritual healing in its application of an intuitively guided, kinesthetic sense of the patient through sensations in the hands.[6] More recently, in acknowledging such interrelated phenomena as touch, emotional contact, and assertions by CAM practitioners regarding the possibility of non-biologically mediated healing mechanisms, the National Center for Complementary and Alternative Medicine has established a program for "frontier science," seeking scientific explanations regarding the mechanism of observed phenomena as well as methodological approaches to study them.[7]

Spiritual Healing and Epilepsy

The historic relationship between the study of epilepsy and religious experience suggests particular, potential associations between CAM therapies (and especially spiritual healing) and care for epileptic patients. There are at least two dimensions to this exploration: first, the widespread use of spiritual healing for treatment of epilepsy and, second, the hypothesized connection between epileptic seizures and mystical states.

A corollary to the latter inquiry is the question as to whether some seizures provide access to states of consciousness in which the patient glimpses an aspect of the divine, or whether the reported, numinous experience can simply be reduced to a series of biochemical responses. This simple corollary has been the subject of intense debates. Weighing in on one side, William James articulated his view that "whatever our organism's peculiarities, our mental states have their substantive value as revelations of the living truth; we wish that all this medical materialism could be made to hold its tongue." James argued that medical materialism "finishes up Saint Paul by calling his vision on the road to Damascus a discharging legion of the occipital cortex, he being an epileptic."[8]

Whether or not the view espoused by James is correct, the debate as to whether mystical experience is primarily transcendental and beyond the body (though it may, perhaps, also be understood to include the body) or merely a flash of neuronal or other physiological activity extends throughout philosophy as well as in psychology and offers one window into the study of disease conditions such as epilepsy and religious experience. This debate also is echoed in controversies concerning the validity of ideologies and approaches taken in CAM therapies to effectuate healing,[9] methodological and study design issues,[10] and discussions about hierarchy, supervision, status, and autonomy in integrative teams that include biomedical and CAM providers.[11] In particular, perspectives differ as to whether spiritual healing involves any readily identifiable, biological mechanism or embodies a more nebulous concept of "organizing principles of vitalism and life force which bring about a harmonizing of the whole person."[12]

Meanwhile, patients are turning to spiritual healing for treatment of epilepsy, particularly in cultures that value spiritual healing as part of their heritage. For example, a study in Nigeria evaluated the use of alternative treatment methods, in various forms, by epileptic patients who had used these therapies before seeking hospital treatment. Among the 265 epileptic patients, 47.6 percent used African traditional medicine alone, 24.1 percent combined traditional medicine with spiritual healing, 20.4 percent used spiritual healing alone, and 7.5 percent used other forms of alternative medicine.[13] Another report described the work of a neurologist affiliated with Michigan State University who spends three months a year treating epileptic patients in Zambia, where she works with native healers and combines her biomedical approaches with theirs.[14]

But even in the United States, patients increasingly are turning to complementary care approaches to help self-manage an epileptic condition. The CAM therapies used in this context include relaxation techniques, such as yoga, meditation, and biofeedback, to help control stress and thus reduce potential seizure activity; acupuncture and acupressure; and various nutritional therapies.[15] While patients can easily find self-help resources on the Internet, the medical evidence is not yet robust; for example, a 1999 systematic review to assess the efficacy of yoga in the treatment of people with epilepsy stated that no reliable conclusions could be drawn regarding the efficacy of yoga as a treatment for epilepsy.[16]

At the same time, while the medical evidence remains in flux, many proponents of CAM therapies and of religious healing in general suggest spiritual etiologies and treatments. For example, some Christian fundamentalists point to a passage in the New Testament in which Jesus healed an individual afflicted with epilepsy by casting out a spirit that had possessed him; the scriptural text points to faith, prayer, and fasting for treatment.[17] Shamanism, an ancient set of practices involving mediation between the physical world and the spirit world, also applies a kind of exorcising practice to help treat epilepsy, though practitioners are careful to point out the difference between voluntarily entering trance states to control spirits and possession or "mad" states, in which persons are hypothesized to be subject to involuntary control by spirits.[18] Doubtless, the phenomenon of access to trance states deserves much deeper study, as the spiritual healer's claim to enter such states at will and receive information through nonordinary, intuitive senses[19] may have parallels to the notion that a patient with temporal lobe epilepsy may imagine sounds or smells that do not come from the surrounding environment.

Legal Considerations in Spiritually Based Therapies

The legal issues relating to clinical inclusion of CAM therapies for conditions such as epilepsy are different from the legal issues
typically associated with epilepsy as a disability. The latter involve
such considerations as discrimination in employment, applicability
of the Americans with Disabilities Act, legal rules pertaining to state
driver licensing requirements, and family law considerations.[20]

Clinical inclusion of CAM therapies raises legal and regulatory
issues such as licensure and credentialing of appropriate CAM providers and therapies, malpractice liability considerations, informed
consent obligations, relevant food and drug law concerns, and issues
of third-party reimbursement.[21] While previous chapters also have
suggested various frameworks to help clinicians decide which CAM
therapies to recommend, avoid and discourage, or accept and monitor, legal concerns may be heightened when contemplating therapies
that have an overt or explicit spiritual dimension. In such situations,
the boundaries between medicine and religion can blur, and patients
may have heightened sensitivity to conversations about spiritual dimensions of illness, as well as to suggestions concerning spiritual
therapeutics.

Patients also may wish to discuss with their physicians concerns
about their interactions with spiritual healers. The spiritual healer
acts not only as a confidant and therapist but also as a medium that
purportedly channels the energies of the divine.[22] As such, the client
may be especially vulnerable to abuse of power and authority, "by
virtue of claimed access to specialized, intuitive information—that
is, access to the shamanic worlds of non-ordinary consciousness that
give the healer a privileged glimpse into the client's condition and
potential mechanisms to resolve the client's health care issues or
crisis."[23]

Boundaries may be more permeable, and therefore more difficult
to maintain, when CAM therapies cross into spiritual realms and
invoke insights and healing energy from spiritual beliefs and traditions. While legal rules exist to address potential boundary violations (see Chapter 6), a beginning entry into boundary control is

recognizing that some CAM therapies—like disease states such as epilepsy—may move the clinician into the borderland, medicine's gray edge, where belief systems and the nondual, nonmaterial world of spirit may hold the patient's physical, mental, and emotional allegiance. It is through this difficult in-between zone that the clinician often must navigate when venturing into the new dimensions that "integrative care" can present.

From an autonomy perspective, it becomes even more important in these situations to attempt to honor patient choices and preferences and see their value in possible religious as well as clinical dimensions. Maintaining open communication and respecting patients' perspectives and preferences also can help diminish liability risk and can keep patients open to conventional intervention when medically necessary because CAM therapies fail or pose undue risks.

At the same time, from the perspective of nonmaleficence, it becomes critical to caution and monitor patients who may place undue reliance on spiritual experience to the exclusion of healthy grounding in medical (and psychological) realities. Mystical states should not be dismissed as epileptic fits; neither should epilepsy fail to be diagnosed and treated as a solely religious phenomenon. Here the negotiation in the borderland of medicine and religion requires a practitioner to have sufficient openness to a pluralistic perspective to acknowledge experiences that may partake of both worlds, while maintaining sufficient boundaries to intervene with conventional medical and mental health care when necessary.

A recent study discussed the importance of navigating this gray zone. The study noted that although patients often disagree with medical recommendations for religious reasons, most physicians intuitively navigate the tension between patient preferences and medical judgment.[24] The study also found that conflict introduced by religion is common and occurs in three types of settings: those in which religious doctrines directly conflict with medical recommendations, those that involve an area in which there is extensive controversy within the broader society, and settings of relative medical uncertainty in which patients "choose faith over medicine." The study found that, in response to such conflict, physicians first seek to accommodate patients' ideas by remaining open-minded and flexible in their approach. However, if they believe patients' religiously informed decisions will cause them to suffer harm, then physicians make efforts to persuade patients to follow medical recommendations.

The study's results and conclusions accord with those of the frameworks presented earlier. If there is a direct conflict between patient preferences for CAM (or religion) and medical recommendations, and medical intervention is imminently necessary, the clinician's ethical stance (and liability management strategy) must be to try to persuade the patient to accept conventional intervention. On the other hand, if the clinical situation involves an arena where there is no strong evidence for the conventional therapy or the treatment is invasive or toxic, the clinician's ethical stance (and liability management strategy) can include accepting the patient's choice of CAM therapies (including spiritually based treatments) while continuing to monitor conventionally.

In short, while CAM therapies generally offer unique legal and regulatory as well as clinical issues, concerns often are heightened when the new health care moves into spiritual realms. Although historically, healing in the religious and spiritual realms has co-existed with medicinal healing on the physical level, in modern times, there appears to be increasing convergence among different systems of knowledge and in consumer (as well as clinician) interest in bridging these various approaches to health and healing. Thus the frontier between material and spiritual presents a major hurdle for those seeking to move beyond rhetoric and toward integration.

Awareness of arenas in which medicine and religion seem to converge may help clinicians empower patients toward greater self-knowledge and self-care in the management of disease and their healing. Such awareness and tolerance on the clinician's part may offer greater possibility for the kind of negotiated exchange that supports a respectful pluralism.

CHAPTER FOUR

Healing, Environment, and Ecology

Reassembling the Broken Fragments

The emergence of the holistic health movement in the 1960s coincided with other social movements, such as feminism, protest against the war in Vietnam, reactions to endemic racism, experimentation with mind-altering drugs, and other more liberalized attitudes and behaviors that loosened the ideological and behavioral strictures of the preceding decade. The expanded consciousness representing exploration of a more open society included greater awareness of links between wholeness of the person—attention to health at the micro level—and wholeness of the society, or health at the macro level. Proponents of bodywork, meditation, and so-called Eastern spirituality tended to identify with social movements reacting against their more conservative, "square" counterparts as holistic health, too, assumed an antiestablishment bent. This identity as "other than" persisted as the movement morphed into "alternative medicine" in the 1970s and 1980s, with the distinguishing feature being its status as other than the medicine that had been accepted as dominant, orthodox, or mainstream. The decade of uns and nons reflected this status of being defined as other.

Yet even as the new label, "complementary and alternative," began to reflect greater penetration of CAM therapies into the mainstream,[1] and "integrative medicine" expressed acceptance of CAM therapies and providers within major academic medical centers, links between notions of "vital energy"—the philosophical thrust behind many of these therapies—and the liberalizing social movements of the 1960s remained. This association made eminent sense (although ironically, the old polarity is breaking down, with groups such as the Defense Department, for example, interested in CAM therapies such as guided imagery to calm and center troops and facilitate group cohesion). In general, meditation, acupuncture, chiropractic, naturopathic or natural medicine, yoga, nutritional practices such as juicing, and somatic therapies including reflexology and shiatsu all reflect emphasis on encouraging the individual's inherent balance and wholeness, a process of stimulating the best of what lies within, rather than using pharmaceutical products, surgery, or invasive technological interventions aimed at acute cures. Makers of commercial products try to capitalize on this orientation toward what is "healing" or "natural" by pitching advertising toward the movement's consciousness of honoring nature.

The orientation toward notions of health and wholeness within resonates with efforts to seek harmony in the outer environment as well—hence connections between healthy living through CAM practices such as yoga and nutritional therapies and, for example, the "green" environmental movement to use alternative fuel sources (such as solar energy) or natural building materials (such as rammed earth or straw bales rather than concrete). Similarly, there is a liaison, for instance, between mindfulness as a therapeutic technique and attention to mindfulness regarding our environmental stewardship. Healing has macroscopic as well as microscopic implications, and negotiating the new health care territory, in which conventional and CAM therapies are interwoven, might influence other social movements and institutions other than those involved with health care.

In its 2001 report titled *Crossing the Quality Chasm*, the Institute of Medicine (IOM) had observed that fragmentary, incremental change would be insufficient to achieve levels of quality improvement in health care. Rather, "fundamental redesign" was required. The report stated that current models of health care were "broken" and that the system needed to be fixed. In part, the IOM's 2005 report, *Complementary and Alternative Medicine*, posed integrative health care as one approach to mending the broken system and as embodying the earlier report's recommendations for change—more specifically, as presenting evidence-based, patient-centered solutions focusing on a process of shared decision making.[2] At the same time, one can fairly argue that negotiating integrative health care offers possibilities beyond mending communication failures, improving systems, or otherwise enhancing the quality of care; rather, the radically different philosophical premises of CAM therapies such as acupuncture, Ayurvedic or Tibetan medicine, or energy healing pose new models for conceptualizing health and healing.

The contradictory, broken world of either/or explored earlier in this book includes such questions as

- Can we accept acupuncture's efficacy in the face of traditional oriental medicine's insistence on the existence of chi, yet without a mechanistic explanation satisfactory to contemporary science?
- Can we accept Tibetan pulse diagnosis as a valid means of detecting imbalance—albeit through a medical system foreign to biomedicine—without reducing its power to relationship, empathy, and placebo?
- Can we integrate spiritual therapies for conditions such as epilepsy without understanding the biological basis for their purported operation, yet without dismissing them as magical mumbo-jumbo?
- Can we accept pluralism without imposing hegemony, on one hand, yet without sacrificing standards, on the other?

In this chapter, the inquiry continues:

- How do we handle the frontier zones without lapsing into critical dismissal, on one hand, and uncritical acceptance, on the other? What is the role of our understanding of consciousness in negotiating these diverse worlds, in mediating the biological and the transpersonal, the material and the spiritual? Is there a connection between our relationship to nature and our understanding of healing?

All these questions squarely force the epistemological question: Is reality only what we know as proven to the satisfaction of present, prevailing scientific and medical communities, or can health care embrace alternative, complementary, and frankly foreign or even antithetical, parallel, or intellectually challenging and disruptive paradigms? How does our collective response to this question shape other considerations, such as our relationship to the environment in our quest for health? This chapter broadens the inquiry from consideration of therapies at the frontier to consideration of the frontiers of the therapeutic process itself, through emerging links between healing, wholeness, consciousness, and the environment. Such links flow from the nature of spiritually based (or spiritually oriented) CAM therapies, which occupy the place of "frontier medicine," including the notions that intention and consciousness affect the healing process.[3]

The latter are particularly controversial, especially in medical contexts in which proof of safety, efficacy, and mechanism normally are viewed as prerequisites to clinician recommendations involving such therapies. For many within the biomedical community, these therapies are clinically unacceptable. In regulating physician use of CAM therapies, one state medical board (Kentucky) classifies all of these therapies into three categories: invalidated, nonvalidated, and validated. It includes as invalidated any therapy that "is implausible on a priori grounds (because its implied mechanisms or putative effects contradict well established laws, principles, or empirical findings in physics, chemistry or biology)."[4]

Yet despite the argument that "implausible" therapies cannot be valid, many CAM therapies are premised on epistemological assumptions that challenge current biomedical canons. The idea that intention matters in healing is linked to notions of vital energy or spiritual energy in many CAM therapies, from chiropractic to acupuncture.[5] Non-Western medical traditions (such as acupuncture and traditional oriental medicine, Tibetan medicine, and Ayurvedic medicine) may be premised on such broader notions of an underlying, unifying structure behind and through material reality and thus claim to occupy a larger sphere than medical science has, to date, been able to prove (e.g., the notion of chi in acupuncture being broader than the limited acceptance by biomedicine of acupuncture as safe and effective for the treatment of nausea following chemotherapy). The concept of spiritual energy has correspondences in numerous cultures. Words such as *chi*, *ankh*, *gana*, *ki*, *prana*, *pneuma*, and *waken* all refer to a flow of vital force from a realm of Spirit that infuses the material world with healing capacity.[6]

Further, the understanding of CAM therapies involving spirituality has profound implications for regulation and policy. If such therapies are considered medically implausible and politically unacceptable, they are less likely to reach consumers through legislative mechanisms such as licensure and hospital mechanisms such as credentialing for relevant providers.[7] On the other hand, to the extent the regulatory system embraces and allows consumer access to such therapies, the consumer's experience of health care may be transformed in unexpected ways. Consider, for example, the impact that the availability of hospice has had on quality of care and decision making at the end of life, or the impact on patients of the use of healing rituals in hospitals.[8]

At the least, adding the notion of healing to the goal of curing suggests the possibility of expanding definitions of health beyond mechanistic and reductionistic views of human life, to embrace transformative aspects of the care process.[9] Such expanded definitions of healing and health are the subject of two important books whose themes concern, respectively, the ecology of awareness and the awareness of ecology. The selected publications epitomize an emerging tension around the role of science in understanding healing. The two books highlight conflicts around what we know, how we know it, and how we use what we think we know to judge what is valid in health care.

In *Healing, Intention, and Energy Medicine*, editors Wayne B. Jonas and Cindy C. Crawford bring together extensive research on spiritual healing, mind-body phenomena, and the role of intentionality in health. In so doing, they credit the "frontier" area of spirituality in health care with scientific underpinnings and thus help validate the notion that spiritual approaches have some efficacy, or at least impact, on the material plane.[10] On the other hand, Derrick Jensen, in *A Language Older Than Words*, describes the preverbal, universal connectivity that binds all species in the ecology web underpinning our technocratic social order. Jensen, trained in physics and psychology, disclaims the hegemonic power of science to order our conception of reality and freeze our ideology into a consciousness of dominance and exploitation.[11]

These books are contrapuntal. One uses science in service of human healing; the other disclaims science in service of planetary healing. Metaphorically, they are the counterparts of Tennyson and Basho. Jonas represents the effort to understand spiritual healing by taking it apart, like Tennyson's rose, and subjecting it to rigorous clinical trials; Jensen represents Basho in understanding spiritual healing by the satori experience of encountering a duck in his yard. Both books, one might argue, represent extraordinary contributions to the quest for understanding health and disease at their most fundamental levels—for example, ecological as well as individual— and for illuminating the possibilities for healing on the planetary as well as individual levels. Both books are particularly relevant to considerations regarding treatment of neurological diseases such as epilepsy, in which links between mind and body (and ways to improve communication or coordination between the domains of each) are of particular concern and study, and in which connections have been proposed between neurological conditions and mystical states.[12]

This chapter highlights common themes in both books and frames them in the context of legal regulation of CAM practices. The chapter places the research on healing and intention in the context of debates around legal regulation of healing; focuses on Jensen's contention that the locus of ecological violence is the urge to dominate and subdue—motivated by the fear to confront wounds and vulnerability; further explores Jensen's notions of ecological and interspecies healing; and offers reflections on links between research into healing and intentionality, Jensen's description of interspecies communication, and regulatory values in health care. The chapter concludes with broader thoughts about links between spirituality in medicine and in law.

Understanding and Defining Healing

IS HEALING REAL? DOES IT WORK?

Jonas and Crawford preface their edited volume with the observation that healing practices using "direct mental or spiritual techniques, such as prayer, ritual, dream work, imagery, direct mental intentions, and laying-on of hands," have been part of "all known cultures." Yet, the scientific community has largely neglected to investigate such practices and their claims.[13] In this light, the editors state that their volume aims to address three important questions: Are the effects of healing "real" as examined by high-quality, independently reproduced experiments? How big are the effects of healing interventions? What clinical impact does healing have in real-life clinical situations?[14]

In attempting to answer these questions, the editors cite (and highlight) relevant literature in six areas they identify as central to the inquiry:

(1) Health correlates of spiritual and religious practices
(2) Intercessory or healing prayer
(3) "Energy" healing approaches
(4) Therapeutic *qigong* (Chinese energy healing)
(5) Direct mental interaction with living systems
(6) Mind-matter interaction studies.[15]

Regarding these six areas, the book's two major sections respectively offer "critical summaries of current research on healing" and "methods and challenges for research on healing."[16] Chapters in the first section summarize research on such topics as the health impact of religious and spiritual practices, intercessory and healing prayer, remote viewing, therapeutic effects of music, and the impact of healing in a clinical setting. Chapters in the second section address such topics as models, measurement descriptors and outcomes measures in healing research, qualitative methods for healing research, and challenges particular to healing research.

The articles in each section are rich with mini-observations. For example, introducing a healer into the clinical care of chronically ill patients dramatically increases doctor-patient openness and communication,[17] or "emotionally engaging situations are the source of an 'active information field' that may be actualized as reduced entropy in appropriately designed random physical systems" (translation: emotionally charged intention can affect random-number generators).[18] There are also many provocative conclusions, such as those in a chapter on "anomalous cognition," or AC, a term to describe "information transmitted from one person to another (commonly known as telepathy), from a non-living source to a person (commonly known as clairvoyance), and from the future to the present (commonly known as precognition)." The authors state that "distance does not dampen AC performance," and "AC performance peaks at about 13.5 hours local sidereal time, when the location of the experiment is orthogonal to the center of the galaxy, and dips at about 18 hours local sidereal time, when the location of the experiment is pointed toward the galactic center."[19]

Finally, the book includes an unusually extensive, annotated bibliography of clinical research on healing[20] and a "comprehensive" bibliography of "spiritual healing, 'energy' medicine, and intentionality research."[21] Even these bibliographies contain much material of potential interest to anthropologists, sociologists, philosophers, students of religion, and other scholars in the humanities, as well as those interested in medicine, public health, ethics, and health care regulation and policy. For example, one trial was designed to "answer the question: Does intercessory prayer to the Judaeo-Christian God have any effect on the patient's medical condition and recovery while in the hospital?" (The conclusion was that "there seemed to be an effect in favor of supplemental prayer, and that effect was beneficial"; among other things, "fewer patients in the prayer group required ventilatory support, antibiotics, or diuretics").[22] Similarly, another trial was designed to "determine the effect of therapeutic touch on people stressed by a hurricane or its after-effects" (results showed a "decrease in perceived stress").[23]

In their preface, Jonas and Crawford summarize the literature as "over 2200 published reports, including . . . 122 laboratory studies, 80 randomized controlled trials, 128 summaries or reviews, 95 reports of observational studies and non-randomized trials, 271 descriptive studies, case reports, and surveys, [and] 1268 other writings."[24] Their key observations include that there is "a positive relationship between religious practices and reduced mortality, better physical health, improved quality of life, and less mental illness and drug abuse"; that 46 percent of randomized controlled trials on prayer reported "significant effects on at least one health outcome"; and that 58 percent of randomized controlled trials of energy healing (usually Therapeutic Touch) reported "positive effects."[25]

Beyond presenting these figures, Jonas and Crawford assign ratings to and comment on the level of evidence for each of these conclusions, offering caveats to any potentially misleading interpretation of results.[26] They conclude that "there is evidence to suggest that mind and matter interact in a way that is consistent with the assumptions of distant healing. Mental intention has effects on non-living random systems . . . and may have effects on living systems." They further conclude that preliminary studies "suggest that chronically ill patients may benefit from spiritual healing," adding that belief in energy healing by *both* patient and practitioner contributes "significantly" to a healing effect. Jonas and Crawford also suggest that further research be pursued.[27] Specifically, they recommend, there is an urgent need to establish "consciousness and healing research laboratories" with multidisciplinary scientific expertise, to develop a "biological model for exploring healing effects," and to "conduct a multicenter healing impact study," including partnering with organizations interested in healing research.[28]

HEALING WITHIN ENERGY MEDICINE

The term "energy medicine" lacks a uniform definition, a unifying body of scientific knowledge, or a coherent professional community that agrees on its meaning. "Energy medicine" sometimes is used to describe approaches to health and healing that rely on use of vital (or "subtle") energies, such as transfer of intention to heal into actual physical healing. In other contexts, the term "energy healing" may be used to describe a specific collection of therapies, such as Therapeutic Touch and Reiki, as opposed to the larger set of approaches including intercessory prayer.[29]

In linking "healing," "intention," and "energy medicine" in their title, Jonas and Crawford note the interrelationship between the domains of research outlined, notions of what "healing" means, the role of one's conscious intention in giving and receiving healing, and the mysterious notion of healing "energy." As Jonas explains, the definition of "energy" in "energy medicine" is "not clear. The concept is ambiguous, holding itself at a mid-point between mind and matter. . . . The concept . . . often has characteristics similar to consciousness or spirit, yet is also treated like a physical substance that can be stored, enhanced, projected, and withdrawn."[30]

Jonas and colleagues also use another term, "focused intention." They explain that the "focused intention" that healers use in the practice of energy healing itself "is known by a number of terms, including: paranormal healing, psychic healing, psychokinesis (PK), laying-on of hands, bio-PK, external hands-on healing, non-contact therapeutic touch, healing with intent, spiritual healing, bioenergy, biofield therapy, telekinesis, natural healing, distant or remote mental influence on living systems (DMILS) or Reiki . . . [or] 'bioenergy.' " The chapter's authors note that many cultures believe that "certain individuals mediate 'supernatural' healing powers"—yet another way of describing the phenomenon.[31]

One of the chapters in Jonas and Crawford's book describes energy medicine within the larger context of the relationship between science and spirituality. In this chapter, David Hufford purports to explain why it is so difficult to describe energy medicine and spirituality within conventional scientific parameters. He proposes that scientific inquiry may be biased against findings that spirituality can affect material events because of the notion that "all paranormal effects . . . break natural law"; he argues that this is a "large claim, and often repeated, though one that is quite dubious."[32]

According to Hufford, healing "has been associated . . . with spirituality and religion" and thereby unfairly considered "obsolete and/or disreputable by mainstream science."[33] Hufford contends that healing must develop "a solid infrastructure of scholarly" data and analysis for "theory and practice to grow in a thoughtful manner" and to counter the "negative stereotypes" that perpetuate misunderstanding (e.g., that healing is based on obsolete historical notions such as mesmerism or relies on notions that are beyond theoretical plausibility).[34]

While Hufford does not entirely resolve the split between science and spirituality, his discussion augments the effort by Jonas and Crawford to describe the role of healing as a common thread between spirituality in medicine and energy therapies. As Jonas and colleagues assert in various ways, both fields have been marginalized at worst and neglected at best. When one considers the larger field of CAM therapies, the energy therapies fall at the more frontier end of the spectrum in terms of scientific understanding and acceptance. On the other hand, while there are many typologies for classifying CAM therapies,[35] one useful way to think of these therapies is in terms of those that are more likely to fall within biomedicine (e.g., proven safe and effective in biomedical terms); those falling within energy medicine; and those straddling both.[36] CAM therapies such as nutritional approaches to healing, for example, might cross over into the biomedical arena, while the healing benefits described for the Native American sweat lodge rely on spirituality and would be difficult to test or understand in a mechanistic fashion.

As suggested, these distinctions are more than academic. They shape scientific research agendas, the politics and ideologies around CAM therapies, acceptance and use within hospitals, decisions regarding third-party reimbursement, and issues of credentialing and licensure.[37] In bringing together a body of scientific research and knowledge concerning therapies involving "healing, intention, and energy medicine," Jonas and Crawford help sculpt a potentially new field of inquiry that cuts across health care fields. They draw together the potential implications of intentionality and consciousness for various forms of clinical care across medical disciplines, as well as for medical research within its numerous domains. The question is whether enhancing the credibility of energy therapies through a careful collection of scientific research and commentary will change the marginal status of such therapies and whether this effort can credibly focus the medical community's attention on the effect of the provider's intention on healing and the therapeutic relationship.

Healing Ecological Violence

Jensen's anguished outpouring concerning ecological violence—and the awareness required for planetary healing—echoes the focus of Jonas and Crawford on the effects of healing, intention, and energy. Two aspects of Jensen's work in particular reflect on the potential critique CAM offers biomedicine generally and on the potential contribution of healing and energy medicine to an emerging synthesis of CAM and biomedicine that touches on neurological and other diseases involving mind-body and brain-body connections. First is Jensen's criticism of Cartesian dualism as a kind of original emotional sin—a deviation from humanness that has led to ecocide and dehumanizing behavior as regards the environment.

Jensen observes that Descartes' famous dictum, "I think, therefore I am," led to a philosophical splitting of mind and body and of thinking and feeling. Even more fundamentally, it located the center of existence in the abstract world of mentation rather than in the living world of felt interconnectedness with all that is. Jensen writes that had he been present when Descartes "came up with his famous quip . . . I would have put my arms around his shoulder and gently tapped, or I would have punched him in the nose, or I might have taken his hands in mine, kissed him full on the lips, and said, 'René, my friend, don't you *feel* anything?' "[38]

Jensen further laments, "Why hadn't he said, 'I love, therefore I am,' or 'I breathe, therefore I have lungs,' or 'I defecate, therefore I must have eaten,' or 'I feel the weight of the quill on my fingers and rejoice in the fact that I am alive, therefore I must be?' " Jensen's analysis goes further than holistic health care's critique of Cartesian dualism as responsible for a split between care for the patient's body and care for the spirit. According to Jensen, Cartesian dualism has led to biomedicine's neglect of life as embodied spirit. The failure to recognize the embodiment of the living soul within flesh, heart, saliva, and alimentary canal represents the fundamental "narcissism" of Western culture and leads to "a disturbing disrespect for direct experience and a negation of the body."[39]

Descartes, according to Jensen, "philosophized [human beings] out of subjective existence," and as a result, his medical and other progenitors "eventually agreed that subjective personhood should . . . not be granted to those . . . whose voices they chose not to hear" and who therefore could be exterminated, robbed, enslaved, or exploited. Jensen concludes with an ominous epitaph: "Searching for certainty, René Descartes became the father of modern science and philosophy. . . . By substituting the illusion of disembodied thought for the experience . . . and most importantly by substituting control, or the attempt to control, for the full participation in the wild and unpredictable process of living, Descartes became the prototypical modern man."[40]

Philosophically, Cartesian dualism opened the way for biomedical mechanism, or the tendency to view the body as a machine composed of isolated parts, and reductionism, or the tendency to reduce the complex phenomenon and experience of illness to a diagnostic category. From the perspective of health care policy and regulation of CAM therapies, an understanding of Cartesian reductionism can help frame the movement toward greater acknowledgment of holism (a stated feature of CAM), the tendency to view human health (and the process of dis-ease) as a whole system involving mind, body, spirit, relationships, and environment.[41]

The second important contribution Jensen makes to consideration of healing—whether ecological or medical—is his emphasis on the need to reverse the consciousness of exploitation and dominance that, he claims, is embedded in our culture. Jensen irreverently muses on whether he should assassinate two senators "whose work may be charitably described as unremittingly genocidal and ecocidal."[42] He then compares this "thought experiment" to an argument about whether it would have been appropriate to attempt to assassinate Hitler.[43] On the latter point, he concludes there is no right answer: "If we fail to fight them we die, and if we fight them we run the risk of becoming them."[44] On the former, he concludes that even were he to assassinate the two senators, "they would simply be replaced by two more people with the same worldview," since "the shared nature of the destructive impulse" embodied in their psyches "would continue, making their replacement as easy as buying a hoe."[45] Jensen morosely concludes that there is "no way" to transition to a culture that is compassionate to the environment—that is, one in which the two senators would not be replaced instantaneously, like the heads of the mythological Greek hydra. "The best we can hope for," he argues, "is that we begin to throttle down our overblown technology, to bring ourselves to a soft landing instead of a full crash."[46]

Jensen assuages his grief, nursing himself through his pessimistic side, by asserting his essential connection with all of nature. He does so by noticing that when he opens himself up to the presence of the pine trees, the flies, and the ants, and to "every grasshopper, every struggling salmon, every unhatched chick, every cell of every blue whale," he realizes "it is no longer possible to be lonely." For Jensen, who is deeply in kinship with Emerson and the transcendentalists, healing means to "hurl ourselves against and through the literal and metaphorical concrete that contains and constrains us, that keeps us from talking about what is most important to us, that keeps us from living the way our bones know we can, that bars us from our home."[47]

Healing, for Jensen, is more than pursuing a specific political agenda or course of environmental activism; it is about recognizing the soul's wholeness in its acknowledgment of relationship with every other subject (and object) in the environment. In other words, sustaining a positive healing intention means relationship and recognition of shared interdependence and interconnection; it is living in the web of life rather than seeking to use and exploit it. In Jensen's view, we are part of the world, realizing ourselves within and through it, and "it is only our own fear that sets us apart."[48]

Jensen's focus on humans' interconnection with nature parallels the scientific research on healing and intentionality and the potential applications of healing intentionality to therapeutic processes. Jensen addresses the macro level at its most expansive: humanity amidst the planetary ecosystem. Jonas and Crawford, at least initially, address a more micro level: healing of the individual within the fragile ecosystem of his or her mind, body, and spirit. The two worlds operate in parallel and are bound by the influence of focused intention.

Healing and Interspecies Communication

One of the more provocative meditations in Jensen's book is his insistence, within the framework of his environmental activism and awareness, that interspecies communication not only is an authentic possibility for the spiritually gifted or aware but may be available to all. Jensen's writing suggests that the ability to communicate deeply with nature is an inherent part of the human birthright, available to anyone who directs attention—intention—to our fellow travelers in the animal and mineral worlds. Further, the notion of interspecies communication is deeply relevant to integrating CAM therapies in conventional care. To the extent that CAM therapies involve spiritual conceptions at the frontiers of biological "plausibility," they presage deeper connections between matter and spirit and self and other, and a blurring between notions of human and nonhuman, individual and cosmos, "animate" and "inanimate," and one's own energy and that of the environment.

Indeed, the genesis of his book, he acknowledges, was a conversation between him and the coyotes surrounding his farm. While at first he was a skeptic and later wondered whether he was crazy, he came to conclude that "pigs, dogs, coyotes, squirrels, even rivers, trees, and rocks: all these . . . were speaking *and listening* if only we too would enter into conversation."[49]

The possibility of such interspecies communication has profound implications for diagnostic and therapeutic processes as well as environmental policy. Already extensive research supports the therapeutic benefits of such activities as pet therapy, suggesting the healing effects of the strong bonds between species. If other species can make their wishes and gifts known to us in direct ways, then our relationship with them may have the capacity to heal at deeper levels than previously assumed. In other words, the relationship between humans and the environment may be a therapeutic one because of a more equal exchange, and not merely a passive, one-way communication between dominant species and mute witnesses to human supremacy.

Jensen emphasizes the importance of such a bilateral relationship, observing that "ownership as practiced by our culture is an expression of a will and capacity to control, and even to destroy." The Western view of nature typically follows the biblical example in which Adam, the progenitor, was invited to name the animals and thereby have "dominion" over them. This is hardly a stance of interspecies equality. Jensen, on the other hand, also provocatively suggests that we "stand the notion of ownership on its head" by asking, "what if I do not own the barn, but instead it owns me, or better, we own each other? What if I do not view it as my right to kill mice simply because I can, and because a piece of paper tells me I own their habitation? What if, because their habitation is near my own, I am responsible for their well-being?"[50]

He calls this a "relationship of mutual care" that involves mutual respect—a view of life as "a web of immeasurably complex and respectful relationships." In this view, the "evolutionary purpose" of life is "for each of us to take responsibility for all those around us, to respect their own deepest needs, to esteem and be esteemed by them, to feed and feed off them, to be sustained by their bodies and eventually sustain them with our own."[51]

Within this paradigm, Jensen observes that the "evidence of interspecies communication and the fundamental *beingness* of nonhumans is so obvious as to render my previous skepticism embarrassing." He even urges that to "attempt a proof" would be "degrading" as well as "silly," and that the proof consists in two words: "*pay attention*" and "*listen*."[52] He offers many instances in which he received information from his animal and insect companions—information revealing their keen awareness of their environment and his role and interaction as well as theirs within that environment. The examples include kinship and cooperation within nature, as well as his perceptions of direct messages or signals from nature to him.

One could critique Jensen as anthropomorphizing nature; his observations, however, go far beyond the mythological attribution of human characteristics to the nonhuman. Jensen summarizes: "There is another kind of revolution, one that does not emerge from the culture, from philosophy, from theory, from thought abstracted from sense, but instead from our bodies, and from the land. It, too, is part of this language older than words. . . . It is not the attempt to seize power or the industrial 'means of production,' but it is actions based upon the instinctual drive to survive, and to live with dignity."[53] Later he adds, "There is a language older by far and deeper than words. It is the language of the earth, and it is the language of our bodies. It is the language of dreams, and of action. It is the language of meaning, and of metaphor. . . . To follow this language of metaphor is to trace words back to our bodies, back to the earth."[54]

Restating his message, he reports a conversation in which philosopher Thomas Berry told him, "The universe is composed of subjects to be communed with, not objects to be exploited. Everything has its own voice. Thunder and lightning and stars and planets, flowers, birds, animals, trees—all these have voices, and they constitute a community of existence that is profoundly related."[55]

As Frances Moore Lappé, author of *Diet for a Small Planet*, observes in a blurb on the back jacket, Jensen's style is "stunningly original, grippingly personal." Jensen combines information, statistics, economics, philosophy, narrative, psychology, and memoir, dropping effortlessly into personal experience to create his web of ideas and stories. Jensen's notion of interspecies communication goes far beyond a metaphorical concordance or synchronicity between events in nature (for example, a stormy sky) and one's moods; he even goes beyond a kinesthetic kind of knowing between humans and animals, or between people and nature. Jensen speaks to literal clairaudient messages that put him in touch with the thoughts and feelings of his fellow creatures.

This kind of awareness is one that many indigenous cultures carry when their members are able to receive such message from trees, ants, spiders, and even foods. In animistic cultures, particularly, everything is alive and carries consciousness; thus, intentionality can be negotiated among species, through a language older than words that may be mediated by words or sacred chants or ritual. By way of comparison, ordinary consciousness has been called "consensus trance," a term that acknowledges the consensual agreement to maintain a certain spectrum of common awareness while blocking other perceptions; hence the use of the term "altered states of consciousness" to describe places of receptivity within the mind that are outside the usual, consensus state.

Jensen understands the importance of food to our identity within the totality of our environment, our awareness, and our values. He writes a lot about food, about the inability of our techno-society to enable either individuals or communities to become sustainable and self-reliant in supplying their own food.[56] He describes how the processes behind any meal in a restaurant are "tied inescapably to pernicious activities across the globe," from the "unspeakable cruelty and debasement of factory farming, and water pollution," to depletion of natural resources, to "the indescribable immiseration and debasement of labor exploitation" internationally, to toxic mining wastes, chemical pollution, and other phenomena.[57] One's relationship to food offers a vehicle for examining and ultimately transcending ordinary consciousness. Jensen writes movingly of animals he has killed for food, of the tender relationship between killer and the being that has become the sacrifice, of the final moments of connection between the two souls: "I finally caught him, and held his large body close, one wing trapped against my chest, the other under my right arm. I remember his eyes were wide, and I could see the black of pupil, blue of iris, white of fear, red of lid, white of feathers, and red of hen's blood."[58]

Jensen's descriptions are vivid, graphic, and powerful, but they also reveal compassion and self-inquiry. While maintaining the relationship between the one offering the sacrifice and the one receiving the fruits of the sacrifice, for example, Jensen asserts that sacrifice for feeding is an inevitable part of the chain of life. The task, accordingly, is to ensure that the process has dignity and manifests respect for the beings involved.[59]

In his description of the vivid encounters between human and animal, he claims to be writing not metaphor but memoir, not invention but experience. He does not ascribe human qualities to animals but, rather, brings out the essential commonality between the human and the animal, in the shared spiritual and emotional dimension of the sacrificial moment. The healing and the understanding of the possibility for energy medicine that Jonas and Crawford carefully put together through scientific explanations find vivid expression in Jensen's intimate portraits of his encounters with life.

A Matrix of Regulatory Goals for Healing

As research continues into healing and intentionality, Jensen's description of the need for a different kind of sensitivity to our environment becomes increasingly relevant to an understanding of how we regulate healing. By supplementing the outcomes and values at stake, experience and narrative, as well as scientific evidence, can enrich consideration of regulatory objectives. As suggested earlier, to date, regulatory efforts surrounding therapies that involve a broader notion of healing than curing have focused primarily on the regulatory interest in controlling deviance by preventing fraud. As suggested, this notion of fraud control has included such areas as licensing (using licensure rules to prevent ignorant and deviant individuals from preying on patient vulnerabilities) and medical discipline (using the power of the state medical board to sanction physicians treating patients through therapies outside medical orthodoxy).[60]

Fraud control is an appropriate goal, and relevant regulation can be effective where truly fraudulent activity is involved.[61] On the other hand, as noted earlier, policy goals additional to fraud control could include the following: quality assurance, health care freedom, functional integration, and human transformation.[62] A movement toward greater emphasis on health care freedom (or consumer autonomy) can be found in new laws, for example, in California, Minnesota, and Rhode Island, allowing nonlicensed health care providers to offer a range of CAM therapies, so long as they make appropriate disclosures to health care consumers and meet other requirements.[63] Similarly, such statutes emphasize the importance of medical pluralism.[64] By shifting the focus from prohibiting access to therapies that lack a significant medical evidence base to allowing access assuming proper disclosures are made, these statutes express a different balancing of medical paternalism and patient autonomy than was previously found in licensing laws based exclusively on an antifraud rationale.

Such a larger set of goals may be highly relevant to contemplation of matters raised by Jonas and Crawford, as well as Jensen, regarding interspecies communication, long-distance healing, and the primacy of intention and relationship in all communication. Jonas and Crawford hint at, and Jensen insists on, the necessary and urgent evolution of human consciousness to move into states in which interrelationship with nature becomes a de facto way of being. In short, the focus is not only on healing existing dysfunction and disease (mental, emotional, and spiritual, as well as physical) but, even more, on evolving to a place in which we become that which we already are but perhaps are too deluded (or preoccupied, particularly in an age in which computerized technology dominates much of our culture) to notice: condensed spirit and spiritual energy on the material plane.

A regulatory focus on the baser aspects of human nature and their potential for distorting therapeutic relationships may be too limiting to address these larger notions of human connectivity with larger ecosystems. As Jonas observes, "While all healing systems involve the use of consciousness . . . modern Western medicine sees most energy emanating off the body as an epiphenomenon of biochemical activity in cells and of no therapeutic value in itself. Spiritual, psychic, and bioenergy healers imagine this energy as directly interacting with the person to facilitate healing."[65]

Both Jonas and Jensen suggest the importance of transformation in connection to the environment and human relationships. From a regulatory perspective, transformation connotes the intent to protect all aspects of human health, including environmental and spiritual values as well as biological integrity.[66] To acknowledge bio-energetic exchanges as a part of health care could have revolutionary consequences for health care in terms of acknowledging the human being as more than the physical body;[67] in fact, acknowledging a regulatory goal of transformation would suggest the importance of using consciousness as a healing faculty.[68]

Jensen is much more direct, as he generalizes beyond medical care to concern for the environment and, ultimately, the soul of our species: "There is another kind of revolution, one that does not emerge from the culture, from philosophy, from thought abstracted from sense, but instead from our bodies, and from the land. It, too, is a part of this language older than words." Jensen clarifies that what he is speaking about is neither political theory nor philosophy nor religion.[69] Rather, "it is remembering what it is to be a human being—an animal. It is remembering what it means to love, and to be alive."[70]

Regulation and the Evolution of Consciousness

How can legal rules and regulation encourage or facilitate the revolution of consciousness of which Jonas and Crawford and Jensen speak, if such encouragement or facilitation is desirable, as the former hint and the latter urges? Environmental law can determine the fates of various animals, plants, landscapes, humans, microbes, insects, and other dwellers of the planet and thereby either encourage or discourage interspecies relations—either preserve or destroy. Environmentalists and industrialists have differing agendas and perspectives on the tradeoffs between commercial development and notions of planetary health. From another perspective, legal rules governing separation of church and state, as well as freedom of expression of religion, aim to balance values so that the ability of individuals and groups to express the spirit they perceive flowing through them is safeguarded in an appropriate manner.

In health care, to the extent that an evolution in consciousness may develop from the movement beyond mechanism and reductionism in biomedicine toward incorporating other insights, approaches, and philosophies from various CAM modalities (for example, notions of chi in acupuncture and traditional oriental medicine, or ideas about a bioenergy field in energy healing), health care regulation in general will have a significant effect on the extent to which such practices—and any corresponding expansion in consciousness—flourish or wither.

Recently, the legal profession has seen a movement toward greater inclusion of spiritual practices—or at least secularized practices from the spiritual domain (such as mindfulness-based stress reduction)—to help lawyers practice with increased clarity and compassion.[71] Similarly, the medical profession has seen explicit acknowledgment of the role of spirituality in clinical care, along with recommendations and guidelines for handling sensitive discussions with patients around spirituality.[72] The shared focus on healing thematically unites these disparate movements—the quest to understand the role of positive intention (or at least, in the case of mindfulness-based stress reduction, the destructive effect of unacknowledged negative emotion) in facilitating and deepening relationship and enhancing positive outcomes—whether within a clinical setting or a negotiation.

Both *Healing, Intention, and Energy Medicine* and *A Language Older Than Words* focus on this common element of healing. The qualities of the authors shine forth in their quest for planetary improvement in the ecology of being, and not simply for health as defined in quantitative terms. The implications of both books for health care and health care policy are significant. Both books implicitly argue for a certain shift in consciousness: from a mechanistic, reductionistic, and dualistic view of the world, in which humanity is seen as the highest rung in the order of nature, born to subdue and dominate all, toward a more unified, integrated harmonization of human creative energies with those of other species as well as the "inanimate" environment.[73]

The authors do take different positions on the role of science in facilitating this shift in consciousness, perhaps echoing Hamlet's observation that inherently, "there is nothing either good or bad but thinking makes it so."[74] In other words, as the research of Jonas and Crawford suggests, intentionality does matter. The intention to use science to subdue, dominate, and control produces one result, whereas the intention to use science in service of openness; in acceptance of our fragmented, wounded, vulnerability; and in recognition of a shared connection with all things produces another. As Jensen puts it, "Our culture's narcissism . . . leads to a disturbing disrespect for direct experience and a negation of the body."[75] But, he urges, "a real world still awaits us, one that is ready to speak to us if only we would remember how to listen."[76] As many philosophers have noted, this is the genius of free will: humans have the choice to make or break the world—to make or break our environment and each other through the ways we choose to interact with ourselves, with each other, and with all that is.[77]

Particularly in an age in which our increasing technological sophistication makes us vulnerable to the very machinery we have built (the not-too-covert subtext of the film trilogy *The Matrix*), it becomes increasingly important to examine intentionality in an honest way. Jonas and Crawford inform us that what we think and feel does make a difference. Jensen repeatedly points out the lies we tell ourselves in order to survive—the psychic accommodation we make at the cost of our souls.

As Jensen observes, the pain of honesty and self-awareness leads many to self-numb. He reports that as he began to open up to his emotions—which he had suppressed for years—he grew "deeply convinced that awareness, and feeling, led inevitably to decreased happiness." He dreamt about baby cranes: "They took off and crashed, took off and crashed. I stopped the car and got out. 'That looks like it hurts. Why do you do it?' One of the cranes looked me square in the eye. 'We may not fly very well yet, but at least we aren't walking.'" Jensen concludes, "I awoke, happy. From that moment, there has been no turning back."[78]

Jensen's description of his dream and his instruction from the cranes is reminiscent of the story about the traveler on the road who saw the radiant Buddha approaching. The astonished individual asked, "What are you, a man or a god?" "Neither," the Buddha replied. "I am awake." In Jensen's terms, awakening means having the fortitude to suffer awareness of the many lies we have told ourselves to numb ourselves, to psychically protect and defend ourselves against the many "atrocities" we inflict on our world.[79] Within the framework of Jonas and Crawford, scientists can join "the good company of adventure-seeking missionaries, venturing travelers and anthropologists" to help bring knowledge of healing "to the bedside, alleviating the symptoms and progression of disease, improving quality of life, and accelerating the recuperation time from illness."[80]

Echoing the desire to translate healing knowledge into universal information, Jensen writes that he dreams of a world in which Buddha or Jesus would present his state of consciousness to the crowd in the marketplace, only there would be no astonishment because each individual would have already incorporated the teaching. In this world, everyone is awake, and everyone shares the "language older than words." This wish for healing expresses a vision unifying mystics of divergent religious tradition—uniting both those who claim to express spirituality through a particular path and those who hope to embody the qualities associated with "spirituality" simply as factors coterminous with their humanity.

Are CAM therapies pointing to an evolutionary development and assumption of these qualities—individually and collectively—with health care and its regulation as vehicles? And can the legal rules of healing support and sustain these processes? Alternatively, are broader aspects of both healing and law implicated by these works? These are not the questions regulation typically has asked. Yet ultimately, by raising these questions, legislators, judges, attorneys, scholars of medicine and public health, clinicians, and others can address the potential future world envisioned by the combination of Jensen's vision and the research collected by Jonas and Crawford.

Between Silence and the Breath

Legal authority sanctions a specific version of health and, in so doing, creates a coercive vision of professional health care.[81] Legal authority, like medical authority, can impose its own violence (e.g., forced C-sections, forced chemotherapy, or forced antipsychotic medication).[82] On the other hand, legal authority, like medical authority, also can foster an environment in which healing between individuals, between communities, between nations, and between species, is possible.

Jensen, focusing on violence sanctioned by law, gives the example of a congressman who calls the police to remove ecological activists from his office. The police promptly spray pepper into the eyes of the "handcuffed and helpless women from a range of less than three inches." Jensen continues: "Over the women's screams they then forced open their eyes and daubed a concentrated liquid form of this substance directly onto their eyeballs." He further reports that the police defended their actions as "cost-effective" and that a judge, denying an injunction against the use of pepper spray or its concentrate, observed that "the hardship to law enforcement in being deprived of the ability to use pepper spray on recalcitrant demonstrators was greater than the discomfort suffered and the risk incurred by those on whom it is used."[83]

Jonas and Crawford, focusing on healing created by intention, also give examples. They devote their collection of research to the opposite of violence at close range: the use of healing at a distance. One of the studies in their book suggests that there is empirical evidence that a remote healing intention can produce physiological changes in a distant subject.[84] Another study concludes that "there is at present moderate scientific evidence supporting the efficacy of various distant healing/intercessory prayer approaches in medicine."[85]

Jensen offers innumerable examples of silently perpetuated violence as an awakening to the potential for recognition, acknowledgment, reconciliation, and healing. Jonas and Crawford offer examples of research in therapeutic effects of intentionality as an antidote to the violence of the world, and of a medical model in which consciousness is neglected. Both take the reader from the suffering world we collectively inhabit and unconsciously re-create to the potential bliss-world in which the transcendental ideals are actualized in mundane life. Like their fellow travelers, these authors acknowledge and encourage the unseen links between matter and spirit, between the incarnate and the disincarnate, between human and other, and between silence and the breath.

CHAPTER FIVE

Renewing the Matrix of Health and Healing

Beyond Pluralism

The notion of pluralism expressed in the Institute of Medicine (IOM) report is radical enough when contrasted against the view that complementary and alternative medicine (CAM) therapies, such as those based on transfers of consciousness or healing energy, are "implausible on a priori grounds" and thus "invalidated" ab initio. Jensen and Jonas and Crawford go even further than the suspension of categorical disbelief urged by the IOM. They suggest not only that the natural environment affects health and healing but that even the intention (consciousness) of the caregiver can be associated with a given intervention. Pluralism in the hands of these writers includes a willingness to shift epistemological assumptions and the hermeneutics of healing and to thereby embrace the possibility that the subtle world can change the physical world and not merely the reverse.

In keeping with the shift toward underscoring the importance of healthy thinking, feeling, and being, the IOM report's chapter on ethics quotes psychologists and religious thinkers such as Abraham Maslow, Robert Thurman, Plato, Mary Baker Eddy, and Frieda Fromm-Reich for the proposition that considerations of health (and health care policy) necessarily must embrace the full spectrum of human (and regulatory) needs:

Thus, although physicians or public health professionals may speak in terms of morbidity, mortality, and risk factors, other kinds of clinicians and therapists may think in terms of healing the shadow self and increasing the capacity for intimacy and mature love or the growth of (and care for) the soul. Some physicians would even link these two domains. In other words, public accountability, like medical pluralism, must include some consideration of the vast array of perspectives that constitute the national (and even international) heritage of healing traditions.[1]

In sum, these perspectives suggest the profound centrality of consciousness in a pluralistic approach to the new health care. Integrative medicine acknowledges that healing is a broader concept than curing, and that although healing can include physiological restoration and an end to a disease state, it also implicates the personal wholeness to which the word "healing" is etymologically related. As the language in the IOM report suggests, such wholeness has many dimensions and can include such aspects of human health as the capacity for love, intimacy, and soul growth. Healing thus can be transformational as well as restorative, transpersonal as well as personal, and embracing of regeneration as well as of physical and emotional recovery. The broadest notion of healing in Jensen's sense includes waking up to new dimensions of consciousness that encompass both the physical and the spiritual and can embrace nature both as the phenomenal world and as a living entity with whom one is engaged in a continual stream of dialogue at multiple levels.

The metaphors for such an expanded consciousness of healing exist in both popular culture and the literature of psychology and religion. For example, the popular film series *The Matrix* offers innumerable metaphors of waking up from the comfortable sleep of delusion to a deeper understanding of human interrelationship with the phenomenal world. The first film in the series takes as its starting premise the notion that humans are encased in rows of jellied cocoons, essentially motionless and incognizant of their true condition, while the world they believe to be true and real is nothing more than an interactive program downloaded into their minds by a giant, worldwide computer.

The Matrix is a clever, modern variation on an ancient tale that bears on deepening notions of integration. Turn to Greek philosophy for Plato's metaphor of the Prisoner in the Cave, to the Russian mystic Gurdjieff for the metaphor of human energies going to "feed the moon,"[2] or to psychologist Charles Tart's notion of consensus trance.[3] Consider Zen, Hinduism, or Kabala: all these teachings assert that humans are blind slaves to a delusional reality from which we refuse to wake up. In the language of Indian scriptural tradition, we are caught in Maya, or delusion—in the Matrix. We are offered the "blue pill" of continuing our pleasant delusion or the "red pill" of recognizing the momentous task of integrating the various sides of our nature and confronting the split between cascading fantasies and dark realities.

In an appropriate continuation of the parallels between *The Matrix* and Eastern religions, the actor Keanu Reeves, the protagonist of the film trilogy, also played the Buddha in a previous role. In both films, he was "the One"—the human being who awakens from delusion and through his own awakening has the power to release millions of fellow beings from this bondage that we call the world. His screen name in *The Matrix* is Neo, a linguistic play on One. According to the film, his unified mind has the power to cut through the false reality and, in the neo-world of the global computer brain, alter time and space.

The film series asks, what is the Matrix and how do we break free? In the film the answer is not a science fiction, techno-gadgetized joyride but, rather, a perennial inquiry on the path to wisdom. The inquiry not only informs the world's major scriptural traditions— and hence the archetypes that fuel the popularity of the film series— but also can help illuminate discussions of integrative health care. In this sense, waking up from the Matrix becomes a metaphor for building a pluralistic system of global care that might possibly be healthier and more expansive than the model that is already familiar through the narrow regulatory lens of fraud control.

The Skirt of Living Souls

Like *The Matrix*, an ancient text from India called the *Yoga Vasistha* tries to answer the question of what lies at the apex of human health (wholeness at all levels, including consciousness) or the frontier of what Maslow termed the "farther reaches of human nature." The text notes that we live within a matrix of delusion and seek ways to achieve freedom from its power. It opens with the following question by Rama, the archetypal deity embodied in human form: "What do people call happiness and can it be had in the ever-changing objects of this world? . . . What is this world? What comes into being, grows and dies? How does this suffering come to an end?"[4]

Rama's question addresses not only Buddha's first Noble Truth—the fact that life includes suffering in many forms, including disease and old age—but also entropy, decay, and the ultimate dissolution of all things. Rama notes, "All enjoyments in this world are delusion, like the lunatic's enjoyment of the taste of fruits reflected in a mirror. All the hopes of man in this world are consistently destroyed by Time."[5] Rama's question, like Maslow's hierarchy of needs, "ups the ante" and moves the issues of disease, health, and healing into new levels at which, as Jensen and Jonas and Crawford suggest, consciousness itself interfaces with the physical world to produce health or sickness, wisdom or folly.

Like the biblical author of *Ecclesiastes*, who proclaims that all is vanity, Rama observes how the world consumes its participants even as they imagine they are in slow motion. Rama compares the world to a "potter's wheel," which looks as if it stands still "though it revolves at a terrific speed"; he compares the cycle of life and death to a "skillful dancer whose skirt is made up of living souls, and her dancing gestures consist of lifting the souls up to heaven, hurling them down in hell, or bringing them back to this earth." All that is accomplished in an earthly body, Rama laments, eventually becomes merely "memory"; nothing material has ultimate endurance.[6]

Having had this partial awakening, Rama is "partly caught and partly freed." He asks whether there exists "a secret that enables one to remain unaffected by the grief and suffering in this world," so that he can be fully freed from grief and befuddlement, the one obfuscation that occludes him from attaining total health.[7] In short, Rama is seeking freedom from the Matrix, from the howling skirt of living souls, and only this freedom will constitute complete healing from the suffering inherent in the human condition.

There are many sacred texts that pose this puzzle, and moving more deeply into this labyrinth could take the question of health and healing far beyond medicine and into other disciplines, such as psychology, religion, sociology, and philosophy. But this book is about the interface—or, rather, a series of interfaces—between these disciplines, at the borderland of law, ethics, biomedicine, and complementary health modalities. So, in a narrower sense, Rama's inquiry moves beyond Jensen's quest and toward a full contemplation of the nature of nature. Jensen has moved beyond negotiation and even medical pluralism toward authentic dialogue with everything surrounding him, an engagement with nature and all beings in an ongoing conversation at multiple levels of awareness, recognizing in each moment the way each party affects the other. Rama sees even this as an illusion and understands that a deeper reality lies behind even this exchange. Negotiating a new understanding of health is nothing short of the quest for liberation.

The Perfected Sages hear Rama's question and respond with admonitions, expositions, and parables. For example, the sage Vasistha advises, "Knowing that the entire universe, including one's wealth, wife, son, etc., are nothing but the creation of the jugglery of the mind, one does not grieve when they are lost, nor does one feel elated when they prosper." Vasistha urges Rama to discover "that which alone is worth knowing," that which "transcends all coming and going, birth and death," namely, knowledge of "the self, which is as subtle as the millionth part of the tip of a hair divided by a million times" and "pervades everything." According to Vasistha, "All things are strung in the self as beads are strung on a thread." A knower of truth, therefore, understands that "I am not the mind."[8]

Returning to popular culture, in *The Matrix*, the One reaches his pivotal illumination, his moment of enlightenment, when he understands that he truly cannot die when the agents of the world computer shoot him. Even when bullets enter his body in the delusional reality of the Matrix, he survives if his mind is strong enough to recognize the illusion. Ultimately, awakening redeems him from the noose of delusion. In the yogic scripture, the sage Vasistha likewise addresses the power of the mind to cut through the knot of physical reality. "To the ignorant, this body is a source of suffering, but to the enlightened man, this body is the source of infinite delight, and when its life-span comes to an end, he does not regard it as a loss at all. . . . The embodied being comes lightly into contact with the body while it lasts but is untouched by it once it is gone, even as air touches a pot which exists, but not one that does not exist."[9]

All this may be quite a mystery to the rational mind, but from the perspective of health care policy, the language of the *Yoga Vasistha* about the nature of the body suggests that words commonly used when discussing integrative health care—such as "integration," "holism," and "pluralism"—may have deeper connotations than simply acknowledging an openness toward paradigms of health outside biomedicine. These terms, while defined in consensus terms in peer-reviewed medical journals and law reviews, may also point toward transcendental states of being that can only be accessed through the tools of complementary therapies such as prayer, meditation, and guided visualization that touch on the "farther reaches" of transpersonal psychology and/or religious teachings.

Thus, healing at the borderland of medicine and religion presents a bridge between integrative medicine and psychology, religion, and the humanities, one that opens gateways to consciousness at the heart of healing. Further, by operating under legal rules that condition what therapies may or may not be offered within the full spectrum of available health care, the regulation of integrative medicine may directly affect the individual's experience of—and access to—not only physical health and wellness but also states of consciousness.

Negotiating Freedom from the Noose of Delusion

The powerful metaphors provided by works such as *The Matrix* and *Yoga Vasistha* suggest that beyond the pluralism of integrative health care lies the possibility for nurturing a deeper awakening about health care policy. That awakening involves peering beyond the delusional matrix of medicolegal reality that binds global medicine to an either/or dualistic view of the human being toward one that, like Maslow's hierarchy, explicitly incorporates notions of consciousness, transcendence, self-actualization, and spiritual evolution into human health.

Pluralism at its outer limits touches on religious teachings—not on a single doctrinal religion, but on a "perennial wisdom" common to world religions and shared by certain branches of psychology that emphasize the transpersonal dimensions of human health. Acknowledging this borderland involves an implicit critique of biomedicine's present limits and the corresponding limits of health care law, even given the emphasis on humanism in medicine and a "good bedside manner."

Like the blue-pill reality of *The Matrix*, the reigning epistemology of biomedicine (and the corresponding regulatory structure) tends to perpetuate a delusional sense that a human being is only material—a three-dimensional substance locked in the physical body, amenable to mechanical interventions that are tightly controlled by a series of carefully circumscribed rules. Biomedicine arguably encourages overidentification with the body. It is fear-based; disease induces desperation in the "race for the cure" rather than focus on "care of the soul." This critique is implicit in the earlier notion of biomedicine as reductionistic and mechanistic—as unduly influenced by limited thinking in Cartesian dualism and Newtonian physics.

As I argued in *Beyond Complementary Medicine,*

Patients' objectification results from a reduction of "care," as a ruling metaphor, to "medical care"; from an overly mechanistic view of their condition; from the denial that they have, at the moment of care, a consciousness of that care. Their dignity, if

you will, is impinged because in treating them as objects of technological intervention, their aliveness is ignored—e.g., the euphe-
mism "reduction" as substitute for "destruction"; the terms
"incompetent" and "noncommunicative" as medical pronounce-
ments rather than functional realities; the reference to the body
part, rather than the person (the "penile implant in O.R. 23").[10]

These kinds of critiques of biomedicine already have penetrated
bioethics: the notion that death, for example, is wrongfully identified in biomedicine as an endpoint rather than a transition for the
human being;[11] biomedicine's failure to assign emotional and spiritual meaning to pathological realities and its insistence on dismissing certain phenomena unknown to contemporary biological science as "spontaneous remissions";[12] and its tendency to relegate
valid, numinous encounters to the realm of psychological dysfunction or improvable mysticism.

  In the purest sense, therapies from hypnosis to meditation aim to
free the dis-eased seeker, and the culture as a whole, from the matrix
of mechanism, reductionism, and other ills to a realm where the
human spirit finds rest. At the level of self-actualization and the
regulatory goal of transcendence, the purpose of integrative medicine includes feeding and freeing by finding a salve for mind and
spirit as well as body; by cultivating the body as sacred garden rather
than as unalterably fixed and mechanical mechanism; and by viewing disease on multiple levels and health as intimating potentially
evolutionary changes in the human organism. As Vasistha says,
"Subdue the mind with the mind. Purify the mind by the mind.
Destroy the mind by the mind," meaning that when the mind is
purified, the real can be grasped.[13]

Health Care's New Medicolegal Matrix

  Purifying the mind may be possible in some transcendental
sense, but in negotiating patient access (and clinician response) to a
fuller range of complementary therapies, one has to integrate the
farther reaches of human nature with real-world issues such as nego-

tiating third-party reimbursement, licensing controls, and the whole panoply of market forces and regulatory tools. These tools can contaminate pure awareness with too much control and bureaucracy, thereby forcing transcendental healing into the container of what is legally cognizable in any given structured interaction between healing professionals.[14] Merely replacing one system of medicine with another, with all the attendant trappings (such as defined educational programs, accreditation, professional regulation, licensure, legally defined scopes of practice, and reimbursement mechanisms) may end up changing neither the status of human health (in an evolutionary sense) nor the way we view one another or build our world. As research progresses and mechanisms are discovered, the practice of herbal medicine, for example, may come to represent replacing one "magic bullet" (the pharmaceutical) with another (the herbal formula).

Legal rules by and large enshrined biomedicine at the apex of legal authority, by initially assigning all healing to licensed medical doctors and allowing prosecution of healers trained in complementary care modalities under statutes prohibiting the unlicensed practice of medicine.[15] But the legal system can move toward more deeply recognizing and empowering integrative medicine in a variety of ways. As I noted in *Legal Boundaries*,

> As complementary and alternative medicine increasingly interpenetrates biomedical practice, the antifraud rationale—the desire to protect patients from dangerous health care practices—will be balanced against the respect for the patient's right to make informed and voluntary health care choices. The law may recognize in equipoise to the antifraud rationale that healing can take many forms: That touch may be beneficial; that support, communication, and emotional contact facilitate well-being; that hypnotic, intuitive and trance states, and prayer, potentially stimulate healing; that personal wholeness, in all its multifaceted richness, is a social good. These perspectives should be included expressly in legislative reform, administrative rule making, and judicial reasoning.

Deeper respect for health care freedom suggests returning to the regulatory perspective that healing is broader than bio-medicine, that nonbiomedical caregivers can nourish the healing process, and that wellness can incorporate not only surgical, pharmaceutical and biochemical realities, but also the vague and shifting contours of the patient's inner world and social environment.[16]

This book's exploration of integrative medicine has moved from negotiation to considerations of pluralism to a broader ecological awareness and, still further, to some of the transformational possibilities that Maslow has called "the farthest reaches of human nature." In a similar way, exploring possibilities for legal reform can acknowledge the movement toward negotiating openness to new therapies and providers.

Legal rules in health care historically addressed the most egregious deviations from the moral good of which providers are capable, such as fraud, misrepresentation, carelessness in treatment (malpractice), failure to honor patient wishes (battery theory of informed consent), and practicing without sufficient training and knowledge (credentialing issues). Such rules seek to control "dark channels," or the shadow side, imposing structure on the healer who comes from ignorance or ego rather than truth, from contempt rather than love, from puffery rather than humility, and from self-involvement rather than compassionate attention to the client's suffering.[17]

Controlling fraudulent practitioners is a public good to the extent that it prevents fraud and provides quality assurance; similarly, licensure and credentialing rules, prohibitions against fraud, and other legal rules can be imposed as light-bearing beacons on healers gone awry. Yet these rules, and those who advocate and/or apply them, also are subject to the same dark forces that affect licentious healers. Fear, jealousy, and control also can govern licensing laws and bodies and manifest polarization by way of such things as unnecessary intraprofessional turf battles, legislative line-drawing in scope of practice conflicts, and attempts by medical boards to revoke licensure and discipline practitioners for deviating from conventional norms.

The problem is not confined to biomedicine or to any one profession but, rather, is the product of a century or more of rivalry between the varying camps and the historic split between biomedical and CAM communities. One might even wonder whether diminishing regulation might bring about the healthiest environment for health care to operate at all levels of Maslow's pyramid. Would legal structures be able to handle not only the notion that healing involves mind, body, emotions, and spirit, but also other dimensions of the human experience such as interspecies communication and a greater sense of Earth-consciousness? How will integrative medicine and the new health care shape alternative dispute resolution and its relation to the resolution of litigation? In addition to negotiation and other forms of conflict resolution, would a legal counselor work on higher planes and levels of the energy field, if such a field indeed exists, to clear destructive energies between disputants? To begin to move in the direction of addressing these questions, it might be useful to explore the uncomfortable borderland between medicine and religion and how this borderland finds expression within the regulatory system.

Healing at the Borderland
of Medicine and Religion

Healing in the New Health Care

Chapters 1 through 5 have discussed the conflict and collision between biomedical understanding of certain conditions as disease states and the understanding in various complementary and
alternative medicine (CAM) therapies of these conditions in terms of
emotional imbalance, distorted consciousness, or a wrecked spiritual orientation. As these chapters have suggested, an emphasis on
healing in spiritual terms presents particular challenges to clinicians
and researchers by bringing the frontier of the new health care to the
fore—the borderland between medicine and religion.

With the penetration of integrative care into modern medicine,
such challenges are increasing, not diminishing. Although historically the phenomenon of spiritual healing emerged as a practice
within the context of specific religions and has traditionally been
ascribed only to mystics, saints, and holy persons,[1] in modern times
a variety of spiritual healing practices unconnected with traditional
religion have entered mainstream health care professions such as
medicine, nursing, dentistry, and other allied health professions.

For example, some physicians either collaborate with (or refer to)
spiritual healers[2] or use " 'healing energy' through touch" without
naming a particular style, school, or technique,[3] and a spiritual healing modality known as Therapeutic Touch is part of the curriculum

in many nursing schools.[4] Use of caring or healing touch may be useful in health care settings from acute care to surgery to obstetrical nursing practice.[5] Reiki, a Japanese form of energy healing, has even been used to help survivors recover from torture.[6]

Additionally, spiritual healing services are offered by practitioners of CAM therapies such as chiropractic, acupuncture, and massage therapy.[7] For example, many practitioners of acupuncture and traditional oriental medicine practice *qigong*, a Chinese system of spiritual healing.[8] Similarly, intuitive use of touch is a central component of chiropractic[9] and of many forms of massage therapy.[10] Overall, at least 50,000 health professionals provide about 120 million sessions of spiritual healing to patients annually.[11]

The prevalence of spiritual healing in the provision of health care services receives extensive attention in the *Chantilly Report*, a 1992 quasi-governmental report to the National Institutes of Health titled *Alternative Medicine: Expanding Medical Horizons*. The report describes spiritual healing as a collection of different practices centering around spirituality and notions of healing used as part of professional health care, not only in the provision of CAM services, but also within medicine, nursing, and the allied health professions. The report does not offer definitive guidance on ways to sort out differences, if any, between spiritual healing, faith healing, laying on of hands, prayer, intentionality, and related practices,[12] but it does highlight the increasing use of these techniques in a variety of health care settings.

The practice of spiritual healing in a secular context, within the provision of clinical care, suggests the possibility of regulating spiritual healing as the professional delivery of a health care service.[13] This chapter argues that those who purport to utilize spiritual healing in clinical care within a secular (and frequently medical) context should be—and in fact, are—subject to an array of regulatory controls similar to those imposed on other health care professionals. The chapter broadly explores how legal rules regulate spiritual healing as a health care (rather than exclusively religious) practice in the United States, conceptualizes the kinds of potential abuse of power in the relationship between spiritual healer[14] and client, and evaluates the extent to which legal rules address—or fail to address—such potential abuse of power in spiritual healing as a professional health care practice.

The chapter first provides preliminary working definitions of spiritual healing and attempts to differentiate spiritual healing in a secular context (i.e., as a professional health care service) from religious healing, which is given a working definition in this chapter as healing in an exclusively religious context.[15] The chapter next examines whether the potential for abuse of spiritual healing in the clinical setting ought to be regulated; it then reviews constitutional and policy arguments both for and against government intervention into a domain of healing still considered by many—correctly or otherwise—to be religious or at the least (in light of the distinctions drawn) spiritual, and thereby still beyond the purview and authority of public policy and legal constraint. The chapter goes on to conceptualize potential forms of abuse between practitioner and client of spiritual healing. Such conceptualization is necessary to determine whether and how legal rules can address issues of abuse. Finally, this chapter reviews the regulatory framework governing the use of professional healing practices generally, and the potential application of these rules to issues of abuse of spiritual healing.

Healing, Spiritual and Religious

Scholars have extensively studied the use of healing rituals in religious, including biblical, contexts.[16] The ancient Israelite priests (or *cohanim*) blessed the people with healing—the blessing, in its biblically recorded form, is still used in synagogues today—and when Moses wished to invest the elders with his power to rule the Israelites, he did so by laying hands on their heads and transmitting to them the *ruach ha-kodesh*, sometimes translated as "holy wind" or "Holy Spirit." Jesus reportedly transmitted healing energy, among other things, through his touch[17] and exhorted his disciples to heal the sick. Catholic saints reportedly had and used associated healing powers. Sacred healing practices in these religious traditions have had both physical and spiritual dimensions, aiming to restore both health of the body and wholeness of the spirit in terms of its unity with God.[18]

While there are numerous scholarly definitions of religion and the religious, some helpful clarifications include these: "practices carried out by those who profess a faith," "subscribing to a set of beliefs or doctrines that are institutionalized," and "the outward practice of a spiritual system of beliefs, values, codes of conduct and rituals."[19] Although religious healing continues today, both in mainline, Western religions and elsewhere, the term "spiritual" has entered the general vocabulary to denote persons who are religious in the sense of having an affinity for religious ritual and practices (including healing practices) or, at the least, for practices involving calming and clarity of mind and emotions, but who do not necessarily wish to be bound to the particular faiths or dogmas of established religious traditions.

Many individuals identify themselves as spiritual rather than as religious. Some would argue that the distinction between spirituality and religiousness is indefensible—the "rose by any other name" argument. And it is true that as many religions refer to the supreme deity as Spirit, the religious impulse—the emotional impetus behind identifying with a larger, more cosmic consciousness than the human personality—may be the same, whether labeled religious or spiritual. Nonetheless, it is useful to distinguish these terms because of the tendency within U.S. law to identify religion as something distinct and apart from secular pursuits, whereas spiritual feeling can occur outside a specific religion and can even persist in a secular context—such as a nurse's application of Therapeutic Touch to a patient within a hospital's intensive care unit, irrespective of membership in any commonly recognized religion. This scenario would be different from, say, a Catholic priest administering last rites to a patient.

Various academic definitions have been proposed for spirituality as a potentially broader category than religion. These include "searching for existential meaning";[20] "a quality beyond religious affiliation that is used to inspire or harmonize answers to questions regarding infinite subjects";[21] being closer to "the source dimension [that the] everyday [awareness often] . . . has moved far from";[22] a "quality that goes beyond religious affiliation, that strives for inspirations, reverence, awe and purpose [and that] tries to be in harmony with the universe, strives for answers about the infinite, and comes into focus when the person faces emotional stress, physical illness or death";[23] and "a belief system focusing on intangible elements that impart vitality and meaning to life events."[24]

Although there are other efforts to differentiate religion and spirituality,[25] one way to conceptualize a distinction is as follows: "People can be spiritual without being religious—and religious without being spiritual. Religion is a belief system organized around a prophet, teacher, or set of human precepts. Spirituality is the ability to discover and use our own unique specialness. . . . Spirituality is the process of becoming a positive and creative person."[26] In other words, spirituality is not necessarily organized around a specific teacher or set of teachings, and spirituality may be but is not necessarily identified with religion. A group of bioethics scholars, attempting to define the physician's role in paying attention to patients' religious and spiritual beliefs within the practice of medicine, has articulated a distinction as follows:

> The term "spirituality" tends to be used as a broader term to refer to that which brings significance, purpose, and direction to people's lives. The person who has spiritual beliefs and interests searches for (usually nonphysical) sources of meaning, life, wholeness, healing, and hope. The various forms of spirituality may be fluid and individual, taking no classical religious form, or they may be crystallized in the beliefs and practices of a specific religious community. . . . The term "religion" . . . tends to be associated with beliefs, practices, and ethical teachings of specific religious bodies and traditions.[27]

In light of these various, proposed definitions, spiritual healing, as opposed to religious healing, draws on the healing power of connectedness to the sacred, without necessarily deriving its authority (or persuasive power of its practitioners and recipients) from the tenets or dogmas of any specific religious tradition.[28]

Spiritual healing is prevalent in the delivery of health care services. Spiritual healing services can be offered in a variety of hospital settings and as rituals intended to help patients heal.[29] Research into links between spiritual practices and health is increasing, as are educational courses in medical schools on the topics of religion, spirituality, and medicine.[30]

In a larger sense, the focus on spiritual care reflects not only interest among health care providers, patients, and others in spirituality but also a broader cultural phenomenon connected to what Mircea Eliade has denoted a "*creative* encounter . . . with archaic—as a matter of fact, prehistoric—spiritual values." This is more than a series of "encounters with oriental spiritualities"[31]—of meetings between Western science and Eastern religion—as is frequently presupposed. The encounter with shamanism,[32] the religious expression of prehistoric humanity, has parallels in theater, literature, poetry, and music as well as health care. It represents a delving into initiatory ordeals to forge a more "structured, stronger personality" that integrates the physical and spiritual worlds.[33]

The prevalence of spiritual healing in health care environments suggests a quiet yet profound cultural revolution, in which the instrument and vessel of divine grace has shifted—at least for many health care providers and their patients—from the exclusive domain of the saint or sage to the province of the ordinary individual.[34] The spiritual gift of offering healing is understood as accessible to many or most persons, and the skills of spiritual healing are considered to be open to anyone who is willing to undergo the requisite training; in short, the gift of healing is no longer seen as emanating entirely from divine dispensation and thereby falling into a particular religious tradition.[35]

Little consensus evidence exists concerning safety, efficacy, or mechanism of therapies in the clinical domain associated with spiritual healing. Further, the evidence validating any claims by spiritual healers concerning the effects of their practices on health or the physical body presently is mixed yet promising.[36] As such, members of the scientific community could argue that these spiritual healing practices should be viewed as religious in the sense that they have not received complete validation through scientific study and, therefore, inevitably must draw on belief and subjectivity. Therapies that do not have satisfactory, objective, *scientific* proof, the argument goes, must rely on subjective belief and hence fall into the realm of faith or religion. The above argument adds to earlier definitions of religion by opposing religious to scientific truth. To the extent that religion involves a set of "practices carried out by those who profess a faith," then the absence of sufficient, reliable scientific data, coupled with the necessity of belief in the modality and its theoretical underpinnings, would suggest that spiritual healing remains in the domain of religion and not medicine.[37]

While the argument has merit, there are several compelling reasons for treating these practices as secular—that is, as capable of operating, and thereby deserving regulation, outside an exclusively religious framework. First, these practices are offered by health care practitioners of many divergent religious faiths, unlike, for example, prayer "treatments" by Christian Scientists, who operate from a common set of enumerated beliefs about God. Similarly, practitioners of spiritual healing in the clinical domain may apply different training and styles of spiritual healing without necessarily ascribing the potency of these methods to a particular form of worship or a particular conception of God. They may not necessarily share among themselves the kind of distinguishing marks of religion, such as a commonly held, "sincere and meaningful belief which occupies . . . in the life of its possessor a place parallel to that filled by the orthodox belief in God [of religious traditions]" (one definition of religion proposed by the U.S. Supreme Court).[38]

Second, unlike the case of religious healing—in which most explanatory models entirely derive from commonly agreed-on, theological constructs—attempts have been made to offer scientific explanations for some of the phenomena reported by practitioners and their clients. Such explanations do not rely on faith or belief any more than scientific hypotheses in general can be said to be faith-based.[39] For example, some scientists have postulated the existence of a unifying, biologically based field of information that can be accessed by practitioners of spiritual healing,[40] while others have looked to electromagnetic explanations and still others to new theories of physics.[41] Irrespective of the apparent success of—and controversy surrounding—such attempts at explanation,[42] they suggest that practitioners and clients can have experiences of these practices without subscribing to a defined religious dogma or creed.

Third, many of the steps in these practices are described in such a generic way that the practitioner who does choose to incorporate a religious practice is free to draw on multiple religious traditions for inspiration. For example, Therapeutic Touch describes several basic steps in the process of healing through spiritual energy. These include centering, focusing on intent, scanning (or assessing the human energy field), directing healing energy to benefit a client, and facilitating release.[43] In the first step of Therapeutic Touch, centering, the practitioner can use his or her preferred meditative practice to attain a quiet, calm, centered space within; no particular religion or religious practice is specified.

Similarly, in describing the preparation for a technique known as pranic healing, the founder of this modality, Choa Kok Sui, describes the most important practice as exerting intentionality. Use of this concept does not depend on religious dogma or faith. Although Kok Sui recommends that practitioners who are religious do incorporate meditation, prayer, and an invocation in their use of pranic healing, he advises the healer who relies on religion to "pray for a few minutes any religious prayer you are used to."[44] Thus, although Kok Sui advocates use of prayer by "the religious," he does not recommend use of any specific prayer or prayer within any particular religious tradition. For Kok Sui, there is no wrong choice and no penalty for invoking the wrong deity or turning to the wrong religion. The optional religious practice is described sufficiently generically that the practitioner can draw on almost any religion; one could say that Kok Sui is not so much an advocate of religious pluralism as an advocate of spirituality by the religious.[45] In like fashion, practitioners of Reiki permit drawing on any, all, or no religious traditions for inspiration and centering.

The blurring of the boundaries between religion and therapy offers yet another reason to view spiritual healing practices that are offered in the clinical domain by nonclerical personnel as falling outside an exclusively religious paradigm. In other words, it becomes difficult to distinguish between religious healing practices centered on affirmations of faith and practices aimed at therapeutic benefit irrespective of whether the patient or provider subscribes to a particular set of beliefs. For example, some evidence suggests a correlation between religious practices and physical health.[46] It has been suggested that even the attitude of the practitioner toward the patient can affect healing;[47] in conventional terms, it is recognized that the patient's attitude toward the therapy—the so-called placebo effect—can have therapeutic benefit.

In light of this work, many have begun advocating a role for the physician in helping the patient access his or her own source of religious practices for potential physical as well as emotional and spiritual dimensions of healing.[48] The profession of psychotherapy also has witnessed a call for integrating spiritual healing approaches and techniques;[49] given these developments, distinctions between psychotherapeutic and spiritual interventions might be difficult to make or might depend not on who is providing the intervention but on how that intervention is framed. Such developments arguably blur the lines between religious and therapeutic use of prayer, as well as between religion and medical use of access to religious practices.

But even more directly, as suggested, attempts have been made to secularize both the learning process for and practice of spiritual healing in various health care professions, particularly in nursing.[50] And like the distillation of various religious traditions of laying on of hands into a reproducible technique that can be taught in the nursing school curriculum (as in Therapeutic Touch), many analogous "religious" practices have been adapted and adopted to yield therapeutic benefit in other secular settings. For example, self-directed "mindfulness meditation"—an attempt to calm the mind and focus on the breath in the present moment—has emerged from Buddhist meditation practices and ripened into a secular practice of potential therapeutic benefit, not only for patients in psychotherapy (as well as medicine),[51] but also in professional relationships such as those between attorneys and clients in alternative dispute resolution.[52]

Similarly, Transcendental Meditation has attracted practitioners who are not bound to religious teachings from the East but, rather, desire techniques to calm and still the mind.[53] Meditation, the "central plank of ancient spiritual disciplines," historically nestled within specific cultural contexts and codes, has been, in many contexts, secularized[54] and, in some cases, reduced to a physiological "relaxation response."[55] The National Center for Complementary and Alternative Medicine (NCCAM) at the National Institutes of Health gave $8 million to fund a research center at the Maharishi University of Management in Fairfield, Iowa, to pursue research involving the health benefits of Transcendental Meditation and other techniques.[56] At some point, the boundary between religious practices and mental health techniques also becomes blurred.[57] It may also be that, as scientific understanding increases, the tendency to dichotomize science and the religious in CAM therapies also changes.[58]

In short, spiritual healing need not necessarily be equated with religion and the religious but can also be viewed as practiced by persons without a specific religious predisposition.[59] Because of the varieties of understanding just described, for purposes of analyzing regulation of healing, this chapter offers a preliminary working definition of "religious healing" as healing in an exclusively religious context and uses "spiritual healing" to denote a wider domain, including religious healing, as well as practices that can be offered in a secular context, such as Reiki or Therapeutic Touch as a nursing service within a hospital.

Energy Healing as a Frontier Health Care Practice

In addition to this distinction between exclusively religious healing and a broader concept of spiritual healing, a further definitional wrinkle is worth noting. In many quarters, the term "energy healing" has come to denote spiritual healing in a secular (health care) context typically offered by providers other than religious personnel (i.e., other than clergy).[60] "Energy healing" is frequently the language chosen by practitioners (and patients) of therapies such as

Reiki, Therapeutic Touch, Polarity Therapy, and other forms of spiritual healing in the context of professional health care services.[61]

"Energy healing," however, also is often used (by some) interchangeably with "spiritual healing," thus confusing the terminology as well as the conceptualization of what energy healing purports to be, how it purports to work, and in what ways its application within a mainstream health care setting partakes of (or fails to partake of) practices classically considered religious. Further, the fact that a member of the clergy—as opposed to, say, a nurse—offers a patient Therapeutic Touch does not transmogrify the practice into the category of religion; similarly, the fact that a nurse prays with a patient does not transmogrify prayer into energy healing. It may be impossible to sort out the definitional confusion at present, since this would require a much deeper understanding of the scientific mechanism, if any, of the various practices and a resolution of larger, perhaps multidisciplinary issues, such as the relationship between meditation, prayer, and the theoretical transmission of mental energy or consciousness for the purposes of healing.

A conceptualization that may help clarify these issues describes energy healing as "a set of therapies based on the projection of spiritual or mental energy through intentionality and consciousness."[62] In this definition, the term "intentionality" refers to mental processes and is free from connotations of attachment to a specific religion. And as noted, the "projection of spiritual or mental energy through intentionality or consciousness" may be performed by physicians[63] and allied health professionals as well as by CAM providers such as acupuncturists and massage therapists, irrespective of religious affiliation or training.[64] Theoretically, an atheist, an agnostic, a person of indeterminate religious affiliation, and a person with multiple religious proclivities could offer such practices.

Unlike CAM therapies such as chiropractic and acupuncture—and to a lesser extent, massage therapy[65]—there are no uniform standards for education, training, and practice of energy healing. Energy healing also lacks a strong, unifying, national body that can translate theory and practice into a health care profession capable of attaining candidacy for licensure in any state.[66] Therefore, energy healing largely remains a covert element in many different health care professions. Furthermore, the training offered to professionals to practice energy healing differs, depending on the school and its philosophy of education. For example, practitioners can receive certificates for weekend classes or take much longer courses, such as four-year programs that attempt to integrate energy healing into other professional health care practices.[67] Schools offering energy healing certificates may include a variety of related items within their coursework, including activities such as spiritual development, meditation and shamanic journeywork, hypnotherapy certification, and modalities such as Reiki. As with other CAM professions, counseling the patient about health issues appears to be an integral part of practice.[68]

Although the experience of energy healing can be individualized, there appear to be common elements, at least as described by patients who received energy healing. These can include sensations of warmth, tingling, and caring. For instance, the *Chantilly Report* describes the experience of energy healing as "a process during which the practitioner places his or her hands either directly on or very near the physical body of the person being treated . . . [and] engages the perceived biofield from his or her hands with the recipient's perceived biofield either to promote general health or to treat a specific dysfunction."[69]

Rather than turning to established religions for explanations of healing, practitioners frequently describe the process in terms of the biofield or human energy field (or aura). Such a human energy field is described as surrounding and interpenetrating the human body and as having multiple layers that express different dimensions of human consciousness.[70] Similarly, rather than turning to concepts within religious traditions, such as prayer, meditation, or grace, practitioners frequently refer to more neutral, secular explanations such as, in Therapeutic Touch, the notion of centering, which can involve prayer or meditation but more fundamentally means "being at a quiet place within ourselves from which we can focus completely on the person before us."[71]

Likewise, Therapeutic Touch uses the concept of assessment to detect imbalances of energies; assessment involves scanning the energy field with the hands and locating imbalances of spiritual energy by sensing "tingling, pressure, shock, pulsation, heat, or coolness."[72] Modalities such as Therapeutic Touch do not necessarily rely on prayer or laying on of hands in the sense of appealing to God to perform the healing but, rather, emphasize a transfer of spiritual energy from (or perhaps through) practitioner to client.[73] The use of such conceptualizations by practitioners of energy healing—resting, as these explanations often do, outside identifiable religious contexts—can offend religious personnel and believers and, in this sense, are even deemed antireligious.[74]

Attempting to bridge beliefs about healing and science, the NCCAM has defined the field as follows: "Frontier Medicine can be defined, for purposes of this initiative, as those CAM practices for which there is no plausible biomedical explanation. Examples include bioelectromagnetic therapy, biofield/energy healing, homeopathy and therapeutic prayer/spiritual healing. Despite the fact that these therapies are used extensively by the U.S. public, there are very little high-quality data available to elucidate or demonstrate the safety, efficacy, effectiveness and/or mechanisms underlying these approaches."[75] Since the definition is for research and not legal purposes, it lumps prayer together with energy healing.[76] NCCAM proposes a more secular purpose for funding: "Exploratory Program Grants will serve to develop the fields in ways that will increase the likelihood that efficacious therapeutic paradigms will emerge from the existing Frontier Medicine approaches, and thus increase the probability that some of these will become integrated with and will make a contribution to interdisciplinary healthcare."[77]

While scientific consensus around mechanistic explanations is lacking, use of the word "energy" in NCCAM and the research literature does not specifically refer to mechanical notions of energy in physics. Rather, the term "energy" probably has "a broader interpretation in spiritual healing and is likened to organizing principles of vitalism and life force which bring about a harmonizing of the whole person." In other words, "energy" suggests "dynamic forces that are channeled or set in motion by the healer, or the patient," to create a transcendent wholeness.[78]

The articulation of energy healing has a secondary import: it also helps describe a subset of CAM therapies linked by this notion of a unifying, healing spiritual energy. The concept of yin and yang in traditional oriental medicine, the idea of the innate in chiropractic, the spiritual vital essence (vital force) in homeopathy, and *prana* in Ayurvedic medicine all reflect the unifying notion of vital energy embedded in consciousness.[79] Thus, while the term "energy healing" refers in a specific sense to therapies aimed, via physical touch or thought, at transmission of intentionality or consciousness to heal, the term captures,[80] in a broader sense, the common, vitalistic worldview underlying many CAM therapies.[81]

In this sense, many CAM therapies share common ground in that they involve spiritual notions of healing that may or may not immediately and directly affect physical health and, thus, in themselves help bridge the present cultural and ideological chasm between medicine and religion. Perhaps for this reason, their introduction into medical care has been highly controversial[82] and has raised issues of power, authority, and legitimacy with respect to who decides what therapies are valid for patient care.[83]

Regulatory Intervention into Spiritual Healing

THE CONSTITUTIONAL SIDE

As suggested, spiritual practices involving healing—on physical and emotional as well as spiritual levels—are central to a variety of religious traditions. Such practices are becoming part of worship services in synagogues and temples, churches, mosques, and other venues for spiritual expression.[84] Religious pluralism and freedom of religious expression are core values in American society, and guarantees of religious pluralism and expression are embedded in the First Amendment to the U.S. Constitution. Yet, while the First Amendment protects religious expression, the Tenth Amendment reserves to the states the power to protect citizens' health, safety, and welfare and thereby to regulate professional health care practices. Under this reserved police power, states decide who may practice and who may be excluded from practice of the healing arts.

This power to regulate professional health care practices includes not only medicine and the allied health professions (for example, nursing, dentistry, physical therapy, and optometry) but also health care practices historically outside biomedicine, such as CAM therapies.[85] But CAM therapies are defined to include chiropractic, massage therapy, herbal medicine, acupuncture, and spiritual healing practices from meditation and prayer to yoga and guided imagery.[86] In other words, irrespective of constitutional protection for religion or even for privacy and due process of law, CAM practices are subject to health care regulation, and practices that cross the boundary into medicine, even if they have religious aspects or infringe on a person's sense of what is best for his or her body, may constitutionally be regulated.

The constitutional collision between individual freedom and the states' rights to regulate pursuant to the Tenth Amendment has received little scholarly attention, largely because, in most instances, states' rights have trumped.[87] For example, in a landmark 1905 case, *Jacobson v. Massachusetts*, the U.S. Supreme Court upheld the state's right to order compulsory vaccination for public schoolchildren and rejected the argument that vaccination violated the individual's "inherent right of every freeman to care for his own body and health in such way as to him seems best." The court observed that "a community has the right to protect itself against an epidemic of disease which threatens the safety of its members."[88] In *Jacobson*, the state's obligation to protect its citizens against public health risks was— and typically has been since—deemed superior to the individual's claim to a right to make autonomous health care choices for his or her own body.

Subsequent cases have reaffirmed the principle.[89] Courts have found that the police power outweighed not only the individual's privacy and liberty interests but also the practitioner's free-speech interests in professional health care practice.[90] Interpreting the practice of medicine broadly—as any activity that could be construed as diagnosis or treatment of human affliction—courts have upheld a variety of cases against spiritual healers for practicing medicine without a license.[91] For example, in *Smith v. People*, the defendant practiced hands-on healing from his living room and claimed that he merely used his hands to deliver a "gift from the Almighty"; yet, because he purported to cure diseases by laying on hands, his conviction for practicing medicine unlawfully was upheld.[92] Similarly, while courts have found constitutional protection for medical choices such as contraception, abortion, and the right to be disconnected from artificial life support, most courts have refused to recognize a constitutional, privacy-based right to obtain the treatment of one's choice (for example, acupuncture) against the objections of a state regulatory body (such as a medical licensing board).[93]

Whether or not such decisions are correct as matters of constitutional interpretation, they do suggest an underlying hierarchy of values when it comes to clashes between the personal choices involving the conflux of religion and medicine. Religious practices involving health are frequently swept into the conceptual category of medicine and its regulation. In this way, the legal system checks individual healing choices and challenges healing impulses in medical as well as religious personnel that represent potential incursions on state determinations of the legally accepted boundaries of healing. Concomitantly, the medical profession itself has adopted an arguably hegemonic definition of its own scope of practice, and the definition tends to sweep spiritual healing choices under medicine's rubric.[94]

Ironically, while the broad, statutory definition of the practice of medicine—and its interpretation by courts—appears to include practices intended as religious, the medical profession seems to exclude rather than embrace religious healing practices in its diagnostic and therapeutic offerings. As one scholar puts it, the scientific basis of modern medicine "often ignores the spiritual factors associated with health. Health invariably becomes defined in anatomical or physiological, psychological or social terms. Rarely do we find diagnoses which include the relationship between the patient and their God."[95] Yet if a nonphysician were to make such a diagnosis—

connecting the patient's health to the relationship between the patient and his or her deity, or between the patient and the cosmos—the nonphysician clinician could conceivably be construed as practicing medicine unlawfully.

This legal opposition between medical healing and spiritual healing sets up a contradiction between the legal definition of practice and the intended practice of some medical professionals. In fact, it could be argued that the actual practice of medicine should—and does—include spirituality: "Patience, grace, prayer, meditation, hope, forgiveness and fellowship are as important in many of our health initiatives as medication, hospitalization, or surgery. . . . It is in the understanding of suffering, the universality of suffering and the need for deliverance from it that varying traditions of medicine and religion meet."[96]

In short, although spiritual healing practices may be an inherent part of health care, when they involve diagnosis or treatment (in the broadest conceptualization of these terms), the legal definition of medical practice makes such practices inherently criminal—unless performed by a medical doctor (or, presumably, by another licensed provider within the legally authorized scope of practice). This is because, as noted, the typical medical licensing statute brings even religious practices into the state's power to sanction unauthorized healing conduct.[97] The rationale has been protection of public health, safety, and welfare, although from a historical perspective, such broad interpretation of medical licensing requirements also reflects the political and ideological triumph of biomedicine over its rivals and competitors. But as noted, medical practice also has been defined as "the humane action of one human [being] toward another to provide comfort, relief and sometimes to cure"—that is, as sometimes constituting practices involving medical training and skill and sometimes constituting practices involving a healing intention.[98]

As suggested, the clash in constitutional values should be noted and clarified but cannot necessarily be resolved without addressing the larger confusion about what is medical and what lies outside the boundaries of medicine; what should be incorporated within medicine and how teams of healing professionals can interact; what are the interlocking layers of health and disease at all levels of being; what is physical, versus mental, emotional, and spiritual (and how these are connected and distinct); which legal rules are anachronistic or the result of historical hegemonies and rivalries, and which legal rules protect patients and further health; and finally, how the complex mix of interlocking aspects of a person's being involving health can be understood and, in some salutary fashion, be regulated.

For now, it is clear from case law that the state has the right and authority, as part of its police power, to regulate spiritual healing practices as one of many health care services offered by providers.[99] The question is whether exercise of such authority unduly (though not necessarily unconstitutionally) intrudes into a domain of healing considered by many to be religious or, at the least, spiritual, and thereby is beyond the purview and authority of public policy and legal constraint.

THE REGULATORY SIDE

With many states licensing a variety of CAM providers, it may seem inevitable that new CAM professions, including those based largely on spiritual healing practices, will seek licensure. But in fact, although a current trend is toward increasing licensure of health care providers[100] and toward administrative involvement in the licensing process, licensing is not uniformly favored as a mechanism to control dangerous and deviant practices. The critique of occupational licensure holds that licensure tends to be ineffective and tends to protect the entrenched interests of those judging candidates for licensure rather than the public, therefore by and large failing to serve the interests it portends to present.[101]

But even if it were effective as a means to control fraud, licensure has other implications in terms of its limits on practitioners' ability to rely on the intuitive aspects of their craft—the so-called dark side of regulation. Licensure presents a potential shadow in terms of increased regulatory control and bureaucratic hurdles and unnecessary intrusion into the therapeutic relationship. For this reason, many CAM providers fear that the "heart and soul" of their profession will be lost once they are subject to professional regulatory boards.[102] If practices involving energy healing remain at the cross-roads of touch, intention, therapeutic contact, and caring—that is, they are practiced in good faith, with genuine regard for patient boundaries—then practitioners might have a genuine fear that regulation would be intrusive and have an overall destructive effect on morale in practice. Many providers, in fact, prefer that practices such as energy healing remain unregulated and beyond the requirements of uniform examinations and educational criteria.[103]

But even in the absence of licensing mechanisms, spiritual healers remain at risk of prosecution when their practices purport to involve (or are understood by the patient to involve) a potential effect on physical health. Once the line between religion and medicine is crossed, the state arguably has the right (and many would argue, the duty) to intervene. Certainly, as noted, the police power pursuant to the Tenth Amendment authorizes such intervention, once practices aim not only at belief, faith, and doctrine but also at facilitating physical health.[104] And states, as noted, have not hesitated to prosecute healers in situations involving the patient's physical health.

At least one court, in *Board of Medical Quality Assurance v. Andrews*, has expressly drawn a line between purely religious care and care sufficiently touching medical concerns as to warrant prosecution.[105] In *Andrews*, the minister of a religious organization purported to have special knowledge of body symptoms and needs, diagnosed ailments, and prescribed treatments to his clients. These included severe and prolonged fasts, which apparently endangered the lives of some of the clients. In reviewing his conviction, a California appeals court found the minister to have engaged in the practice of medicine. The court reasoned that the purpose of the fasts and other treatments was therapeutic and not religious.

Andrews suggests that once a religious figure has crossed the line into recommending therapies that aim at physical as well as spiritual benefit, a court well may find that the practitioner has crossed the line into practicing medicine. The holding of *Andrews* is consistent with the tendency by courts to interpret diagnosis, treatment, and the practice of medicine extremely broadly, sweeping many different kinds of diagnostic and therapeutic activities—whether or not expressly medical—under the medical licensing statute's rubric. As suggested, historically, such broad interpretation helped to maintain the monopoly by biomedicine over professional healing practices.[106] In any event, whether or not spiritual healing practitioners find a way to receive licensure or to find exemptions thereto,[107] their activities will doubtless be seen as affecting physical health and thereby to cross the line into licensed medical (and other health care) practices.

A related arena in which spiritual healing practices are subject to regulatory control involves informed consent. The doctrine of informed consent, as noted, protects the patient's bodily integrity by requiring disclosure of information material to decision making by the patient. The doctrine does not necessarily provide the patient with a protected interest in access to a variety of therapies.[108] Nor have informed consent rules expanded to embrace a patient's right to be informed concerning CAM therapies.[109] Yet, presumably, there are risks and benefits of practices involving energy healing, even though it might be difficult to frame such disclosure, given the relative paucity of practice standards and scientific evidence concerning results.[110] Policy arguments surrounding regulation of energy healing remain in flux.[111]

Conceptualizing Abuse in Spiritual Healing

DEFINING ABUSE

The fiduciary element of the healer-client relationship is ubiquitous, whether that healer is a physician, a mental health care professional, a nurse, or a member of the clergy. Perhaps for this reason, ethical codes among such diverse professions as medicine, chiropractic, and massage therapy contain parallel provisions.[112] Yet because spiritual healing traditionally has been offered within a religious context, it is also useful to begin by looking at definitions of abuse within the relationship between a member of the clergy and a believer. Further, the spiritual authority of the clergy presents unique challenges in conceptualizing the potential for abuse of that fiduciary relationship.

In describing betrayal and infliction of trauma within the setting of the provision of religious services, the term "abuse" has been used almost exclusively to describe sexual abuse between clergy and client.[113] The notion of abuse, however, covers a larger territory, of which sexual misconduct is a subset. More generally, abuse signifies a deviation from the trust and fiduciary responsibility expected by a practitioner of professional health care services. An alternative term in the literature, referring to pastoral care, is "clergy misfeasance"; one current definition is "the exploitation and abuse of a religious group's believers by trusted elites and leaders of that religion."[114]

In legal terms, such malfeasance represents a violation of fiduciary responsibility. Use of the term "clergy malfeasance" recognizes that similar violations also "occur across a broad range of occupations and institutions—for example, in doctors' and counselors' offices, in law firms, and on university campuses"—in short, in other contexts presenting "hierarchies of unequal power."[115] In this usage, clergy malfeasance has been conceptualized as a subset of "elite deviance," broadly defined as "illegal and unethical acts committed by persons in the highest corporate and political strata of society," who "run relatively little risk of apprehension or serious punishment."[116] Examples include manufacturer distribution of dangerous products and political and corporate corruption.[117]

Unlike perpetrators of "secular" elite deviance, whose misconduct frequently is motivated by a desire to further organizational goals, perpetrators of clergy malfeasance frequently are motivated by "lust, greed, or personal problems."[118] The common element is violation of a fiduciary relationship—betrayal of trust in an expert professional to whom the client "has turned for services and assistance and thereby revealed vulnerability."[119]

Clergy malfeasance, as previously defined, takes at least three forms of deviance: sexual, economic, and authoritative. Sexual deviance includes seduction, rape, and pedophilia. Economic malfeasance includes con schemes and diversion of funds for personal enrichment.[120] Familiar examples include economic fraud by televangelists and resemble white-collar crime, with an added overlay of religious manipulation.[121]

Authoritative malfeasance (or "abuse of authority" by a spiritual figure) includes "excessive monitoring and controlling of members' livelihoods, resources, and lifestyles to enrich" the spiritual figure. Essentially, authoritative malfeasance (deviance) means "abuse of authority by a religious leader" and covers a gray zone or continuum of behaviors, from those acceptable (e.g., "shepherding" others) to those clearly identifiable as wrongful (e.g., micromanaging every aspect of followers' lives).[122] A popular term for this kind of abuse from the perspective of the victim is "toxic faith," defined by one author as "a destructive and dangerous involvement in a religion that allows the religion, not a relationship with God, to control a person's life."[123] Notably, the term "spirituality" could equally be substituted for "religion," and a generic term such as "one's spiritual center" could be substituted for the more religiously oriented term, "God."[124] The principle remains the same: ceding personal power and enabling dysfunctional control in the name of higher ideals.[125]

Ultimately, all these forms of misconduct are, in a psychological sense, boundary violations—distortions of the accepted and healthy boundaries of the therapeutic relationship between the spiritual caregiver and the recipient of spiritual care. Boundary violations are a common ethical concern in psychotherapy,[126] and the mental health professions offer an additional model for exploring the potential for abuse between the practitioner of spiritual healing and client. As a baseline, issues of sexual boundaries between therapist and patient and their potential exploration are of deep concern. In addition, the profession has sufficiently evolved to generate a complex set of definitions and rules governing many different kinds of potential abuse between psychotherapist and client.[127]

Ethical rules governing mental health counseling provide a useful analogue for practices involving spiritual healing, because of the attention paid to the therapist's own psychological state (e.g., awareness of transference and countertransference) and the need to respect the client's emotional boundaries as part of the therapeutic process. Furthermore, the ethics of mental health counseling emphasize a holistic view of personal development as a paramount treatment goal. Finally, psychotherapy emphasizes the patient's vulnerability and emotional dependence on the therapist.[128]

Although some connections between ethical issues in the practice of psychotherapy and practices involving spiritual healing have been preliminarily explored,[129] further research is necessary to investigate the intersection of thought (i.e., intention), behavior (e.g., touch), nuances of emotion (e.g., healthy and healing or pathological and abusive), and the extent to which the profession of psychotherapy can or even should, from an ethical perspective, embrace spiritual healing[130] or, alternatively, intensify the psychic boundaries between therapist and patient.[131] In any event, malfeasance in psychotherapy offers a potentially parallel research ground for exploring issues of abusive conduct by health care providers offering spiritual healing.

ABUSE OF AUTHORITY IN SPIRITUAL HEALING

Spiritual healing in the health care context purports to mediate the client's physical, mental, and emotional issues with the spiritual realms,[132] with claimed benefits ranging from curing on the physical level to the broader notion of healing (a sense of spiritual redemption or reclaimed wholeness).[133] The healer acts not only as a confidant and therapist but also as a medium through whom the energies of healing are purported to flow. The relationship between healer and client thus involves an expanded realm of interaction, bridging the physical, mental, emotional, and spiritual realms of being. In other words, the relationship involves not only the client's trust, vulnerability, and surrender to the healer's care but also the perception of a flow, or exchange, of spiritual energy. The healer purportedly anchors the sacred[134] and thereby literally claims to draw on a universal field of spiritual energy to self-charge and then transmit the resulting "voltage" to the patient.[135] The healer can be viewed as a shaman—bridging worlds and helping individuals transcend their normal, ordinary definition of reality by moving easily between ordinary and nonordinary states of consciousness.[136]

Further, the healer ostensibly is empowered with spiritual gifts to which the client presumably lacks access. These are self-reported, among some healers, to include from among the following: clair-voyance (the ability to access information through visual means), clairaudience (auditory access), clairsentience (access through sens-ing or feeling), long-distance perception, and direct access and pre-cognition (ability to predict possible futures).[137] Given such reports, the "unequal power" thus includes "claims to possess disproportion-ate spiritual wisdom, experience, or charisma of office," as well as "theological authority."[138] This very imbalance of power—of stated ability in the arena of spiritual access and discernment—creates a potential for abuse of authority.[139]

Therefore, while both sexual and economic deviance may be pos-sible in the realm of spiritual healing, this chapter focuses on the category of authoritative abuse. Given the above claims of spiritual power by healers, the exchange between healer and client arguably is just as heightened and intensified, and the client is just as vulnerable and dependent, as in the clergy-confidant relationship.[140] Yet the healer's role purports to bridge that of physician and clerical coun-selor: to mediate physical and spiritual and to make the unmanifest manifest, thereby bringing gifts from divine realms—or at least the most sublime dimensions of human awareness—into the human condition.

Thus, whereas in the context of pastoral care, authoritative abuse may involve controlling recipients of care (e.g., through microman-aging or manipulating behavior through expressions of spiritual dogma), the potential authoritative abuse in spiritual healing is likely to involve abuse of the healer's position of authority by virtue of claimed access to specialized, intuitive information—that is, ac-cess to the shamanic worlds of nonordinary consciousness that give the healer a privileged glimpse into the client's condition and poten-tial mechanisms to resolve the client's health care issues or crisis.[141]

Although at its basest level, abuse of power may include inciting the client (or follower) to engage in criminal behavior,[142] at a basic level, the abuse involves deception, a transfer of authority to the healer, and the potential for physical (and emotional) injury arising from relinquishing appropriate self-care.[143] The same instrument of healing—the human form, with its consciousness of caring, loving intentionality, and sacred touch—also can be used for destructive exploitation. In short, the potential for abuse of authority in spiritual healing presents unique conceptual challenges, precisely because it is potentially ubiquitous among spiritual health care providers and simultaneously promises to bridge medicine and religion.[144]

Regulating Abuse in Clinical Delivery of Spiritual Healing

Legal rules governing (and attempting to control) potential abuse of authority by health care professionals are extensive. They are subsumed under five categories: medical licensure, scope of practice, professional discipline, malpractice, and fraud.[145] These legal rules often operate together as limitations on potential abuse of authority by a variety of health care professionals.

MEDICAL LICENSURE

Medical licensure is one of the earliest forms of regulation recognizing professional delivery of health care services, and subjecting the conduct of health care professionals to statutory proscriptions.[146] Medical licensure originated in New York in 1760 as a means to prevent "ignorant and unskillful persons" from "endangering the lives and limbs of their patients, and many poor and ignorant persons, who have been persuaded to become their patients."[147] Thus, medical licensure neatly fits the police power rationale of protecting public health, safety, and welfare.

By requiring a license to practice medicine and defining the practice of medicine in its broadest sense—as any act constituting diagnosis or treatment for any disease or ailment—medical licensing laws, as interpreted by courts, resulted in convictions of chiropractors, naturopaths, massage therapists, hypnotists, nutritional counselors, and spiritual healers for unlicensed medical practice.[148] Thus, although they were initially weakly enforced, by the late nineteenth century, medical licensing laws had become a powerful tool for enforcing dominant medical paradigms.[149] Medical licensure had evolved from the attempt to control lay practitioners of the healing arts into the consolidation of a medical establishment, with extensive political and economic control,[150] and the ability to condemn anyone who opposed dominant medical perspectives as "an 'enemy of physic and all learning.' "[151]

While medical licensure has been variously criticized as self-serving, ineffective, and tending to incite litigation over practice boundaries,[152] its ostensible purpose—to protect the public from unscrupulous and untrained providers—arguably deters those who practice medicine under the statutory definitions from delivering health care services that could injure the public. Medical licensure thus serves the regulatory goal of fraud control.[153]

Courts have followed legislatures in conceptualizing the practice of medicine broadly, so as to include many different kinds of practitioners and practices within the proscription against practicing medicine without a license. This interpretation has resulted in litigation involving allied health providers—such as psychologists, physician assistants, and nurse practitioners—as well as osteopaths, midwives, and other providers of therapies outside conventional medicine (including lay practitioners of spiritual healing).[154] Criminal convictions of spiritual healers in the past have shown courts' willingness to construe diagnosis and treatment sufficiently broadly to cover laying on of hands, especially in cases where healers have purported to use their spiritual gifts to cure disease as well as to bring spiritual wholeness.[155]

Notably, most state medical licensing laws typically contain an exemption for spiritual healers. These healers, however, usually are exempt from medical practice acts so long as they limit their activities to praying over their clients or to delivering their services in a religious context.[156] This is because treatment by prayer alone has been held to constitute religion and not medicine.[157] Since energy healing often purports to operate in a secular context—and often involves centering, mindfulness, or similar techniques without necessarily invoking prayer to God—the statutory exemption for religious healers arguably is unavailable or at the least, as a matter of policy, inappropriate.[158]

Parenthetically, because medical licensing laws have resulted in convictions of spiritual healers and other providers for unlicensed practice of medicine, grassroots movements have grown in a number of states seeking to free such providers from the threat of prosecution for unlicensed medical practice. For example, California, Minnesota, and Rhode Island have enacted legislation permitting (with specified limitations) practice of health care by persons who are not licensed by the state.[159] Rhode Island, for example, defines "unlicensed health care practices" as

> the broad domain of unlicensed healing methods and treatments, including, but not limited to: (i) acupressure; (ii) Alexander technique; (iii) aroma therapy; (iv) ayurveda; (v) cranial sacral therapy; (vi) crystal therapy; (vii) detoxification practices and therapies; (viii) energetic healing; (ix) rolfing; (x) Gerson therapy and colostrum therapy; (xi) therapeutic touch; (xii) herbology or herbalism; (xiii) polarity therapy; (xiv) homeopathy; (xv) non-diagnostic iridology; (xvi) body work; (xvii) reiki; (xviii) mind-body healing practices; (xix) naturopathy; and (xx) Qi Gong energy healing.[160]

The legislation provides that subject to certain restrictions, persons in Rhode Island "are authorized to practice as unlicensed health care practitioners and receive remuneration for their services."[161] Restrictions include a posting that the state has not adopted any educational and training standards for unlicensed health care practitioners.[162]

The registration requirements provided by such laws, intended in large part to protect such providers from unlicensed medical practice, may still leave them vulnerable to claims of exceeding competence and thereby crossing the line into unlicensed medical practice, if courts continue the historical tendency to interpret medical licensing statutes and the concepts of diagnosis and treatment broadly.[163] Further, such laws allow providers to be prosecuted if they commit fraudulent acts[164] or are found to be engaging in contact that "may be reasonably interpreted by a client as . . . engaging in sexual exploitation"[165] or are shown unable "to engage in unlicensed health care practices with reasonable safety to . . . clients."[166] Providers also may not offer a medical diagnosis,[167] although that term, while it is more specific than "diagnosis," is not defined further.

SCOPE OF PRACTICE RULES

Scope of practice rules refer to services that licensed non-physicians (as opposed to physicians or laypersons) are authorized to provide pursuant to their own licensing statutes. Such services typically are defined more narrowly than the broad authority granted to physicians to diagnose and treat disease.[168] For example, in the allied health professions, licensure to practice psychology or physical therapy does not authorize the licensee to diagnose and treat in the medical sense.

As an example that may be relevant to the limits of healing by CAM providers, licensed chiropractors typically are authorized to use spinal manipulation and adjustment to readjust the flow of "nerve energy" in their patients; licensed acupuncturists may use techniques of traditional oriental medicine to help adjust the "flow and balance of energy in the body"; and licensed massage therapists can use "rubbing, stroking, kneading, or tapping" the muscles to promote relaxation and affect well-being.[169]

None of these providers are authorized to diagnose and treat disease in the medical sense. For this reason, frequently, the licensing statutes delineating scope of practice provisions for nonphysicians include an express prohibition against the unlicensed practice of medicine.[170] Such providers have a duty to refer the patient to a physician whenever the patient's condition exceeds the scope of their training, education, and competence, and violation of the duty can lead to malpractice liability.[171]

Despite these statutory attempts to draw distinctions, the line between authorized practice of a nonmedical profession (e.g., chiropractic) and unauthorized medical practice can be difficult to draw. For example, chiropractors who have offered nutritional advice have been prosecuted for practicing medicine unlawfully, despite the argument that nutritional care is part of chiropractic education and training. Courts have tended to interpret scope of practice narrowly, in the same way they have tended to interpret the practice of medicine broadly and inclusively.[172]

In addition to the rationale of preserving public health, safety and welfare, one reason for this blurring of lines is that any distinction between a holistic notion of wellness care (adopted by many CAM providers) and the actual diagnosis and treatment of a disease is difficult to conceptualize. The difficulty increases when the latter terms are taken in their broadest sense to incorporate any attempts to help patients heal.[173] In either case, many modalities such as nutritional care occupy the borderline between the two poles of "wellness care" and "disease care."[174] A further problem is that scope of practice rules "reflect the notion that the enterprise of healing can be carved into neatly severable and licensable blocks," whereas many CAM practices aim to be holistic—to address the whole person, not an afflicted body part.[175]

One implication of these definitional conundrums is that, to the extent that licensed health professionals are using spiritual healing as part of professional care, they may offer such services only if acting within their legally authorized scope of practice. Thus, for example, nursing professionals would have to ensure that Therapeutic Touch is within the scope of nursing practice authorized by the licensing statute within their state.

A further complexity arises since spiritual healing services may be provided by any number of health professionals—physicians and allied conventional health professionals (such as nurses and dentists) as well as CAM providers (such as chiropractors, acupuncturists, and massage therapists). Scope of practice thus may overlap. Yet, state licensing statutes do not always expressly state whether spiritual healing can be offered. Sometimes regulations by the relevant state professional board may delineate what the licensing statute omits. For example, in Massachusetts, the Board of Registration in Nursing has provided that it is within the scope of practice for a registered nurse or a licensed practical nurse to employ complementary therapies including "Massage, Therapeutic touch, Reiki, Reflexology, Imagery, Hypnosis, Music therapy, Shiatsu, and Aromatherapy" as "part of an overall plan of [nursing] care for which clients have granted informed consent."[176] In the absence of such regulation, providers may argue that spiritual healing, if not expressly prohibited in the statute, is permitted (so long as it is part of their education and skill set);[177] the state, however, may argue just the opposite—that what the statute fails to expressly authorize, it prohibits.

PROFESSIONAL DISCIPLINE

Licensing statutes for health care professionals typically include a set of provisions specifying under what circumstances the licensed professional may be disciplined, with sanctions ranging from fines to loss of licensure. Unprofessional conduct (also known as professional misconduct) that provides a basis for such discipline typically includes such acts as obtaining the license fraudulently, practicing the profession fraudulently, practicing with gross incompetence or gross negligence, practicing while impaired by drugs or alcohol, permitting or aiding an unlicensed person to practice unlawfully, or failing to comply with relevant rules and regulations.[178]

Presently, no independent licensure exists for practitioners of spiritual healing.[179] As a result, in most states, health care providers arguably must seek licensure in another category or profession (such as nursing or chiropractic) that incorporates modalities such as Healing Touch or Reiki into its regimen. In such cases, these providers are bound by the provisions governing professional discipline that are contained in their respective licensing statutes.

Presumably, for example, a nurse practicing Therapeutic Touch in an extremely unskillful manner conceivably could be considered to be practicing with "gross incompetence," and thereby be subject to professional discipline. However, it may be difficult to define what constitutes gross incompetence to the extent that the profession itself may have failed to establish practice standards for the modality in question (e.g., Therapeutic Touch).

Even if the profession has set such standards, they may be less tangible than parallel standards for a medical or nursing procedure, since such acts as centering, assessing, and directing energy—even if taught as part of the nursing school curriculum and applied in a hospital setting—inherently cross the boundary between medicine and religion and perhaps suggest untested (or untestable) metaphysical propositions. In other words, if there are no objective criteria to measure whether a practitioner has met the standard, it may remain difficult to interpret and enforce the norms contained in professional discipline provisions of the licensing statute.

In recent years a number of states have enacted statutes protecting health care providers—particularly physicians—from professional discipline based on therapeutic recommendations involving CAM therapies. For example, Alaska's statute, enacted in 1990, states that the medical board "may not base a finding of professional incompetence solely on the basis that a licensee's practice is unconventional or experimental in the absence of demonstrable physical harm to a patient."[180]

Similarly, according to Colorado's statute, "The board shall not take disciplinary action against a [physician] solely on the grounds that such a [physician] practices alternative medicine."[181] The language contained in these statutes varies by state.[182] In most states, it remains to be seen whether such language would, in fact, protect providers incorporating controversial therapies considered by a given regulatory board to be within a domain that is beyond testing or, in the minds of some, beyond plausibility.[183]

MALPRACTICE

Malpractice liability rules protect patients against negligence by health care providers. Negligent practice is defined as practice below the standard of care, which conduct injures the patient. Since CAM therapies historically have been defined as outside conventional standards of care, the potential arises for courts to label use of such therapies as malpractice per se—that is, irrespective of any wrongdoing.[184]

As noted earlier, at least one court (*Charell v. Gonzales*) has articulated the proposition that a physician's inclusion of CAM therapies conceivably could itself be negligent, given the current definition of CAM therapies.[185] The danger increases with a therapy such as energy healing, which has theoretical underpinnings about which many similarly situated providers would be skeptical. Thus, an expert witness from the defendant's profession might be able to persuade the jury, as in *Charell*, that the defendant's use of the modality in question was "bogus" and "of no value."[186]

Several defenses to medical malpractice might be available to the provider who uses a CAM therapy, even though the therapy has not been adopted as part of the standard of care within the jurisdiction. These defenses include the "respectable minority" defense—the idea that a significant segment within the profession accepts the modality—and assumption of risk, the notion that the patient knowingly, voluntarily, and intelligently assumed a risk of injury from the chosen therapy.[187]

The respectable minority defense, however, is especially complicated in regard to use of CAM therapies, since it may be difficult to determine what constitutes the requisite quantity of providers and what level of evidence of safety and/or efficacy would make them sufficiently respectable to trigger the defense. Similarly, the assumption of risk defense does not allow providers to act negligently—in other words, there are some risks that courts will not allow patients to assume. This caveat to the defense triggers a circular argument as to what is negligent and whether, in cases involving novel and controversial therapies, negligence can, like fraud, become a label that is applied based on a biased view of those therapies.

A second theory supporting malpractice liability is the failure to provide adequate informed consent. To date, no patient has successfully argued that a provider's failure to disclose the possibility of using a CAM therapy instead of a biomedical therapy caused injury and constituted malpractice. At least one court has, however, observed that such an argument would succeed if the therapy in question had a sufficient level of professional acceptance.[188]

The implication is that if energy healing were to gain significant acceptance within a given profession—say, nursing—then failure to disclose its availability to a patient if the patient were thereby injured would constitute an actionable violation of informed consent and allow the patient to recover for malpractice. On the other side, an energy healer who fails to inform the patient concerning material, medical alternatives to energy healing probably would have violated the duty of informed consent and—particularly if such alternatives are considered standard care within the provider's legally authorized scope of practice (e.g., medicine or nursing)—thereby be liable in malpractice.

FRAUD

The tort of fraud is triggered when a health care provider deceives the patient and does so with the intent to so deceive.[189] To the extent the provider offering spiritual healing intentionally deceives the patient into expecting a result that lacks sufficient scientific evidence, the prosecution would have a viable argument that fraud has occurred if that result is not achieved. The deception would have to be intentional and not negligent or the result of an honest mistake.

Providers of spiritual healing face arguably less legal risk if they describe potential results in spiritual rather than physical terms—alluding to the distinction between healing and curing. The argument is that the description of healing work as spiritual helps deflect perception that the conduct falls within diagnosis and treatment of disease. On the other hand, this definitional strategy dichotomizes medicine and religion—the physical and the metaphysical—and eviscerates the notion of a borderland between the two. As noted, various practitioners in a variety of settings incorporate different kinds of spiritual healing practices and frequently do so with the intent to produce more than relaxation, palliation, or spiritual comfort.

Ultimately, the language of fraud may be inadequate to the task, except under egregious circumstances meeting the requisite legal definitions. The law, perhaps, has not yet adequately learned to address the uncomfortable borderland between science and faith, medicine and religion—between accounts of the world considered objective and those by and large regarded as subjective. By definition, energy healing, when it is practiced in good faith—with the intent to heal, not to dupe—makes a charge of fraud appear as an ideological label rather than as a conclusion of law. Fraud, an intentional tort, is among the most extreme forms of abuse and potentially the most difficult to prove, since a distinct mental state must be alleged and proved. This is ironic since, as noted, spiritual healing purports to draw on a clear and healing intentionality (i.e., a positive and beneficial mental state) on the part of the practitioner.

Categorizing Potential Abuse

As suggested above, legal rules that could apply to the practice of spiritual healing within a secular context, such as the modern medical center, are extensive, even if not explicitly directed at spiritual healing practices. Whether such rules are in fact effective is an empirical question, requiring data beyond the scope of this chapter.[190] What this chapter can suggest, however, is that these rules, taken as a whole, help conceptualize abuse of authority and thus create a conceptual web that helps curb potential abuse by providing legal sanction for specific kinds of violations. For illustration, consider the following scenarios:

(1) D, who lacks any health care licensure but has several certificates from various schools teaching certain CAM modalities, offers energy healing to individuals, purporting to cure various ailments.

(2) D, who is a licensed nurse, offers energy healing to individuals, purporting to cure various ailments.

(3) D, a licensed family physician, offers energy healing to help a patient access his or her own inner resources for smoking cessation.

(4) D, a licensed family physician, offers energy healing to a cancer patient and, making the assumption that these methods will help shrink a tumor, neglects to perform or recommend accepted mainstream treatment.

(5) D, a licensed family physician, offers energy healing to a cancer patient and, assuring her that these methods will help shrink a tumor, neglects to perform or recommend accepted mainstream treatment.

These hypothetical situations, respectively, illustrate major potential arenas of abuse of authority in healing as follows: (1) lack of professional competence; (2) exceeding professional competence; (3) exceeding professional boundaries; (4) professional negligence; and (5) intentional deception (including exaggeration of claims and diversion from conventional care).[191] This is not an exclusive and comprehensive or even systematic map of potential areas of abuse, but it does provide a working framework for assessing the extent to which legal rules capture and address abuse of spiritual authority.

In this light, one can draw a parallel between the major legal rules governing delivery of healing services, identified above, and the potential arenas of abuse just mentioned. In the first scenario, D lacks the education and professional training necessary to cure various ailments. Because D arguably holds himself or herself out as being able to diagnose and cure disease, D could be criminally liable for practicing medicine without a license. Perhaps for this reason, hospitals may rely on licensed providers (e.g., licensed nurses or massage therapists, if massage therapy is licensed within the state) rather than unlicensed personnel (e.g., lay practitioners trained in Reiki) to offer energy healing services.[192]

In the second hypothetical situation, D in some (but not all) jurisdictions (particularly those with officials adverse to energy healing) might be considered to be exceeding professional competence and thus the scope of practice authorized in the licensing statute.[193] This would subject D to criminal charges of practicing medicine without a license.

The third hypothetical scenario presents a situation in which a licensed physician employs energy healing. Since physicians typically are said to have an "unlimited" scope of practice to diagnose and treat disease—as opposed to the more limited range of practice allocated to allied health professionals and CAM providers[194]—the issue is not one of legal authority over practice but, rather, of professional boundaries. In other words, the relevant professional regulatory board (i.e., medical board) could argue that physicians should not include energy healing in clinical practice because energy heal-

TABLE 6.1. Form of Abuse and Corresponding Legal Rule

Form of Abuse	Corresponding Legal Rule
Lack of competence	Licensure
Exceeding professional competence	Scope of practice
Misconduct	Professional discipline
Negligence	Malpractice
Deception	Fraud

ing lacks a sufficient evidentiary base.[195] The physician's claim about energy healing (e.g., for cure, support, or stress reduction) could be relevant to the board's ultimate response, however, especially if the physician continued to offer conventional care, since the physician then could not be accused of forgoing necessary medical care for untested alternatives.[196]

In the fourth scenario, the physician neglects necessary conventional care, and thus is negligent in failing to meet the standard of care, and commits malpractice. The fifth hypothetical case presents an unwarranted claim that deceives the patient. If the deception has been intentional, then the patient can sue for fraud, and criminal fraud charges can be brought as well.[197]

The noted correspondence between forms of abuse and applicable legal rules is summarized in Table 6.1.

In short, the relevant legal rules—whether or not directed in a comprehensive, rational manner toward such practices—do provide a preliminary conceptual map for major arenas of dysfunction. Whether or not completely adequate to the task, when taken together, legal rules governing licensing, scope of practice, professional discipline, malpractice, and fraud do constrain the practitioner and begin to address major arenas in potential abuse of authority. Questions remain, however, as to how deeply these rules—historically rooted in the biomedical health professions—penetrate into future problems likely to arise from use of spiritual healing in mainstream health care settings.

Future Regulation of Abuse

Historically, of the above categories, the label of fraud has been most commonly ascribed to CAM therapies[198] and perhaps most strongly resonates with impressions of energy healing for many in the scientific and medical communities. Fraud, however, requires a mental state—an intention to deceive—as well as deception itself and therefore should not be used as a conclusory label for liability.[199]

As different kinds of CAM providers receive licensure, scope of practice becomes an area of increasing legal attention.[200] In cases of energy healing, this can result, for example, in attendant debates over whether Therapeutic Touch is properly within the scope of nursing, whether such therapies as network chiropractic are appropriate for professional practice in integrative care settings in hospitals, and the extent to which "noncontact touch" therapies are within the legally authorized scope of practice for some massage therapists.

Similar debates are likely to erupt in the arena of professional discipline, as emerging uses of energy healing challenge political structures within each profession—like earlier debates concerning use of homeopathy by physicians.[201] Such debates already have erupted within institutions, for example, attempting to define policies determining which providers can lawfully practice energy healing and under what circumstances.[202] In addition, debates may erupt as to what constitutes efficacy, given that spiritual healers may be competent in their own terms while failing to meet a biomedical paradigm of effectiveness.[203]

Finally, ethical codes within a healing profession may help delineate gray zones of conduct where legal rules fail to reach. These might include, for example, referring patients to chaplains or other ministers when significant spiritual needs are identified, and ensuring that patients can exercise the right to refuse spiritual healing, counseling, or inquiry.[204]

One arena that the above scenarios fail to address is the abuse of power that results in emotional injury but without any physical consequences. For example, consider the following scenario:

P, a thirty-year-old woman, inexplicably grows deaf in one ear. Her physician has no explanation other than reporting that some people grow prematurely deaf. P visits an "intuitive helper" who says she is "learning a lesson on a soul level: you haven't been listening to God," and advises her that "with prayer, meditation, and opening your heart to God's wisdom, the deafness will heal." P leaves the session, feeling bewildered, guilty, and morally imperiled, as well as frightened by her new physical status. She visits her physician who reassures her that all standard diagnostic and therapeutic procedures have been performed.[205]

In one sense, the dogmatic, black-and-white thinking articulated by the healer in this scenario, combined with the ascription of a physical condition as punishment from God, exemplifies the notion of religious abuse—of "adopting a rigid belief system that specifies only one right way, which you feel you must force onto others by means of guilt, shame, fear, brain-washing, and elitism."[206] An individual who buys into such abuse may have a toxic belief—for example, that she is being punished for failing to listen to God, or that if she has real faith, a cure is guaranteed.[207] On the other hand, one need not label the individual who is prey to the healer's misconduct a spiritual addict in order to understand the heightened vulnerability, propensity for dependence, and intense trust such a person may come to place in the healer.

Legal rules would address a physical injury if the healer were to make a recommendation to ignore or neglect medical advice or to substitute spiritual advice for medical diagnosis and treatment. But legal rules may incompletely address the explicitly emotional aspect of malfeasance by spiritual healers. Historically, the tort of negligent infliction of emotional distress could be met only when physical injury was shown, although more recently the requirement has been relaxed so long as the plaintiff can show that the defendant has breached some other duty recognized by law as being owed to the plaintiff.

Thus abuse of trust, without more measurable physical injury, might not be actionable, especially if the relationship was based on spiritual caregiving and advice, the healer steered away from giving an opinion on medical problems or issues concerning physical health, and there were no agreed standards of professional conduct in such a relationship (making negligence difficult to show). If, on the other hand, the healer, as suggested, were to advise P to disregard her physician's advice and to substitute a prescribed, ritualized regimen for healing, issues of scope of practice, malpractice, professional discipline, and fraud doubtless would arise.[208]

The lacuna between spiritual and physical injury—between infliction of a wound to the heart and soul of the patient and injury that can be concretized in material terms—raises novel policy issues. It may well be that the law, having opened up through licensing and other rules the possibility of allowing health care professionals to deliver exclusively spiritual (and not physical) healing to patients, has failed to recognize legal harm consisting exclusively of spiritual (and not physical) injury.

Of course, it is debatable whether this has do with evolution in consciousness among those who give and interpret the law,[209] or whether it is difficult to concretize spiritual injury sufficiently to make such injury comprehensible to a jury, and thereby compensable. At the very least, the thrust of modalities historically considered religious into realms historically considered scientific, medical, and outside the purview of religion may augur reconsideration of fundamental assumptions about what sorts of conduct are comprehensible as forbidden, socially condemnable, and monetarily compensable.

Reconceptualizing the Law

The presence of spiritual healing in clinical care centers, within a secular (and frequently medical) context challenges the legal boundaries of professional health care practice. More specifically, energy healing therapies, whether they are practiced by physicians, nurses, or other licensed health care providers such as (in many states) massage therapists, are subject to an array of legal rules.

Such rules proscribe (and ideally constrain) certain specified categories of professional misconduct and simultaneously circumscribe attempts by providers to portray diagnostic and therapeutic practices as religious rather than as medical. More importantly, such rules attempt to delineate the major categories of potential abuse of power in the relationship between the energy healer and the patient.

Perhaps most significantly, in considering such rules and their impact on conceptualizing malfeasance, policymakers confront practices that occupy the borderland between regulatory categories. In other words, energy healing therapies, like other CAM therapies, can blur the distinction between realms considered by many to be distinct as religion and medicine, and thus force a reconceptualization of legal categories previously thought to be less permeable.

Finally, although present legal rules address issues of abuse of power in the practice of energy healing, the practices themselves may lead to profound rethinking of fundamental legal principles. As one example, one of the exceptions to the informed consent doctrine— the therapeutic privilege—protects the physician from liability for failure to disclose to the patient information that could result in the patient's suffering physical or emotional harm.[210] Yet some forms of energy healing assert that consciousness is nonlocal (i.e., not limited to the body and mind of a particular individual), thereby permitting providers who are appropriately trained to gain intuitive access to information concerning a patient's health and prognosis.[211] The suggestion is that in the future, some healing professionals will have intuitive diagnostic as well as therapeutic tools of consciousness (rather than medical or scientific instruments) at their disposal that may enable them to reach information not available to the patient in question.[212] Thus, the reach and extent of therapeutic privilege may need to be reconsidered, should physicians be able to access information intuitively and have to wrestle with legal and ethical obligations surrounding such knowledge.

In a similar fashion, as suggested in Chapter 5, theories of malpractice liability may need to take into account the provider's mental, emotional, and spiritual effect on the patient, as well as physical injury. Likewise, in conceptualizing battery, questions may arise as to what constitutes impermissible touch in a world where individuals are conscious not only of the physical body and a zone of privacy around it but also of threads of spiritual energies connecting persons.[213] In other words, if safety, efficacy, and mechanisms of energy healing ultimately receive sufficient scientific proof to garner general medical acceptance, expanded use of these controversial therapies in clinical care may suggest the need to extend legal paradigms to include expanded ideas, not only about different therapeutic modalities and domains of training and knowledge, but also about the nature of healing and human consciousness.[214]

In sum, spiritual healing touches the boundary between medicine and religion, science and faith, and intellect and uncertainty. Legal rules, in addition to safeguarding the public health, also codify political attempts to preserve professional monopolies. In so doing, such rules crystallize cultural belief systems about what professional healers can or should be able to do. Thus, it is important to explore the nexus between legal rules, ethical codes, religious values, and medical culture. Probing the regulatory edges of abuse of power at the borderland of religion and medicine begins to tease out unstated assumptions about the ultimate meaning of human affliction and the health care professional's role in the process of healing.

Toward the Future

Unresolved Issues in the New Health Care

In giving a legal opinion or advice, lawyers make educated guesses based on the state of current law as applied to specific factual situations. With integrative medicine, the task is not easy. State legislation licensing practitioners of the healing arts emerged in the late nineteenth century, favored biomedical doctors, assigned all legislatively authorized healing to these providers, and changed little for almost a hundred years.[1] While chiropractors and practitioners of acupuncture and traditional oriental medicine, massage therapy, and naturopathic medicine are licensed in various states, the case law surrounding complementary and alternative medical (CAM) therapies is rudimentary and still reflects an antipathy to diagnostic and treatment theories foreign to currently accepted biomedical authority.[2] This means that emerging statutes, administrative regulations, and cases concerning CAM therapies will continue to change the legal landscape for liability, authorized professional practice, and consumer access to CAM therapies. Such changes will affect providers and institutions as well as patients.

This shifting legal and regulatory status of CAM therapies also reflects the larger boundaries of the new health care as it assimilates notions of pluralism and the frontiers of accepted medical science. As health care institutions, regulators, providers, and patients fully confront the borderland between medicine and religion, the contradictions and paradoxes doubtless will continue to mount. Meanwhile, unresolved issues lurk in at least five overlapping domains: clinical practice, ethics, hospital policy, insurance reimbursement, and legislation.

- *Clinical Practice*: How will providers across institutions work out clinical pathways for integrative care? For example, should a patient complaining of tennis elbow see the acupuncturist first? Or the chiropractor, the massage therapist, or a physical therapist? Should the first provider of choice be a conventional or CAM professional? How can teams consisting of physicians, allied health professionals, and CAM providers resolve conflicts and translate diagnostic and therapeutic categories across medical traditions?
- *Ethics*: How will institutions meet the ethical obligation of justice if access to CAM therapies within the institution remains dependent on who can pay for these therapies out of pocket (and is thus limited to the wealthy)? How will governments meet the ethical obligation of justice as regards CAM therapies, particularly given renewed calls for universal health care and the need to wisely allocate limited resources?[3]
- *Hospital Policy*: How will hospitals propose to limit the scope of practice of individual providers when competencies overlap (for example, when chiropractors and physical therapists can legally provide the same service for the same patient population)? How will providers respond to institutional policies that purport to restrict their practice authority (for example, acupuncturists forbidden from using herbs)?
- *Insurance Reimbursement*: Which CAM therapies will be proven cost-effective (as well as effective) and hence lead to more widespread third-party reimbursement? Will successes in the reimbursement arena stymie the personalized delivery of certain CAM therapies (such as massage therapy), increase the bureaucratization (real or perceived) of services, and diminish the power of the therapeutic relationship? On the other hand, will most CAM therapies remain outside reimbursement schemes and also outside systems of inpatient care and billing?

- *Legislation and Regulation*: How many new states will adopt statutes authorizing practicing for nonlicensed providers (such as energy healers, naturopaths, and homeopaths who lack independent health care licensure)? Will such statutes protect these providers or still leave them vulnerable to charges of practicing medicine (or another licensed health care profession) unlawfully, or even to allegations of mail and wire fraud? Will such a movement for "health care freedom" mean the end of licensure, or at least diminishment of its significance as an arbiter of who may legally offer professional health care services?

Yet another missing piece is the connector between CAM therapies and disciplines in the humanities such as psychology and religion. Perhaps the battle that will determine the frontiers of health care is not the generic one widely conceptualized as between religion and science. Rather, the battle, to be fought within academic medicine as well as health care institutions and their many constituents and representatives, may be between the tendency to maintain a hegemonic epistemology and the need to stretch currently accepted epistemological frameworks in an effort to understand medical traditions that lie outside biomedicine on their own terms. Such an effort has been accomplished, for example, in the field of integrative mental health in a preliminary effort to map similarities and differences between psychiatric diagnoses in biomedicine and mental health categories in traditional Chinese medicine.[4]

Politically, the language used to describe CAM therapies has positioned the field to garner increasing acceptance (i.e., moving from "holistic" to "alternative" to "complementary and alternative" to "integrative"). Further language shifts are likely to continue shaping acceptance at all levels in institutions and governments. And lawyers and legal scholars, like politicians, lobbyists, philosophers and poets, work with language as a tool for shaping consciousness.

This sculpting of consciousness by choice of language renders law a powerful tool for social transformation in terms of health care norms and clinical practice. While medical research continually aims to gather scientific evidence in efforts to definitively prove or disprove the safety and efficacy of individual CAM therapies, the research community is beginning to recognize the complexity of translation across CAM therapeutic disciplines and scientifically validated, investigative techniques. The Institute of Medicine (IOM), among others, has recognized the existence of gaps in research as well as in appropriate research methods.[5] Law also fills in the lacuna. Research efforts are not always tethered to legislative movement, which often depends on local state politics rather than on the results of clinical trials. Larger questions of institutional policy as well as public policy tend to frame whether and how integrative care is or should be practiced, in nonscientific terms, such as the ethical clash between patient autonomy interests and biomedical paternalism.[6]

At the same time, both research and legislation may neglect the potentially transformational aspects of various CAM therapies and, as suggested, the implications of such therapies for future health, health care policy, and bioethics, including the potential to influence such disparate fields as diplomacy and environmental advocacy. To address all these dimensions of the new health care, this book has endeavored to offer new ways of conceptualizing the emerging synthesis between conventional and CAM therapies at the intersection of clinical, financial, institutional, legal, ethical, and spiritual concerns.

Six Degrees of Separation

While the future shape of the new health care remains to be fully envisioned, designed, and implemented, one general feature is clear: global health care no longer relies exclusively on the biomedical dominance of the late nineteenth and early twentieth centuries but, rather, is beginning to accommodate a broader pluralism that is capable of embracing—in whole or at least in part—some of the theory, epistemology, and practice of other traditions. Like Callahan's book, the formation of a committee within the IOM to study American use of CAM therapies, as well as the committee's final report, suggests such a transition toward greater acknowledgment of the potential benefits of a more pluralistic approach than historically allowed. A concomitant development is the establishment of the

Consortium of Academic Health Centers for Integrative Medicine, a collection of highly esteemed academic medical centers (twenty-seven at present) that have dean-level support to "transform medicine and health care through rigorous scientific studies, new models of clinical care, and innovative educational programs that integrate biomedicine, the complexity of human beings, the intrinsic nature of healing and the rich diversity of therapeutic systems."[7] Such developments suggest movement within academic medicine toward consideration of perhaps a more open stance toward CAM therapies, one still based in rigorous scientific method yet able to reflect creatively on other paradigms of medical thought.

Three brief anecdotes may help further illuminate this shift-in-progress. The first concerns a talk by David S. Rosenthal, the medical director for the Leonard P. Zakim Center for Complementary and Alternative Medical Therapies at the Dana Farber Cancer Institute, a Harvard-affiliated hospital. In a recent address to a professional group, Rosenthal described the evolution of his interest in the field as beginning with his participation in a group within the American Cancer Society known as the Committee on Quackery. That committee later was named the Committee on Unconventional Medical Practices and, still later, the Committee on Complementary and Alternative Medicine. Rosenthal had once sat on a committee that vilified doctors incorporating CAM modalities and whose very name suggested such a mandate; now he leads a Harvard-affiliated hospital center that is dedicated to devising credible and effective models of integrative oncology.

The second tale involves a colleague who served as a member of the IOM committee that drafted the *Report on Complementary and Alternative Medicine*. I had the privilege of serving as a consultant to that committee. During an early meeting, this colleague was quizzed by other committee members, who learned that while publicly known as a skeptic regarding CAM therapies, this conservative physician had coauthored a paper with a practitioner of Tibetan medicine. Our colleague quipped, "I'm a closet CAM sympathizer." As Freud noted, jokes sometimes disclose truths too difficult for the conscious mind to bear openly.

The third involves *Wilk v. American Medical Association* (AMA),[8] the historic case in which chiropractors proved a conspiracy by the AMA to stamp out their profession. I had learned that, long ago, a member of the IOM committee had been named as one of the defendants in that historic lawsuit. Some weeks later, I gave a talk to the Greater Detroit Area Health Council and was approached by an individual who told me that he had served as the chiropractors' expert witness in the case. In other words, the former *Wilk* defendant now served on a prestigious committee within academic medicine charged with exploring to what extent (and how) the medical profession should accommodate therapies such as chiropractic, while the former *Wilk* expert witness for the plaintiffs now was part of a conference to explore collaborative approaches between conventional medical professionals and CAM caregivers (such as chiropractors) in mainstream medical institutions and clinics.

Integration had arrived in the person of these former foes who were joined across cities in a shared exploration. Although these two individuals did not, to my knowledge, meet in their new incarnations, I felt somehow that they were linked—embodying "six degrees of separation" (if not one degree) between the present and the past, a kind of entanglement of particles in the world of future medicine.

A World beyond Languages

If Jensen writes of a language older than words, then the "integration" in "integrative medicine" also suggests a world beyond languages. That world is the shared knowing in the intuitive enterprise of healing, the art that accompanies the science of clinical care. This book has emphasized the rich possibility of an enhanced attention to the many dimensions of pluralism as a central feature of integrative health care. As the IOM report notes, "Without rejecting what has been of great value and services in the past, it is important that these ethical and legal norms be brought under critical scrutiny and evolve along with medicine's expanding knowledge base and the larger aims and meanings of medical practice. The integration of CAM therapies with conventional medicine requires that practitioners and researchers be open to diverse interpretations of health and healing, to finding innovative ways of obtaining the evidence, and to expanding the medical knowledge base."[9]

Experience can inform professional attitudes. Objectivity sometimes presents the mask behind which lies a deeper synthesis of the objective and subjective sides of our being; in such a way, therapeutic practice integrates outer and inner, and scholarship merges the professional and the personal.[10] Acknowledging such an approach can "bring the covert into the overt" and can "validate subjectivity, intuition, and mystery in equipoise to science and law," so that "the field of knowing may be broadened and enriched."[11]

To critique the limitations of biomedicine is not to deny biomedicine's diagnostic and therapeutic power. Rather, a truly pluralistic approach potentially can add open-minded inquiries to Jensen's notion of a "language older than words": a preverbal understanding that includes such facets of therapeutic experience as body wisdom, spirit knowing, intuition, sensation, and emotion. Hamlet's retort, "There are more things in heaven and earth, Horatio, than are dreamt of in your philosophy,"[12] could have been critiqued as unscientific or antiscientific; yet while Hamlet's approach to the ghost of his father may have lacked the empirical rigor of evidence-based medicine, it had other meaning for his own troubled spirit.

The argument for pluralism, as the authors of essays in Callahan's book and the IOM report suggest, is deeper than a critique of biomedical dominance. To quote the U.S. Supreme Court, "If there is any fixed star in our constitutional constellation, it is that no official, high or petty, can prescribe what shall be orthodox in politics, nationalism, religion, or other matters of opinion."[13] The "fixed star" in my own interest in complementary and integrative medicine has been the respect for pluralism and the individual's autonomous, empowered search for all dimensions of health and healing, including those at the borderland of medicine and religion. I have argued for interpretations of law and of ethics that liberate patient choices from historic notions of medical paternalism and move toward a more informed autonomy. I have suggested that while controlling fraud serves as an important regulatory objective, the goal of mass self-actualization, based on individual human transformation, may be at the pinnacle of regulatory values. I have sought an acknowledgment within narrow legal rules of larger notions of healing and spiritual evolution, alongside treatment and cure.[14] On an ethical level, when paternalism and autonomy clash, and when clinicians are called to make sensitive yet important ethical decisions, I have suggested that patients' ways of "knowing" about medical choices may be valid even if they conflict with what clinicians feel may be reasonably supported by the current, consensus medical evidence.[15]

The synthesis between science and spirit is emerging and, as it pertains to medicine, may well reach beyond medicine to disciplines within the humanities such as transpersonal psychology. It is in this sense that the delusional matrix of medicolegal reality arguably shapes future medicine in the wrong direction, errs when it perpetuates a delusional sense that a human being is only material, and, in my view, needs to expand to wisely assimilate portions of foreign (and sometimes competing) worldviews.

In sum, this book's essential argument has been that, like the age-old story of several blind men who examine an elephant and, on holding various parts of the animal, come to different conclusions regarding the nature of the beast, biomedical materialism sometimes gropes blindly within its own predetermined (albeit powerful) parameters and so comes to limited conclusions regarding CAM therapies based on notions of spiritual energy, chi, transmission of subtle information through pulse diagnosis, and related concepts. In the same way, without an appreciation of scientific method, including current research tools, proponents of CAM therapies can grope blindly within the limitations of their own speculative frameworks. To return to the introduction to this book, and to the initial metaphor of D. T. Suzuki regarding "West" and "East,"[16] the "rose" of human health, in all its multifaceted splendor and challenge, can be grasped both in the penetrating analysis of its components and in its illuminated totality. Some combination is necessary of the "analytical, discriminatory, differential, inductive, individualistic, intellectual, objective, scientific, generalizing, conceptual, schematic, impersonal, legalistic, organizing, power-wielding, self-assertive, disposed to impose its will upon others" and the "synthetic, totalizing, integrative, nondiscriminative, deductive, nonsystematic, dogmatic, intuitive (rather, affective), nondiscursive, subjective, spiritually individualistic and socially group-minded."[17]

It is, perhaps, not only medicine that is being integrated, but also these two facets of human nature—two different ways of knowing. Hence, we may enrich understanding of integrative medicine by exploring CAM therapies through the mental health disciplines, anthropology, sociology, and other fields of study. To invoke Callahan, bridges must be built from a place of open inquiry; we should not view health care through a curved lens that only sees back on itself. As this book asserts, such open inquiry may change much, in health care and elsewhere. We are thus not at the end but at the beginning of the beginning, and even with the best of tools, our task of negotiating the new health care may be much more complex and multifaceted than initially realized.

State of the Evidence Regarding Complementary Therapies

The Institute of Medicine (IOM) report on complementary and alternative medicine (CAM) use showcased the best available evidence regarding CAM therapies in its chapter titled "State of Emerging Evidence on CAM." Summarizing Cochrane Reviews with "positive effects," the report listed a number of conditions for which specified CAM therapies may be effective.[1]

The Cochrane Library is an international collaboration to review therapies and modalities. The Cochrane Complementary Medicine Collaboration, based at the University of Maryland Center for Integrative Medicine, coordinates CAM-related activities, including development of a database with information on more than 7,000 controlled trials of CAM therapies. Cochrane Reviews apply the same standards of evidence to conventional and CAM therapies. The Cochrane Collaboration defined its conclusion category of "positive effect" to mean that "treatment is more beneficial/effective than control for the positive outcome."

The IOM report on complementary and alternative medicine concluded, "Although CAM therapies are often criticized for being used despite a lack of evidence, hundreds of systematic reviews have, in fact, evaluated specific CAM therapies; of these, some have been well conducted and have shown that the CAM therapy offers a clear benefit."[2]

TABLE AP. I. Conditions for Which Specified CAM Therapies May Be Effective

Indication	Therapy
Age-related macular degeneration	Antioxidant vitamin and mineral supplements
Anxiety	Kava
BPH	Saw palmetto and other dietary supplements
Cystic fibrosis	Omega 3 fatty acids
Depression	Folate and St. John's Wort
Headache	Acupuncture
Low-back pain	Massage
Jet lag	Melatonin
Knee osteoarthritis	TENS
Osteoarthritis	Electromagnetic fields
Preventing urinary tract infection	Cranberries
Type 2 diabetes mellitus	Fish oil

Key Arenas of Legal and Policy Intervention

The following table suggests a variety of potential arenas of legal/policy intervention and offers examples and case studies to show how such intervention can change the map for integrative health care.

The answers do not all lie within Congress but are spread across a variety of domains, including state law and the regulatory power of health care professional organizations and institutions.

TABLE AP.2. Arena of Legal/Policy Intervention

	Federal Legislation	State Legislation	Administrative Regulation
Example	Federal food and drug law, including the Dietary Supplements Health Education Act	State licensing laws for physicians, allied health, and complementary care providers	Federation of State Medical Board Guidelines for Physician Use of Complementary and Integrative Medical Therapies
Case Studies	Should patients be required to get physician prescription for dietary supplements? How can adulteration be prevented?	Should naturopathic physicians receive licensure in every state? Can they call themselves "primary care providers"?	Should state medical boards be able to strip physicians of their licenses for offering therapies such as homeopathy?

Judge-Made Law	Professional Self-Regulation	Institutional Policy	Multidisciplinary Scholarly Contribution
Malpractice liability rules (cases) for practitioners and institutions; scope of practice rules for practitioners	Ethical codes for the profession; baseline educational requirement for entering the profession	Policies governing patient use of dietary supplements; credentialing practitioners within the hospital	Medical ethics (bioethics) and CAM; multiple perspectives on spirituality in health care, including use of energy healing
Will institutions be liable for allowing their physicians to recommend CAM therapies? When should clinicians recommend or discourage use?	How can professions increase members' level of ethics and responsibility? Should acupuncturists be required to have doctoral-level study for entry?	Should hospitals routinely confiscate patients' dietary supplements (such as an elderly patient's ginkgo or St. John's Wort)?	Do CAM philosophies and theories have a unique contribution to make to bioethics? What professional boundaries apply to healers?

Introduction

1. A program from the First International Congress on Tibetan Medicine: Revealing the Art of the Medicine Buddha, held in Washington, D.C., in 1998, is available at <www.tibetmed.org/ictm.htm>. According to the organizer of this conference, the seventh century

marks the beginning of two centuries of Tibetan dominance of Upper Asia. King Songtsen Gampo (617–650) invited physicians from India, Nepal, Persia and China to Tibet to discuss their medical systems. The result is believed to be a collection, in Tibetan, of their combined medical knowledge. . . . During the reign of King Trisong Deutsen (755–795), the first International Medical Conference was held at Samye, in Tibet. Physicians skilled in the medical systems of India, Persia, Nepal, Greece, China and other neighboring countries debated and shared their knowledge. After the conference, the elder Yutok Yonten Gonpo synthesized the essence of the various Asian medical systems and rewrote the Four Tantras, known as the Gyud-Zhi (pronounced Goo-shee). He founded the first Tibetan medical school in Kongpos Menlung, Tibet in 762. [Anna Souza, personal correspondence, January 2004]

2. Kaptchuk and Eisenberg, "Varieties."

3. James, *Varieties*.

4. For regulation regarding "implausible" complementary and alternative medicine therapies, see Kentucky Board of Medical Licensure, "Policy Statement."

5. Byrant, *Wheel of Time*.

6. This is the main theme of Derrick Jensen in *Language*. See Chapter 4.

7. This theme is continued in published conversations involving the Dalai Lama and facilitated by writers such as Daniel Goleman of the *New York Times*. See, e.g., Goleman, *Healing Emotions*.

8. See Snyderman and Weil, "Integrative Medicine."

9. A project funded by the National Library of Medicine surveyed at least twenty integrative centers in the United States. More than fifty interviews were conducted to explore the institutional and legal obstacles the centers faced in bringing integrative care into conventional medical settings (such as academic medical centers). These centers have developed a number of common strategies for overcoming such hurdles. See Cohen and Ruggie, "Integrating" and " Overcoming Legal and Social Barriers."

10. See, e.g., Ernst, *Desktop Guide*; Fulder, *Handbook*; Kohatsu, *Complementary and Alternative Medicine Secrets*.

11. See, e.g., Lewith and Aldridge, *Clinical Research Methodology*; Vincent and Furnham, *Complementary Medicine*.

12. See, e.g., Morton and Morton, *Five Steps*.

13. Dillard and Ziporyn, *Alternative Medicine*.

14. See, e.g., Crelling and Ania, *Professionalism and Ethics*; Humber and Almeder, *Alternative Medicine and Ethics*.

15. Suzuki, Fromm, and DeMartino, *Zen Buddhism*.

16. Ibid., 2.

17. Ibid., 3.

18. Ibid., 5.

19. Ibid.

20. Cohen, *Legal Boundaries*, 2.

21. Chapter 4 will revisit the detrimental impact of Cartesian dualism on health and healing, focusing on the effect of this worldview on the state of our environmental stewardship.

22. See Cohen, *Legal Boundaries*, 2 (citing sources). See also Chapter 4.

23. See Cohen, *Legal Boundaries*, 2–8 (citing sources). The notion of holism as articulated by Jan Smuts in the early 1920s—the idea that nature expresses itself in wholes—provided the philosophic fuel for the holistic health movement that powerfully resurged in the 1960s; see ibid.

24. Ibid.

25. Such a suggestion has, in fact, already been made by government commissions in both the United Kingdom (House of Lords, *Sixth Report*) and the United States (White House Commission, *Final Report*).

26. See Riskin, "Mindfulness."

27. For an early definition of alternative medicine, see Eisenberg et al., "Unconventional Medicine." For a brief description of the history of movement toward incorporating alternative therapies into conventional, clinical care and of the evolution of terminology such as "CAM" and "integrative medicine," see Cohen and Ruggie, "Integrating." See also

Kaptchuk and Eisenberg, "Persuasive Appeal"; O'Connor et al., "Complementary and Alternative Medicine."

28. See White House Commission, *Final Report*.

29. The Dietary Supplements Health Education Act regulates dietary supplements as foods and not drugs; accordingly, manufacturers can market dietary supplements without prior proof of safety and efficacy, so long as the supplement is not intended for use in the "diagnosis, cure, mitigation, treatment, or prevention of disease" (21 U.S.C. §§ 321[g][1], 321[ff]). For a discussion of the debate around the enactment of this act and its impact on consumer access to herbal medicine, see Cohen, *Legal Boundaries*, 73–86. For a discussion of legal issues more generally concerning CAM therapies, see Cohen, *Legal Boundaries*; for a discussion of malpractice issues, see Studdert et al., "Medical Malpractice Implications."

30. See CA SB 577; Minn. Stat. § 146A; R.I. Gen. Laws § 23-74-1(3). The statutes are described in greater detail in Chapter 6.

31. Institute of Medicine, *Complementary and Alternative Medicine*.

32. White House Commission, *Final Report*.

33. See Cohen, *Legal Boundaries*, chap. 3.

Chapter 1

1. Rothstein, *American Physicians*; Cohen, *Legal Boundaries*, 15.

2. Cohen, *Legal Boundaries*, 15–20.

3. Ibid., 2.

4. Ibid.

5. Ibid., 2–7.

6. Ibid., 2.

7. Ibid.

8. Callahan, *What Kind of Life*.

9. Cohen, *Legal Boundaries*, 2–6.

10. Smuts, *Holism and Evolution*; Cohen, *Legal Boundaries*, 6–7.

11. Cohen, *Legal Boundaries*, 4.

12. Ibid., 20.

13. Ibid., 29–31; *Stetina v. State*, 513 N.E.2d 1234 (Ind. Ct. App. 1987).

14. *Wilk v. American Medical Association*, 719 F.2d 207 (7th Cir. 1983), cert. denied, 467 U.S. 1210 (1984), on remand, 671 F. Supp. 1465 (N.D. Ill. 1987), aff'd, 895 F.2d 352 (7th Cir. 1990). The quotation is from the Seventh Circuit opinion and is found on 895 F.2d at 362.

15. American Medical Association, *Alternative Medicine*, 16–17 (citing C. Krauthammer, "The Return of the Primitive," *Time*, 20 January 1996).

16. Fontarosa and Lundberg, "Alternative Medicine."

17. Beyerstein, "Alternative Medicine."

18. Astin, "Complementary and Alternative Medicine."

19. Cohen and Ruggie, "Integrating."

20. Eisenberg et al., "Unconventional Medicine."

21. Eisenberg et al., "Trends."

22. Cohen, *Legal Boundaries*, 39–44.

23. Eisenberg et al., "Unconventional Medicine," 246.

24. Eisenberg et al., "Trends."

25. American Hospital Association, *Survey*.

26. Straus, "Complementary and Alternative Medicine."

27. American Medical Association, "Policy."

28. American Academy of Family Physicians, "Policy."

29. National Center for Complementary and Alternative Medicine, "What Is Complementary and Alternative Medicine?"

30. Cohen and Ruggie, "Integrating."

31. One of the concepts in *Difficult Conversations* may be helpful here in framing what could be a next step in integrative medicine: the notion of the "And Stance," a way of recognizing complexity and that both views (e.g., conventional and CAM) may have validity. See Stone, Patton, and Heen, *Difficult Conversations*.

32. Cohen and Ruggie, "Integrating"; Ernst, Cohen, and Stone, "Ethical Problems"; Kemper and Cohen, "Ethics."

33. Kaptchuk and Eisenberg, "Varieties."

34. Eisenberg et al., "Credentialing."

35. Weintraub, "Legal Implications."

36. See Cohen and Ruggie, "Integrating."

37. Walker, "Evolution of a Policy."

38. Eisenberg, "Advising Patients."

39. See Cohen, *Beyond Complementary Medicine*, 37–45.

40. Angell and Kassirer, "Alternative Medicine."

41. Ernst, "Harmless Herbs?"; Piscitelli et al., "Indinavir."

42. *Charell v. Gonzales*, 660 N.Y.S.2d 665, 668 (S.Ct., N.Y. County, 1997), affirmed and modified to vacate punitive damages award, 673 N.Y.S.2d 685 (App. Div., 1st Dept., 1998), reargument denied, appeal denied, 1998 N.Y. App. Div. LEXIS 10711 (App. Div., 1st Dept., 1998), appeal denied, 706 N.E.2d 1211 (1998).

43. Cohen, *Beyond Complementary Medicine*, 25.

44. Adams et al., "Ethical Considerations."

45. Cohen and Ruggie, "Integrating."

46. Stone, Patton, and Heen, *Difficult Conversations*.

47. Fisher, Ury, and Patton, *Getting to Yes*, 4–5.

48. From actual cases experienced by or reported to Dr. Karen Adams; the quotations are from Adams et al., "Ethical Considerations."

49. Fisher, Ury, and Patton, *Getting to Yes*, 6.

50. These choices are discussed but not explicitly spelled out in the same fashion in Adams et al., "Ethical Considerations."

51. This scenario was described by Fisher during a talk titled "Negotiating Complementary Medicine" at the Dispute Resolution Forum of the Harvard Law School Program on Negotiation in November 2003.

52. Fisher, Ury, and Patton, *Getting to Yes*, 21.

53. There also may be subgroups within each of the enumerated constituents, each with different interests. For example, among policymakers and regulators, the FDA may view an issue involving consumer access to specified CAM therapies differently from a particular state legislature. Similarly, among CAM providers, chiropractors (or chiropractic associations) and massage therapists may have different interests (particularly if they have overlapping scopes of practice (see Cohen, *Legal Boundaries*, 55). Likewise, allied health providers may disagree about the best care algorithm (e.g., nurses and physical therapists) or may disagree about the kind of intervention (e.g., nurses versus psychologists) or whether the intervention should involve pharmaceutical prescription (e.g., a psychiatrist's prescription for depression) or a behavioral process (e.g., a recommendation from a cognitive psychologist).

54. Cohen, *Legal Boundaries*, 73–77.

55. Ibid.; Cohen, *Future Medicine*, 81, 86–88.

56. Cohen, *Legal Boundaries*, 115–16.

57. Ibid., 56–59.

58. See Ernst and Cohen, "Informed Consent."

59. See Eisenberg et al., "Credentialing."

60. See Cohen, *Legal Boundaries*, 24–38.

61. See ibid., 39–55.

62. See Eisenberg et al., "Credentialing."

63. See Cohen, *Legal Boundaries*, 87–95.

64. See Cohen and Ruggie, "Integrating."

65. See Cohen and Eisenberg, "Potential Physician Malpractice."

66. See Chapter 6. In addition, the different domains give rise to a variety of arenas of legal and policy intervention; see Appendix B.

67. See, generally, Cohen, *Legal Boundaries*.

68. Fisher, Ury, and Patton, *Getting to Yes*, xviii.

69. Cohen, *Legal Boundaries*, 56.

70. Cohen and Eisenberg, "Potential Physician Malpractice."

71. I am grateful for this observation to participants in the Dispute Resolution Forum of the Harvard Law School Program on Negotiation.

72. Snyderman and Weil, "Integrative Medicine."

73. Adams et al., "Ethical Considerations."

74. The clinician who finds this approach unacceptable, who sees this strategy as "giving tacit approval to an irresponsible decision," should refer the patient to "a more like-minded" physician (ibid.). This is one of the options Fisher and Fisher advise when the patient and clinician disagree on the proper medical choice. The patient should seek (and the clinician should help the patient find) another provider who is more amenable to the patient's perspective. See Fisher and Fisher, "What Is a Good Decision?"

75. Weiger et al., "Advising Patients."

76. Adams et al., "Ethical Considerations."

77. Fisher, Ury, and Patton, *Getting to Yes*, 4, 15.

78. See Cohen, "Reckoning."

79. See Astin, "Complementary and Alternative Medicine."

80. Fisher, Ury, and Patton, *Getting to Yes*, 21.

81. Ibid., 23–39.

82. Astin, Harkness, and Ernst, "Distant Healing."

83. Fisher, Ury, and Patton, *Getting to Yes*, 48.

84. Ibid., 43.

85. Katz, *Silent World*.

86. Fisher and Fisher, "What Is a Good Decision?," 190.

87. Fisher, Ury, and Patton, *Getting to Yes*, 4.

88. Becker, *Denial of Death*.

89. Brody, *Healer's Power*.

90. Cohen, *Beyond Complementary Medicine*, 37–45. In this regard, the AMA cautions that patients who choose CAM therapies "should be educated as to the hazards that might result from postponing or stopping conventional medical treatment" (American Medical Association, "Policy").

Chapter 2

1. CAM adherents have criticized the stance of biomedicine toward requiring proof of efficacy through randomized, double-blind trials for every CAM therapy as a "double standard," given the lack of such proof for surgical and other conventional interventions. This critique can also be restated as mistakenly pursuing a regulatory agenda of "fraud control" to the exclusion of other regulatory values, such as that of facilitating health care freedom (or choice) as well as the possibility for deeper human transformation. See, generally, Cohen, *Future Medicine*.

2. Kaptchuk and Eisenberg, "Varieties."

3. National Center for Complementary and Alternative Medicine, "What Is Complementary and Alternative Medicine?" Such language goes beyond the dichotomization of what works/what doesn't, proven/unproven, validated/quackery, or even plausible/implausible, but it does not necessarily capture the entire balance to which the Dalai Lama alluded; nor is the ideal even universally shared.

4. Callahan, *Accommodating Pluralism*.

5. Humber review.

6. See, generally, Cohen, *Legal Boundaries*; Cohen, *Beyond Complementary Medicine*; and Cohen, *Future Medicine*. Academic discussions around integration of CAM therapies are open to an array of hermeneutics and need not necessarily preclude advocacy of critical thinking and self-inquiry, of being as well as doing, of taking responsibility for one's actions, of doing no harm but taking professional and interpersonal risks, of friendship and of solitude, and of integrating head, heart, and soul.

7. Eisenberg et al., "Unconventional Medicine."

8. Callahan, *Accommodating Pluralism*, 38. The citation is to O'Connor et al., "Complementary and Alternative Medicine."

9. See, e.g., Cohen and Eisenberg, "Potential Physician Malpractice" (citing examples and correlating clinical scenarios with potential liability).

10. Callahan, *Accommodating Pluralism*, ix.

11. Ibid., viii. In addition to Callahan's introduction, the book contains eleven chapters from different authors on a broad range of topics, including "methodological pluralism" (1–14); CAM and cultural diversity (15–35); the role of science in assessing CAM therapies (36–53); epistemological issues (54–73); implications of the placebo effect for study and practice of CAM therapies (74–83); the role of spirituality in clinical care (84–106); the interpretation of results of trials (107–21); the evaluation of global

medicine (122–47); the nature of evidence (148–62); medical culture and CAM therapies (163–71); and the quest for holism in medicine (172–89).

12. Schaffner, "Assessments of Efficacy," 1–3.

13. Ibid., 4–5. Schaffner distinguishes several different types of evidence, which he calls experimental, clinical practice, safety, comparative, summary, rational, demand, satisfaction, cost, and meaning. See ibid., 5, citing John W. Spencer, "Essential Issues in Complementary/Alternative Medicine," in Spencer and Jacobs, *Complementary and Alternative Medicine.*

14. Schaffner, "Assessments of Efficacy," 5–6, 8.

15. Ibid., 12.

16. See, e.g., Angell and Kassirer, "Alternative Medicine," 839–41 ("What most sets alternative medicine apart . . . is that it has not been scientifically tested. . . . Alternative medicine also distinguishes itself by an ideology that largely ignores biologic mechanisms, often disparages modern medical science, and relies on what are purported to be ancient practices and natural remedies. . . . With the increased interest in alternative medicine, we see a reversion to irrational approaches to medical practice. . . . It is time for the scientific community to stop giving alternative medicine a free ride.").

17. Humber review, 1655.

18. Jonas, "Evidence, Ethics, and the Evaluation of Global Medicine," 123. Jonas argues that while biomedicine "succeeds dramatically in many areas, such as the control of acute and infectious disease, it also fails in others, such as the management of chronic conditions with complex etiologies" (ibid., 122). He notes that randomized controlled trials are more likely to succeed when "a disease occurs over a short period of time and involves single domains so that multiple confounding factors have little time to influence the outcome" (ibid., 126); he calls, however, for a more explicit balance in research and evaluation strategies "between the criteria of internal validity (focused on identifying causal links) and external validity (focused on clarifying impact and utility)" (ibid., 127). Jonas argues for less reliance on causal models that look for specific treatments ("the magic bullet") and greater reliance on probabilistic models (that look for "wide and general medical effects") and acausal models (that "look for methods of altering these associations—often by creating new meanings (causal links) that are not dependent on classical time and space relationships") (ibid., 131). Core research methods in his model would include a balance of (1) qualitative research, (2) laboratory and basic science approaches, (3) observational studies, (4) randomized controlled trials, (5) methods for

assessing the accuracy of the above methods (such as meta-analyses and systematic reviews), and (6) health services research (ibid., 135–36).

19. Kopelman, "Role of Science," 48. Kopelman goes on to state that within such frames, "scientific assessments of CAM may even be regarded as incomplete, biased, or irrelevant" (ibid., 47); as an example, she cites healing rituals within certain religious frameworks that do not rely on the kind of causal explanations used in scientific inquiry (ibid.).

20. Ibid., 48. She concludes, "Although limited, science has a genuine and important role in assessing . . . CAM by the same or best available methods. Scientific methods explanations may have a different force in some framework when their goals, values, and presuppositions differ, yet science will at least have an important role in evaluating certain claims, such as in settling disputes over the value of some interventions to fulfill certain goals of health or avoidance of disease" (ibid., 49).

21. Humber review, 1655.

22. See, generally, Cohen, *Legal Boundaries*, 20–21 (citing sources).

23. See ibid.

24. 719 F.2d 207 (7th Cir. 1983), cert. denied, 467 U.S. 1210 (1984), on remand, 671 F. Supp. 1465 (N.D. Ill. 1987), aff'd, 895 F.2d 352 (7th Cir. 1990).

25. See, generally, Cohen, *Legal Boundaries*, 21, 134–35 n. 34 (citing Cassell, "Sorcerer's Broom").

26. Humber review, 1655.

27. See, e.g., Cohen, *Legal Boundaries*, 107–8 (applying tort of fraud to scenarios involving provision of CAM therapies).

28. The Federal Trade Commission provides various guidelines for businesses and consumers that include references to relevant legal rules and regulations. For example, for guidelines relating to advertising involving dietary supplements, see Federal Trade Commission, *Dietary Supplements*. See also Peeler and Cohn, "Regulation." Regarding rules about advertising on the Internet, see Federal Trade Commission, *Advertising and Marketing*.

29. Humber review, 1655–56.

30. Jonas, "Evidence, Ethics, and the Evaluation of Global Medicine," 132–33, 140.

31. Humber review, 1656.

32. Ibid.

33. See, generally, Cohen, *Legal Boundaries*, 17–20 (summarizing these developments and citing sources).

34. See ibid., 26–31.

35. See ibid., 21–23, 26–31.

36. Ibid., 23.

37. Cohen, *Future Medicine*, 19. For a different but parallel reflection, see Adams et al., "Ethical Considerations."

38. Cohen, *Future Medicine*, 86–91 (offering in-depth examples).

39. See ibid., 93–94.

40. See ibid., 96–97.

41. Ibid., 98–99.

42. Institute of Medicine, *Complementary and Alternative Medicine*, 172. Some CAM therapies "may have less kinship with technologically oriented, biomedical interventions and greater kinship with therapies at the borderland of psychological and spiritual care that are offered in professions such as pastoral counseling and hospice" (ibid.).

43. Ibid., 2.

44. Institute of Medicine, *Complementary and Alternative Medicine*, 172.

45. Ernst and Cohen, "Informed Consent."

46. See Cohen, *Future Medicine*, 251–76 ("Beyond Living and Dying") and 277–303 ("Reproductive Technologies and Spiritual Technologies").

47. Ibid., 113.

48. Ibid. (quoting Maslow, *Psychology of Being*, 114).

49. "The goal of empowering transformation is likely to challenge a regulatory system premised on biomedical notions of health and disease and the marginal role assigned to both the individual's emotional life and spiritual consciousness" (ibid.).

Chapter 3

1. See, e.g., Kaptchuk and Eisenberg, "Varieties."

2. The typology indicated in the *Chantilly Report* is reviewed in Cohen, *Legal Boundaries*. Chapter 1 of the present book classifies CAM therapies according to the four most commonly licensed providers, although these may have overlapping scopes of practice (for example, homeopathy may be variously provided by naturopathic physicians, licensed veterinarians, and licensed nurses in some states, while only a handful of states license M.D.-homeopaths). See Cohen, *Legal Boundaries*, chap. 4, for a discussion of scope of practice.

3. Cohen, *Beyond Complementary Medicine*, chap. 6, explores this in terms of therapies for which the scientific community has or reasonably may be able to find mechanistic explanations and therapies that purport to operate based on "subtle energy," "bio-energy," and the like. These catego-

ries may overlap; for example, there may eventually be a mechanistic explanation for the way acupuncture works, although traditional oriental medicine uses explanations based on chi, or vital energy (life force).

4. The term "spiritual healing" here is used to encompass a number of practices, including healing practices within the context of specific religious traditions (for example, anointing of the Spirit and laying on of hands in Christian ministry) as well as healing involving intentionality or consciousness that is connected with teachings that followers consider to be "scientific" rather than "religious" (as in, for example, Christian science) or are taught in secular settings (such as Therapeutic Touch within the nursing school curriculum). (Chapter 6 returns to distinctions between "spiritual" and "religious" healing.) For the present, such a definition of spiritual healing can help frame discussion for the clinician who is interested in patient beliefs and practices, not only to offer proper medical counseling and satisfy any informed consent obligation, but also to help facilitate and augment the therapeutic relationship.

5. Krieger, *Therapeutic Touch*; see also Chapter 6.

6. Jamison, "Chiropractic's Functional Integration."

7. National Center for Complementary and Alternative Medicine, "Exploratory Grants."

8. James, *Varieties*, 29.

9. Kaptchuk and Eisenberg, "Varieties."

10. See Chapter 2.

11. Cohen and Ruggie, "Integrating."

12. Aldridge, *Spirituality, Healing, and Medicine*.

13. Danesi and Adetunji, "Use of Alternative Medicine."

14. Michigan State University, "Doc's Work."

15. Devinsky, Schachter, and Pacia, *Complementary and Alternative Therapies*.

16. Ramaratnam and Sridharan, "Yoga for Epilepsy."

17. *Mark* 19:14–29 (King James edition [available from the Electronic Text Center, University of Virginia Library, at <http://etext.lib.virginia.edu/toc/modeng/public>]).

18. Eliade, "Waiting for the Dawn," 11.

19. Bruyere, *Wheels of Light*; Schwartz, *Human Energy Systems*.

20. The Epilepsy Foundation of America, 4351 Garden City Drive, Landover, MD, 20785, publishes a number of helpful texts on these subjects for patients and their families.

21. Cohen, *Legal Boundaries*; Cohen and Eisenberg, "Potential Physician Malpractice"; Ernst and Cohen, "Informed Consent"; Studdert et al., "Medical Malpractice Implications."

22. Cohen, *Future Medicine*, chap. 6. Chapter 6 of this book explores in detail legal mechanisms to control against abuse.

23. Cohen, "Healing at the Borderland," 340. Cohen, *Future Medicine*, chap. 6, explores parallels between boundaries in psychotherapy and in spiritual counseling.

24. Curlin et al., "When Patients Choose Faith."

Chapter 4

1. See, generally, Ruggie, *Marginal to Mainstream*.

2. Institute of Medicine, *Crossing the Quality Chasm*; Institute of Medicine, *Complementary and Alternative Medicine*.

3. The National Center for Complementary and Alternative Medicine includes within its definition of "frontier medicine," "systems that use 'subtle energy' fields in and around the body for medical purposes. Examples include Therapeutic Touch, Reiki, Huna, laying-on-of-hands, external Qi-Gong, etc.; Homeopathy; or Therapeutic Prayer; Spiritual Healing; Distance Healing; or other examples of prayer and/or spirituality as direct clinical interventions" (National Center for Complementary and Alternative Medicine, "Exploratory Grants").

4. Kentucky Board of Medical Licensure, "Policy Statement." The term "invalidated" also includes any therapy that "(b) lacks a scientifically acceptable rationale of its own; (c) has insufficient supporting evidence derived from adequately controlled outcome research; (d) has failed in well-controlled studies done by impartial evaluations and has been unable to rule out competing explanations for why it might seem to work in controlled settings."

5. See Cohen, *Beyond Complementary Medicine*, 71 (citing sources).

6. See ibid.

7. See White House Commission, *Final Report*, chap. 6. In observing that the "present state of evidence concerning the safety and effectiveness of various CAM practices precludes any final assessment of their contributions to and limitations in addressing these broader health issues," the report cautions that "the process of gathering evidence is on-going, however, and as evidence increases concerning ways that various CAM approaches do or do not affect health, processes of living and dying, and costs

for other care, access to and delivery of some CAM practices and services are likely to become more pressing public policy issues."

8. See, e.g., Roche, "Creative Ritual"; Kaptchuk, "Placebo Effect."

9. See Cohen, *Legal Boundaries*, 11–12: "Finally, because healing, as opposed to curing, includes growth or transformation, the relief of symptoms which is provided by biomedicine does not necessarily indicate a successful or complete treatment in holistic terms."

10. Jonas and Crawford, *Healing, Intention, and Energy Medicine*.

11. Jensen, *Language*.

12. See Chapter 3.

13. Jonas and Crawford preface, xv.

14. Ibid.

15. Ibid.

16. Ibid., 5.

17. Harlow, "Impact of Healing," 175.

18. Nelson and Radin, "Research on Mind-Matter Interactions," 56.

19. Utts and May, "Non-sensory Access," 60, 70.

20. Jonas and Crawford, *Healing, Intention, and Energy Medicine*, 309–39.

21. Ibid., 343–91.

22. Ibid., 312.

23. Ibid., 320.

24. Jonas and Crawford preface, xv.

25. Ibid., xv–xvi.

26. Ibid.

27. Ibid., xvii.

28. Ibid., xviii–xix.

29. Cohen, *Beyond Complementary Medicine*, 81.

30. Jonas and Crawford, *Healing, Intention, and Energy Medicine*, 83–84.

31. Sparber, Crawford, and Jonas, "Laboratory Research on Bioenergy Healing," 140.

32. Hufford, "Challenges for Healing," 298.

33. Ibid.

34. Ibid., 300–301.

35. See, e.g., Kaptchuk and Eisenberg, "Varieties."

36. Cohen, *Beyond Complementary Medicine*, 81.

37. Ibid., 81–87.

38. Jensen, *Language*, 8.

39. Ibid.

40. Ibid., 9, 10.

41. Cohen, *Legal Boundaries*, 2–3.

42. Jensen, *Language*, 220.

43. Ibid., 221.

44. Ibid., 222.

45. Ibid., 220.

46. Ibid., 74.

47. Ibid., 75.

48. Ibid.

49. Ibid., vii.

50. Ibid., 113.

51. Ibid.

52. Ibid., 248.

53. Ibid., 287.

54. Ibid., 311.

55. Ibid., 361.

56. Ibid., 279.

57. Ibid., 280–81.

58. Ibid., 195–96.

59. Ibid., 32. He writes that killing for food, with respect for the creature sacrificed, "can be accepted and even celebrated, with respect, and in full cognizance of the loss, as a requisite part of a beautiful dance which necessarily ends in death for all of us." Such an act, he writes, is "deeply emotional . . . a form of intimacy," in which the life taken is celebrated and seen in its significance; see ibid., 35–36.

60. Cohen, *Future Medicine*, 84–85.

61. Ibid., 107–8.

62. Ibid., 86.

63. See Cohen, "Healing at the Borderland" (citing and describing statutes).

64. See, generally, Kaptchuk and Eisenberg, "Varieties."

65. Jonas, "Energy Healing Research."

66. Cohen, *Future Medicine*, 91.

67. As previously noted,

Yet another area of potential contribution—or stimulus and provocation—from practitioners of energy healing involves medical ethics, particularly at the boundaries of birth and death. Whereas Western medicine, and thus bioethics, tends to split science and religion, energy healing regards sentient beings, from animals to patients in a "persistent vegetative state," as having consciousness on some level— irrespective of whether such consciousness can be measured through medical concepts and instruments. Because secular humanism regards attempts to describe consciousness, outside of medical measurement, as speculative and futile, Western medicine and medical ethics frequently strive to perpetuate biological existence at all costs; to draw artificial boundaries between life and death; and to assume that animals, pre-embryos (who can be "selectively terminated"), anencephalic infants (who are born without a brainstem thus presumed to have only a reflexive response to painful stimuli), and other life forms lack consciousness, or do not deserve our respect and freedom from undue or undignified invasion. . . . Perspectives from energy healing can enrich and inform such topics as multifetal pregnancy reduction, decisions regarding termination of life support, and organ donation. [Ibid., 77]

68. Ibid., 156.

69. Jensen, *Language*, 286, 287.

70. Cohen, *Beyond Complementary Medicine*, 287.

71. Riskin, "Mindfulness."

72. See, e.g., Koenig, *Spirituality in Patient Care*.

73. Jensen, echoing indigenous and shamanistic perspectives, argues that the Western perspective, dichotomizing animate and inanimate, is fundamentally flawed. He quotes his friend, a traditional Okanagan Indian, in arguing that " 'listening to the land is . . . not a metaphor. It's how the world is' " (Jensen, *Language*, 24). He critiques the understanding of experience as metaphor as follows: "The *other* remains a case study onto which we project whatever we need to learn. That's an entirely different circumstance than listening to the other as it has its say, reveals its contents, and does all this *on its own terms*" (ibid., 24–25).

74. Shakespeare, *Hamlet*, act 2, scene 2.

75. Jensen, *Language*, 8. This is the "culture's overemphasis of the logical and physiological and its denial of the analogical and psychological . . . a collective consciousness that medicalizes life and death and denies the language of the body, the wisdom of feeling, the truth of inner experience" (Cohen, *Beyond Complementary Medicine*, 139).

76. Jensen, *Language*, 7. Another way to view this is as "transcending hierarchical relations and dependencies through the immediate, body-

and feeling-centered awareness of our shared vulnerability" (Cohen, *Beyond Complementary Medicine*, 143).

77. Regarding the difference between the approaches of Jensen and of Jonas and Crawford, my own approach is to synthesize, the task being to "validate subjectivity, intuition, and mystery in equipoise to science and law" (Cohen, *Beyond Complementary Medicine*, 144).

78. Jensen, *Language*, 60.

79. Ibid., 4.

In order for us to maintain our way of living, we must, in a broad sense, tell lies to each other, and especially to ourselves. . . . The lies act as barriers to truth. These barriers to truth are necessary because without them many deplorable acts would become impossibilities. . . . When we do allow self-evident truths to percolate past our defenses and into our consciousness . . . we try to stay out of harm's way, afraid they will go off, shatter our delusions, and leave us exposed to what we have done to the world and to ourselves, exposed as the hollow people we have become. And so we avoid these truths, these self-evident truths, and continue the dance of world destruction. [Ibid., 2]

80. Sparber, Crawford, and Jonas, "Laboratory Research on Bioenergy Healing," 149.

81. Cohen, *Legal Boundaries*, xi.

82. See ibid., 21–25 (citing cases).

83. Jensen, *Language*, 366, 367.

84. Schmidt, "Direct Mental Interactions," 23–35.

85. Astin, "Intercessory Prayer," 21.

Chapter 5

1. Institute of Medicine, *Complementary and Alternative Medicine*, 172.

2. For a readable introduction to Gurdjieff's work, see Vaysee, *Toward Awakening*.

3. Tart, *Waking Up*.

4. Venkatesananda, *Yoga Vasistha*, 9.

5. Ibid., 16.

6. Ibid., 19.

7. Ibid., 20–21.

8. Ibid., 132, 146.

9. Ibid., 133.

10. Cohen, *Beyond Complementary Medicine*, 141.

11. Callahan, "Peaceful Death."

12. See, e.g., Dossey, *Meaning and Medicine*.

13. Venkatesananda, *Yoga Vasistha*, 412.

14. See, e.g., Eisenberg et al., "Credentialing" (referring to the "dark side" of CAM provider credentialing).

15. Cohen, *Legal Boundaries*.

16. Ibid., 113.

17. See, generally, Cohen, *Future Medicine*, chaps. 5–6.

Chapter 6

1. For examples, see the descriptions of healing ministries of Catholic saints in Butler, *Lives of the Saints*.

2. See, e.g., Myss and Shealy, *Creation of Health*, 72–76.

3. Janiger and Goldberg, *Different Kind of Healing*, 123, 128–32.

4. See, generally, Krieger, *Therapeutic Touch*.

5. See, e.g., Weaver, "Nurses' Views"; King, "Healing Pathways"; McSweeney, "Midwifery"; Umbreit, "Healing Touch"; Villaire, "Healing Touch Therapy"; Wilkinson et al., "Clinical Effectiveness."

6. See, e.g., Kennedy, "Working with Survivors."

7. Alternative medical practices initially were defined as therapies not commonly used in U.S. hospitals or taught in U.S. medical schools. See Eisenberg et al., "Unconventional Medicine." However, as these therapies gained greater footing in U.S. hospitals and in medical school curricula, and consumer use of such therapies dramatically expanded, "complementary and alternative medicine" gained recognition as a consensus term for a broad range of therapies that historically had fallen outside biomedicine. See Cohen, *Future Medicine*.

The reasons for defining modalities as "CAM therapies" are not only scientific but also "political, social, or conceptual" (Jonas, "Policy," 33). Such reasons include lack of a generally accepted explanatory model and/or the fact that the origin of the practice is outside the dominant system (e.g., acupuncture); that the amount of data or type of data is considered insufficient or otherwise inadequate (e.g., herbalism or megavitamin therapy); that the use of the practice is marginalized in that it is not available within conventional hospitals (e.g., relaxation techniques); that the teaching of the practice is marginalized in that it is not generally taught within medical, nursing, or graduate schools of the dominant institutions (e.g., nutritional therapy); that the amount of research funding, infrastructure, and capacity for investigating the practice is low (e.g., cancer or chiropractic); that the practice is not reimbursed by insurance companies and third-party payers; that the practice is not readily used for feasibility, acceptability, or other reasons (e.g., clinical ecology or complex lifestyle programs); that the practice is not regulated or licensed in most states (e.g., naturopathy); and that an aspect of the therapy is marginalized though it is studied under other names or subdivisions (e.g., antineoplastons and shark cartilage). See Jonas, "Policy," 33.

8. See, e.g., Guorui, *Qigong*; Aung, *Medical Qi Gong*.

9. See, e.g., Jamison, "Chiropractic's Functional Integration."

10. See, e.g., Rexilius et al., "Therapeutic Effects."

11. *Chantilly Report*, 136–37. The report helped catalog the nature and extent of the field of "alternative medicine."

12. For some of the unresolved definitional conundrums, see below.

13. See Cohen, "Fixed Star," 134–37 (discussing applicability of tort rules for fraudulent conduct by healers).

14. The term "healer" is in customary use among providers, and such usage informs this book, although the term, "facilitator of healing" might be more accurate.

15. Despite attempts by numerous scholars (as discussed below) to provide rigorous definitions for terms such as "religion," "spirituality," and "healing," such definitions are subject to critique as ultimately ambiguous, overlapping, and/or circular. Even the U.S. Supreme Court has had difficulty defining religion—and has even "avoided attempting to define 'religion' and the 'religious'" (Jefferson, "Strengthening Motivational Analysis," 644). Further, definitions of religion seem to change according to the context. For example, the Free Exercise Clause and the Establishment Clause of the First Amendment seem to demand incongruent definitions, so as to "maximize individual liberty, protect individual religious conduct, and limit the constraints on government" (ibid.). Even the attempt to assess whether something is "religious," according to whether the activity is associated with prevailing doctrines of a particular religion, is problematic, because religion is "essentially a personal experience and one may have individual beliefs outside the canon of a particular religion" (ibid., 645).

Not only does a monolithic interpretation seem impossible, but also, more generally, "defining the term 'religious,' especially at the fringes of its meanings, is an almost Sisyphean task" (ibid., 644). Moreover, from a psychoanalytic perspective, some would argue that religion is merely a "socially constructed and maintained system of internal objects" and that, moreover, such internal objects have "no material existence" but, rather, are "elaborated over time to meet the experience of practitioners" (Black, "Religion," 624; see also Paul, "Cultural Resistance"; West, "Law, Rights," 869 [arguing that religion, conscience, and rule of law are social constructs]). To denote religion as a "social construct" suggests, perhaps, that religious beliefs are erroneous, trivial, or at the least, beyond scientific proof and therefore not subject to serious debate. See Bonnie B. O'Connor, personal communication, 20 November 2002.

Further, even to denote a particular healing practice or set of health care practices as "religion" or "religious" may be imposing a Western, medical bias on particular modes of existence, since practitioners may experience themselves as "being" rather than subscribing to a particular, identifiable set of beliefs. For example, while Hmong culture does not have a separate category for religion, a Hmong shaman is certainly recognized within the community as practicing a specialized knowledge of certain spiritual matters. In many cultural frameworks one does not, or need not, identify as "religious" or "spiritual" in a way that is separate from one's cultural or ethnic identity, because the latter identity *entails* religious and/or spiritual worldviews, interpretations, and actions. This is true even in those cultures whose languages may not have a word for "religion" or that do not consider religion a separate "department" of culture in the way so-called Western cultures do. All sorts of disciplines seem to have their own approach to the definition of religion, and such definitions generally reflect each discipline's particular orientation and foundational assumptions.

Despite the above caveats, and without attempting to craft definitive responses to the above conundrums, this chapter attempts to draw preliminary, working distinctions to help frame the way health care practices once considered religious or spiritual are penetrating mainstream clinical care; hence the title's emphasis on practices at the borderland of what historically has been considered, in many camps, medicine as opposed to religion. In so doing, the chapter in no way advocates particular practices or beliefs but, rather, evaluates some legal, regulatory, and ethical conundrums arising out of the integration of beliefs and practices into contexts that generally are considered predominantly secular and mundane.

16. See, e.g., Sered, *Women as Ritual Experts* and *Women of the Sacred Groves*.

17. See, e.g., *James* 5:14: "Is any sick among you? Let him call for the elders of the church; and let them pray over him, anointing him with oil in the name of the Lord" (King James edition [available from the Electronic Text

Center, University of Virginia Library, at <http://etext.lib.virginia.edu/toc/modeng/public>]).

18. Aldridge, *Spirituality, Healing, and Medicine*, 32–33. Aldridge traces the historical rise of medicine and consequent decline of church authority over understandings of life, birth, death, and the body—a "rift in the ecology of ideas"—and the recent return, in holistic notions of health, "to the idea that body, mind and spirit are not separate" (ibid., 34).

19. Ibid., 56 (quoting, respectively, D. Doyle, "Have We Looked beyond the Physical and Psychosocial," *Journal of Pain Symptom Management* 7, no. 5 [July 1992]: 302, 303; D. Lukoff, R. Provenzano, F. Lu, and R. Turner, "Religious and Spiritual Case Reports on MEDLINE: A Systematic Analysis of Records from 1980 to 1996," *Alternative Therapies* 5, no. 1 [January 1999]: 65; and M. King and S. Dein, "The Spiritual Variable in Psychiatric Research," *Psychological Medicine* 28, no. 6 [November 1998]: 1259).

20. Aldridge, *Spirituality, Healing, and Medicine*, 27 (quoting D. Doyle, "Have We Looked beyond the Physical and Psychosocial?," *Journal of Pain Symptom Management* 7, no. 5 [July 1992]: 303).

21. Aldridge, *Spirituality, Healing, and Medicine* (quoting J. Emblen, "Religion and Spirituality Defined According to Current Use in Nursing Literature," *Journal of Professional Nursing* 8, no. 1 [January–February 1992]: 41, 43).

22. Aldridge, *Spirituality, Healing, and Medicine* (quoting Michael Lerner, *Choices in Healing* [Cambridge, Mass.: MIT Press, 1994], 115).

23. Aldridge, *Spirituality, Healing, and Medicine* (quoting W. McSherry and P. Draper, "The Spiritual Dimension: Why the Absence within the Nursing Curricula?," *Nurse Education Today* 17, no. 5 [October 1997]: 413).

24. Aldridge, *Spirituality, Healing, and Medicine* (quoting M. Joseph, "The Effect of Strong Religious Beliefs on Coping with Stress," *Stress Medicine* 14, no. [October 1998]: 219, 220). Aldridge draws the distinction this way: "Where spirituality is seen as subjective, religion is seen as being social and means subscribing to a set of doctrines that are institutionalized. Thus some people may be spiritual in that they have a sense of being related to the sacred but do not take part in any organized religion. Conversely, others may perform the expected rituals of religious observance but have no personal experience of the divine" (ibid., 66).

25. See, e.g., Benedikt, *Spirituality versus Religion* (proposing that many "get caught in nationalistic slogans or doctrines or religious creeds and dogmas which cause rather painful and violent disturbances and even warlike antagonisms in our already deeply shaken world," but that it is only

through "a spiritual understanding which goes to the root and source of religion itself, which is God, that we can discover the goal of our quest."

26. Booth, *When God*. The author is a "recovering" Anglican priest and alcoholic who has recognized within himself an addictive propensity to use religion "to escape loneliness, low self-esteem, and fear of reality . . . [as a] drug" (ibid., 9). He has created programs to help individuals recover from religious addiction and abuse. He attributes spiritual abuse and addiction, among other things, to the "growing awareness of the spiritual emptiness felt by many people—the alienation and shame produced by the negative messages religion often gives," and his model draws on the Alcoholics Anonymous system of healing. See ibid., 23.

27. Cohen et al., "Walking a Fine Line," 31–32.

28. This chapter draws working definitions to clarify analysis of legal rules, acknowledging that many define religion and spirituality in terms of each other.

29. Increasingly there is recognition that healing rituals may have powerful, therapeutic effects. See, e.g., Roche, "Creative Ritual"; Kaptchuk, "Placebo Effect." On the other hand, exclusive reliance on rituals—to the exclusion of conventional care—can be destructive. See, e.g., Pfeifer, "Belief in Demons and Exorcism" (finding that although patients experienced rituals as positive, a negative outcome, such as psychotic decompensation, was associated with exclusion of medical treatment and coercive forms of exorcism). The destructive possibilities of too much reliance on spiritual healing, to the exclusion of medical healing, is a subtheme of this chapter. It also informs abuse and neglect law in pediatric care. See Cohen et al., "Pediatric Use of Complementary Therapies."

30. Koenig foreword.

31. Eliade, "Waiting for the Dawn," 13, 12.

32. The shaman travels through realms of consciousness to bring healing. See Harner, *Shaman*.

33. Eliade, "Waiting for the Dawn," 15–16.

34. See, e.g., Smith, *Called into Healing*.

35. See, e.g., Kok Sui, *Pranic Healing*. Kok Sui "does not believe that any special, inborn healing power is needed to perform paranormal cures. . . . All that one needs is the willingness to heal" (ibid., xv).

36. See Astin, Harkness, and Ernst, "Distant Healing," 533 (concluding that 57 percent of trials of distance healing showed a significant effect on at least one outcome).

37. Eliade likely would insist that irrespective of the level of scientific

evidence for a given therapy, one studying such a therapy should have an actual "encounter" with it and thus have "passed beyond the stage of pure erudition—in other words, when, after having collected, described, and classified his documents, he has also made an effort to understand them *on their own plane of reference*" (Eliade, "New Humanism," 38 [referring to study of religious phenomena by the historian of religion]). Eliade adds, "Works of art, like 'religious data,' have a mode of being that is peculiar to themselves; they *exist on their own plane of reference*, in their particular universe. The fact that this universe is not the physical universe of immediate experience does not imply their nonreality" (ibid., 39).

38. *United States v. Seeger*, 380 U.S. 163, 166 (1965).

39. Of course, arguments have been made that scientific inquiry can be faith-based, in the sense of assuming certain premises and dismissing worldviews incompatible with these assumptions. See, e.g., Wolpe, "Professional Authority." Thus, for example, when acupuncture came to the forefront of medical attention in the United States in the early 1970s, physicians and medical societies dismissed its principles as "'Oriental hocuspocus'" (ibid., 587–88 [quoting George A. Ulett, "Acupuncture Treatments for Pain Relief," *Journal of the American Medical Association* 245, no. 7 [20 February 1981]: 768, 769]).

40. See, e.g., Rubik, "Energy Medicine." Similarly, the Samueli Institute is a nonprofit organization, with links to laboratories in academic research centers internationally, that is attempting to elucidate scientific explanations for mechanisms underlying healing phenomena, including those associated with healing. The Samueli Institute defines healing as "those physical, mental and spiritual processes of recovery, repair and renewal that increase order, coherence and wholism in the individual, the group and the environment" (Samueli Institute for Informational Biology, "Exploring").

41. See, e.g., Talbot, *Holographic Universe*.

42. See, e.g., Frohock, "Moving Lines" (summarizing some of the relevant clinical trials and challenges posed by some current, explanatory propositions).

43. See, generally, Krieger, *Therapeutic Touch*.

44. Kok Sui, *Pranic Healing*, xvii.

45. Cf. Eck, *New Religious America* (exploring how Americans of all faiths and beliefs can engage with one another to shape a positive religious pluralism).

46. See, e.g., Koenig, McCullough, and Larson, *Handbook* (citing studies); Koenig and Cohen, *Link between Religion and Health*; Chamberlain and Hall, *Realized Religion*.

47. See, e.g., Dossey, "Dark Side."

48. See, e.g., Koenig, *Spirituality in Patient Care*, n. 52.

49. See, e.g., Sollod, "Integrating Spiritual Healing."

50. One could also argue that professions such as osteopathy, which have become mainstream and comparable to the medical profession in status and legal authority, represent the gradual secularization of practices initially based in spiritual discoveries. See Cohen, *Legal Boundaries*, 140 n. 67 (noting shift from AMA policy of forbidding physician association with osteopaths to judicial criticism of a state board rule that attempted to perpetuate a distinction between M.D.'s and D.O.'s); Kaptchuk and Eisenberg, "Varieties," 198 (noting that osteopathy has "reconfigured itself and has become 'conventional,' in the sense of D.O.'s having 'equivalent status' to M.D.'s"). Ironically, the discoveries of Andrew Taylor Still, the founder of osteopathy, had roots, like those of Palmer, the founder of chiropractic, in magnetic healing.

51. See, e.g., Santorelli, *Heal Thy Self*.

52. For example, Pepperdine School of Law held a workshop on mindfulness in mediation and alternative dispute resolution, as did Harvard Law School. See Harvard Law School Program on Negotiation, "Mindfulness in the Law."

53. See, e.g., Frew, *Management of Stress*; Kory, *Transcendental Meditation Program*.

54. Aldridge, *Spirituality, Healing, and Medicine*, 94–95.

55. Ibid., 95 (citing the work of Harvard Medical School professor Herbert Benson).

56. The funding helped establish the Center for Natural Medicine and Prevention, with a proposed research agenda to include "basic study of mechanisms of meditation on atherosclerotic CVD (arterial vasomotion, cardiac autonomic tone, and psychosocial risk factors); a clinical trial of effects of meditation on carotid arteriosclerosis, CVD risk factors, physiological mechanisms, psychosocial risk factors, and quality of life in older Black women with CVD" (National Center for Complementary and Alternative Medicine, "NCCAM Research Centers Program Description").

57. See, generally, Pargament, *Psychology of Religion* (reviewing the literature on use of religion in coping with crisis); Koenig, *Handbook of*

Religion and Mental Health (examining the relationship between religion and stress, depression, anxiety, schizophrenia, and substance abuse); Shafranske, *Religion and the Clinical Practice of Psychology*.

58. One recent attempt involves using complexity theory to explain phenomena previously understood only through the lens of CAM disciplines. See Jianping and Rose, "Chinese Medicine."

59. Theoretically, an atheist or agnostic could practice Therapeutic Touch, although this assertion would be debated by those who believe that to practice a technique such as Therapeutic Touch is to adopt a particular set of beliefs akin to those adopted by the religious. In a sense, this harks back to the earlier tautology (if it is not scientific, it is religious) and to the earlier argument as to what is religious, both of which may be essentially unsolvable. A similar problem arises when one tries to define Spirit or spirit, or what it means to be spirited or to practice mind-body-spirit medicine. The definition might differ depending on who is invoking the definition (for example, a practitioner of Christian Science, a Navajo healer, a minister, a practitioner of Japanese acupuncture, or a physician in the emergency room). The problem is compounded by the fact that some practices involve laying on of hands, whereas others do not necessarily require contact with the physical body and, according to proponents, can even be done from a distance (as in so-called distant healing, which relies, according to some theorists, on "nonlocal consciousness," the notion that information and healing that are accessed through consciousness do not depend on limitations of space and time).

60. Much of the discussion also uses the words "spiritual healer" and "spiritual healing" to denote healing practices by both religious and secular personnel.

61. Cohen, *Beyond Complementary Medicine*, 72.

62. Cohen, *Future Medicine*, 129. This can be conceptualized as including at least three different, but somehow linked, kinds of phenomena: potentially explainable transmissions of informational patterns between humans in the form of bio-electromagnetic energy; transmissions of informational patterns that are physically, emotionally, and spiritually mediated between individuals in close proximity—for example, by laying on of hands—that presently cannot yet wholly be accounted for in material or physical terms; and nonlocal phenomena such as distance healing that may or may not be phenomena of body, mind, or spirit (however one defines each of these concepts). See ibid., 10. Along these lines, the Samueli Institute for Informational Biology sponsored a symposium that organized a

list of working definitions and terms, ranging from "attention," to "biofield," to "nonlocality" in healing, to "healing" ("those physical, mental, social, and spiritual processes of recovery, repair, renewal, and transformation that increase wholeness, and often [though not invariably], order and coherence"), to "spirituality" ("feelings, thoughts, experiences, and behaviors that arise from a search for that which is generally considered sacred or holy") (Dossey, "Samueli Conference").

63. A separate set of issues arises regarding the ethical implications of clinicians discussing religion with patients as part of medical diagnosis and treatment. These include, for example, questions regarding potential imposition of the provider's beliefs on the patient, potential coercion, violation of therapeutic boundaries, and management of intraprofessional boundaries. See Koenig, *Spirituality in Patient Care*. Asking patients questions about their spirituality and taking their responses into account is "not 'alternative medicine' " (King, "Healing Pathways," 7) and thus differs from using energy healing as a diagnostic or therapeutic modality. Rather, assessing patients' religious beliefs and practices can help clinicians understand patient interpretation of disease and therapy. On the other hand, praying with patients may overlap with energy healing practices, since conceptually, energy healing includes accessing nonphysical forces of healing to improve health or wholeness. See Cohen, *Future Medicine*, 134–36.

64. Several tools and indexes have been adopted to take a patient's "spiritual history," either as part of a social history or in response to various events in the patient's medical life and/or the therapeutic relationship. See King, "Healing Pathways," 56–62; see also Cohen et al., "Walking a Fine Line," 34–37 (offering guidelines for professional inquiries by physicians regarding patients' spiritual beliefs). Yet, although such tools may be useful, it must be remembered that medicine "is not a form of religion, and physicians are not priests"; thus, counseling patients inappropriately or invasively concerning spiritual care "opens wide the door to coercion," and physicians (and other health care providers) must "walk a fine line between the practice of medicine and the practice of religion and between sympathetic response to patients' spiritual needs and professional coercion" (Cohen et al., "Walking a Fine Line," 36–37).

65. See Eisenberg et al., "Credentialing," 965, 968, 969.

66. See, generally, ibid. (suggesting importance of strong, national professional organizations for licensure).

67. The *Chantilly Report*, 134–42, catalogs various modalities, their theory and practice, and their sponsoring educational institutions.

68. See, e.g., Brennan, *Hands of Light*, 81–88.

69. *Chantilly Report*, 134. As noted, the report uses the term "biofield therapeutics," which has not been widely adopted. Interestingly, the report classified biofield therapeutics as a manual therapy, while it puts prayer in another classification (i.e., mind-body therapy). The typical presence (or absence) of human touch appears to be the reason for these classifications, although the report does observe that "mental healing, psychic healing, distance healing, nonlocal healing, and absent healing" are part of biofield therapeutics. See ibid., 135.

70. See, e.g., Brennan, *Hands of Light*, 5, 49–54.

71. Wytias, "Therapeutic Touch, 93."

72. Ibid., 93–94.

73. In Therapeutic Touch, this step is known as "directing and modulating energy" (ibid., 94).

74. See Aldridge, *Spirituality, Healing, and Medicine*, 16 (discussing how Larry Dossey has been "criticized by churchgoers for his support of psi phenomena" and how an English bishop interested in laying on of hands was criticized for importing "Eastern spirituality").

75. National Center for Complementary and Alternative Medicine, "Exploratory Grants," describing the center's "frontier medicine" program in a request for grant applications.

76. NCCAM further defines the program areas within "frontier medicine" as (1) Bioelectromagnetic Therapy (e.g., diagnostic and therapeutic application of electromagnetic [EM] fields, including pulsed EM fields, magnetic fields, Direct Current [DC] fields, artificial light therapy, etc. Note: This category does not include the study of electromagnetic fields as risk factors for disease.); (2) Biofield (e.g., energy healing, etc. Note: This category involves systems that use "subtle energy" fields in and around the body for medical purposes. Examples include Therapeutic Touch, Reiki, Huna, laying on of hands, external *qigong*, etc.); (3) Homeopathy; or (4) Therapeutic Prayer, Spiritual Healing, Distance Healing, or other examples of prayer and/or spirituality as direct clinical interventions. See ibid.

77. Ibid.

78. Aldridge, *Spirituality, Healing, and Medicine*, 42.

79. Cohen, *Beyond Complementary Medicine*, 81.

80. Aldridge, *Spirituality, Healing, and Medicine*, 43 (defining healing as "the intentional influence of one or more persons upon a living system

without using known physical means of intervention") (quoting Daniel Benor, "Spiritual Healing in Clinical Practice," *Nursing Times* 87 [1991]: 9).

81. "The names of the energies change—life force, universal innate intelligence, psychic, parapsychological, psi astral, spiritual vital force—but they inevitably elude scientific detection" (Kaptchuk and Eisenberg, "Varieties," 199). The authors' taxonomy distinguishes such "New Age healing" from "mind-body medicine," "religious healing" (use of "religion for salutary effects on . . . health"), "folk medicine practices," "ethno-medicine," and categories such as non-normative scientific enterprises, popular health reform, and professional or distinct medical systems.

82. Kaptchuk and Eisenberg, "Persuasive Appeal."

83. See Kaptchuk, "Placebo Effect," 821–22 (suggesting that "the question of enhanced placebo effects raises complex ethical questions concerning what is 'legitimate' healing, and what kinds of measurement embody cultural judgment on what is 'correct' healing").

84. See, e.g., Klotz, "Jewish Healing Services"; see also O'Connor, *Healing Traditions*.

85. Cohen, *Legal Boundaries*, 39.

86. *Chantilly Report*, xi–xiii.

87. Cohen, *Legal Boundaries*, 24–26.

88. 197 U.S. 11, 26, 27 (1905).

89. See, e.g., *Rutherford v. United States*, 438 F. Supp. 1287 (W.D. Okla. 1977), remanded, 582 F.2d 1234 (10th Cir. 1978), cert. denied, 449 U.S. 937 (1980), later proceeding, 806 F.2d 1455 (10th Cir. Okla. 1986); Cohen, *Legal Boundaries*, 23–24.

90. Cohen, *Legal Boundaries*, 25–26.

91. Ibid., 22.

92. 117 P. 612 (Colo. 1911).

93. Cohen, *Legal Boundaries*, 81–82.

94. See ibid.

95. Aldridge, *Spirituality, Healing, and Medicine*, 9.

96. Ibid.

97. See Cohen, *Legal Boundaries*, 15–23 (citing cases and observing that "references to chiropractic and other modalities as 'sorcery' and 'voodoo' have continued to find their way into biomedical and legal discourse"). More recently, the increasing prevalence of CAM therapies also has resulted in calls for a more "pluralistic system of health-care delivery" that includes "spiritual, as well as physical, psychological and social"

definitions of illness, health and healing. See Aldridge, *Spirituality, Healing, and Medicine*, 10.

98. Aldridge, *Spirituality, Healing, and Medicine*, 30 (citing E. van Leeuwen and G. Kimsma, "Philosophy of Medical Practice: A Discursive Approach," *Theoretical Medicine* 18, no. 1–2 [March–June 1997]: 99-112).

99. See Cohen, *Legal Boundaries*, 15–23.

100. At least in the arena of CAM therapies, acupuncturists and massage therapists are increasingly finding themselves subject to state licensure. See Eisenberg et al., "Credentialing," 967, 969.

101. See Blevins, *Medical Monopoly*.

102. Eisenberg et al., "Credentialing," 971–72.

103. See Cohen, *Legal Boundaries*, 35.

104. Some have argued that since the Medicare Act allows Christian Science faith healers to receive Medicare benefits, the patient's visit to a Christian Science faith healer is "primarily . . . a medical one, not a religious one, or arguably both" (Greenberg, "In God We Trust," 469). Greenberg argues that Christian Science faith healers therefore should be "held accountable under the medical licensing laws, be regulated under the provisions regarding health care providers, and be liable for medical malpractice for negligence" (ibid.). Alternatively, she argues, if such faith healers are to be exempt from licensing laws and other regulation, their patient visits should not be covered under Medicare.

105. 211 Cal. App. 3d 1346, 260 Cal. Rptr. 113 (1989).

106. Cohen, *Legal Boundaries*, 22–23.

107. See the discussion later in the chapter of new state laws regulating nonlicensed CAM providers.

108. See Schultz, "Informed Consent"; Cohen, *Legal Boundaries*, 60–61.

109. See, generally, Karpman, "Informed Consent."

110. In the faith healing context involving a practitioner of Christian Science, an early case noted that the applicable standard would be the "standard of care, skill and knowledge of the ordinary Christian Scientist, in so far as he confined himself to those methods" (*Spead v. Tomlinson*, 59 A. 376, 378 [N.H. 1904]).

111. Countering the trend toward increasing licensure of health care providers is a movement to reduce the bureaucracy, restrictiveness, and professional turf battles caused by licensure, by creating a new class of "unlicensed" CAM providers who are regulated largely by registration. By creating a large group of providers not subject to the more rigorous criteria for state licensure (as opposed to mere registration), such statutes may

counteract a historical trend of using state licensing laws to maintain professional monopolies and exclude undesirable competitors. See Cohen, *Legal Boundaries*, 15–23 (describing use of licensing laws to maintain economic control over professional health care services).

112. See Cohen, *Future Medicine*, 72–78. In medicine, physicians "hold a near monopoly on a sort of power that can make the difference between sickness and health to persons who have been made vulnerable by pain, uncertainty, grief, anxiety, or simply by their dependence on others for care. . . . Fidelity to patients requires that physicians use their power in ways that avoid inadvertent or deliberate coercion" (Cohen et al., "Walking a Fine Line," 36). While informed consent has been heralded as a limitation on the potential for physician abuse of power, misconduct can infuse more subtle dimensions of the therapeutic relationship and arguably require vigilance beyond the sanction of legal and ethical rules. See, generally, Brody, *Healer's Power*.

113. "Over the past decade clergy malfeasance has been discussed largely within a narrow sexual paradigm—the sexual exploitation of youth by pedophiles or of vulnerable females by male clerics" (Shupe, "Introduction," 2).

114. Ibid., 1.

115. Ibid., 1–2.

116. Ibid., 3 (citing David R. Simon and Stanley Eitzen, *Elite Deviance* [Boston: Allyn and Bacon, 1990]).

117. Ibid.

118. Ibid., 4. Psychotherapists who violate sexual space with clients tend to have unmanageable levels of personal vulnerability, fear of intimacy, crises in personal relationships, feelings of failure, low self-esteem, poor impulse control, professional isolation, and depression. See Cohen, *Future Medicine*, 175–80 (citing Patricia Keith-Spiegel and Gerald P. Koocher, *Ethics in Psychology: Professional Standards and Cases* [New York: Random House, 1985], 256).

119. Shupe, "Introduction," 4.

120. Ibid., 5, 6.

121. Shupe, "Economic Fraud."

122. Shupe, "Introduction," 7.

123. Arterburn and Felton, *Toxic Faith*. The authors, like Booth, agree that "people broken by various experiences, people from dysfunctional families, people with unrealistic expectations, and people out for their own gain or comfort seem especially prone to . . . abusive and manipulative

and . . . addictive" involvement with spirituality. The authors list four common characteristics of "religious addicts": having had rigid parents, having a deep wound from a major disappointment, feeling low self-worth, and being a victim of abuse; see ibid., 20. They include as forms and variations of toxic faith compulsive religious activity, laziness, giving to get, self-obsession, extreme intolerance, and addiction to a religious high; see ibid., 24–31. Ironically, they argue, "toxic faith" erects barriers between individuals and genuine spiritual growth, see ibid., 20.

124. Ibid. The book's title, which refers to "Spiritual Abuse," implies as much. Since autonomy is voluntarily relinquished, however, and not invaded, legal rules such as those governing informed disclosure arguably are inapplicable.

125. As suggested, it is not the attribution of physical illness to religious compliance (or lack thereof) alone that is abusive but, rather, the control and manipulation of individuals' expectations, beliefs, and conduct in order to achieve submission to the authority of individual human personalities or to the authority of designated organizations. The religious affiliation, thus, becomes a dangerous and destructive involvement that controls the subject's life rather than enhancing welfare. See ibid.

126. See, generally, Peterson, *At Personal Risk*; cf. Williams, "Boundary Violations," 238 (arguing that although "hugging, dining with, self-disclosing to, or making house calls to patients are among behaviors which have been termed 'boundary violations' in psychotherapy . . . some of the activities in question are consistent with the ethical practice of humanistic and behavioral psychotherapies, as well as with eclectic approaches deriving from those schools").

127. See, e.g., American Psychological Association, "Ethical Principles."

128. Cohen, *Future Medicine*, 175–80.

129. Ibid., chaps. 5–6. American Psychological Association, "Ethical Principles," notes in ethical standard 3.08, "Psychologists do not exploit persons over whom they have supervisory, evaluative, or other authority such as clients/patients, students, supervisees, research participants, and employees."

130. See, e.g., Gallo, *Energy Psychology*.

131. Freud apparently initiated the debate about appropriate use of touch in mental health care and raised "questions that still cannot be definitively answered: Where is the line that demarcates non-erotic touching from erotic contact or sexual intimacy?" See Cohen, *Beyond Complementary Medicine*, 176 (quoting Patricia Keith-Spiegel and Gerald P. Koocher, *Eth-*

ics in Psychology: Professional Standards and Cases [New York: Random House, 1985], 253).

132. See Cohen, *Future Medicine*, 137–42 (citing sources).

133. *Chantilly Report*, ix.

134. This is what Therapeutic Touch denotes as "centering." See, generally, Krieger, *Therapeutic Touch*.

135. Brennan, *Hands of Light*, 185. According to Brennan, healing occurs through "harmonic induction": as long as the healer's "voltage" is higher than the patient's, the healing energy flows from the healer to the patient; but if the healer is tired, weak, and unhealthy, the healer could pick up the patient's negativities or, presumably, drain the patient.

136. Cohen, "Bioethics of Compassion," 685 (citing Harner, *Shaman*, xvii–xix). The health care professional in biomedicine, in contrast, typically helps individuals "by manipulating technological or institutional know-how," though physicians, like other caregivers, may have a dual identity—professional and shaman. See ibid., 685–86.

137. See Brennan, *Hands of Light*, 153–56. See, generally, Bruyere, *Wheels of Light*. Some would critique the assertion of such powers as exercises in "magical thinking," a category of pathological delusion articulated in DSM-IV. Cf. Booth, *When God*, 35–36 (describing the abuse of power by Jimmy Swaggart), though this also may reflect negative bias against religious proclivities. See Cohen, *Future Medicine*, 295–96. Interestingly, some place "messages from God" in the category of delusional or pathological behavior; see Booth, *When God*, 45. Yet, energy healers frequently rely on intuitive information to locate sources of imbalance and attempt to bring healing. The controversy over the epistemological legitimacy of intuition and other such "spiritual gifts," including "messages" from another source, is beyond the scope of this chapter, although it mirrors attempts to distinguish "faith and fanaticism, healthy religiosity and addiction" (Booth, *When God*, 57). Notably, the conflict has been played out historically, perhaps most visibly in the Inquisition's trial of Joan of Arc. See Cohen, *Beyond Complementary Medicine*, 76.

138. Krebs, *Church Structures*, 17. Although Krebs is discussing how institutional structures in the Roman Catholic Church facilitate sexual malfeasance, I extend a part of that analysis to spiritual healing in the secular arena.

139. In the religious context, "the local authority of individual clergy is an extension of a bureaucratic authority that legitimizes it" (ibid. [citing Anson Shupe, "Opportunity Structures, Trusted Hierarchies, and Reli-

gious Deviance: A Conflict Theory Approach" (paper presented at annual meeting of the Society for the Scientific Study of Religion, Raleigh, N.C., 1993), 19]). When spiritual healing is presented in a secular context—such as the hospital—the local authority of the individual practitioner could be viewed as an extension of the profession as a whole (e.g., nursing) that sanctions the technique (e.g., Therapeutic Touch) and/or the institutional bureaucracy (e.g., hospital credentialing committee) that authorizes its use.

140. The potential for the "dark side" presumably is analogous in the physician-patient relationship. See, generally, Brody, *Healer's Power.*

141. See, e.g., Myss and Shealy, *Creation of Health*, 72–76. Powers may include "the ability to prophesy, see and hear at great distances, bend the flame of a candle at will, transmit his emotions to others, change the weather, and heal sickness" (Kisala, "AUM Spiritual Truth Church," 36 [providing description of claims of founder of AUM Shinrikyo]). In the case of destructive religious groups, promises may be made that the client (or follower) will attain the psychic powers the leader already has attained by following the leader's training. See Kisala, "AUM Spiritual Truth Church," 36.

142. Interestingly, in assessing why followers have joined destructive religious groups to the point of engaging in criminal activity, some have rejected theories based on claims of social tension and/or mind control. See Kisala, "AUM Spiritual Truth Church," 34. "Techniques of psychological manipulation," such as fasting, sleep deprivation, isolation, and image training, are "not unique to destructive religious groups and have been found useful in presumably healthy contexts," such as meditation by mainline religious groups and training by athletes (ibid., 42). Instead, it has been argued, "ultimately the dynamics of religious faith, supported by elements" within a nation's indigenous religious and cultural heritage, motivate the criminal activity (ibid., 34). Thus, for example, AUM Shinrikyo was founded by an acupuncturist and masseur convicted of manufacturing and selling harmful and deceptive remedies for various ailments; "in the wake of his conviction his business went bankrupt, and he apparently turned to religion" (ibid., 35).

143. It has been argued that both parties—healer and client—can share some responsibility in abusive situations that occur on a mass scale. See, e.g., *Dushkin v. Desai*, 18 F.Supp.2d 117 (D. Mass. 1998). In *Dushkin*, the court granted motions by the defendant, a yoga teacher, spiritual healer, and leader of a spiritual community, to dismiss claims for intentional

infliction of emotional distress, breach of fiduciary duty, and breach of contract.

144. In another sense, abuse of religious authority parallels abuse in other contexts—and similarly, it has been argued, "religious addiction" parallels addiction to mood-altering behaviors and substances. See, e.g., Booth, *When God*, 2. Religious addiction is defined as "using God, a religion, or a belief system as a means both to escape or avoid painful feelings and to seek self-esteem. It involves adopting a rigid belief system that specifies only one right way, which you feel you must force onto others by means of guilt, shame, fear, brain-washing, and elitism" (ibid.).

145. A contractual relationship between healing professional and patient also may be possible, triggering contract, rather than tort, obligations and potential liabilities. Contracting principles may be especially appropriate when healing practices rely on consensus and mutual responsibility. See Cohen, "Fixed Star," 152 (citing Heidi Rian, "An Alternative Contractual Approach to Holistic Health Care," *Ohio State Law Journal* 44 [1983]: 185, 187). There are limits, however, as to what rights courts will permit patients to contract away, and negligence principles may still apply if practices are below prevailing standards of care. Such cases further blur the borderland between contract and tort. See Cohen, "Reconstructing Breach" (proposing tort remedies, or at the least, expanded contractual remedies, for bad faith and unreasonable breaches involving denial of the existence of a contract, and other situations involving obstruction of the injured party's interest in securing the compensatory value of the agreement).

146. See Cohen, *Legal Boundaries*, 29.

147. Ibid., 15 (quoting T. Romeyn Beck, "A Sketch of the Legislative Provision of the Colony and State of New-York, Respecting the Practice of Physic and Surgery," *New York Journal of Medicine* [1822]: 139).

148. Cohen, *Legal Boundaries*, 22 (citing cases). The statutory definition of practicing medicine varies by state but typically includes (1) diagnosing, preventing, treating, and curing disease; (2) holding oneself out to the public as able to perform the above; (3) intending to receive a gift, fee, or compensation for the above; (4) attaching such titles as M.D. to one's name; (5) maintaining an office for reception, examination, and treatment; (6) performing surgery; and (7) using, administering, or prescribing "drugs" or medicinal preparations. See ibid., 26–29 (citing cases). The third element, involving receipt of compensation for the healing service, is not a necessary requirement in all states.

149. Ibid., 15.

150. Ibid., 17, 34–35.

151. Ibid., 17 (quoting Richard H. Shryock, *Medical Licensing in America, 1650–1965* [Baltimore: Johns Hopkins Press, 1967]).

152. Ibid., 34–35 (citing sources). For a seminal critique of licensure, see Gellhorn, "Abuse."

153. See Cohen, *Future Medicine*, 86–87.

154. See Cohen, *Legal Boundaries*, 35 (citing cases).

155. See Cohen, *Beyond Complementary Medicine*, 117 n. 272 (citing cases).

156. See Nobel, "Religious Healing"; see D.C. Code § 3-1201.03 (2002) (exempting any minister, priest, rabbi, officer, or agent of any religious body or any practitioner of any religious belief engaging in prayer or any other religious practice or nursing practiced solely in accordance with the religious tenets of any church for the purpose of fostering the physical, mental, or spiritual well-being of any person).

157. Greenberg, "In God We Trust," 457 (citing *Crane v. Johnson*, 242 U.S. 339 [1917]). Thus, a faith healer who also prescribed herbal medicine and applied a personally patented medication was held liable for practicing medicine unlawfully, since the healer arguably had exceeded the bounds of religious practice. See ibid., 458 (citing *People v. Vogelgesang*, 221 N.Y. 290 [1917]).

158. Cohen, "Fixed Star," 78–79. Presumably, however, the Native American medicine man and Christian faith healer would retain the exemption, since they purport to practice within a religious tradition.

159. See, e.g., 2002 Cal. Stat. 820, enacting Cal. Bus. & Prof. Code §§ 2053.5, 2053.6 (also stating the purpose of the legislation). The legislation provides that a person is not in violation of specified provisions of the Medical Practice Act that prohibit the practice of medicine without being licensed as a physician, as long as the person does not engage in specified acts and also makes specified disclosures to each client, for which the client must acknowledge receipt in writing.

160. R.I. Gen. Laws § 23-74-1(3). The statute provides that "unlicensed health care practices" do not include "surgery, x-ray radiation, prescribing, administering, or dispensing legend drugs and controlled substances, practices that invade the human body by puncture of the skin, setting fractures, any practice included in the practice of dentistry, the manipulation or adjustment of articulations of joints, or the spine, also known as chiropractic medicine . . . , the healing art of acupuncture . . . , or practices that are permitted under" two other specific statutes.

161. Ibid., § 23-74-1(4)(d).

162. Ibid., § 23-74-1(4).

163. See Cohen, *Legal Boundaries*, 29–31 (citing cases, describing legal action against the nonlicensed CAM provider) and 47–55 (citing cases, describing legal action against the licensed CAM provider).

164. California's legislation allows prosecution if the provider

(1) Conducts surgery or any other procedure on another person that punctures the skin or harmfully invades the body. (2) Administers or prescribes x-ray radiation to another person. (3) Prescribes or administers legend drugs or controlled substances to another person.
(4) Recommends the discontinuance of legend drugs or controlled substances prescribed by an appropriately licensed practitioner.
(5) Willfully diagnoses and treats a physical or mental condition of any person under circumstances or conditions that cause or create a risk of great bodily harm, serious physical or mental illness, or death. . . .
(8) Holds out, states, indicates, advertises, or implies to a client or prospective client that he or she is a physician, a surgeon, or a physician and surgeon. [Cal. Bus. & Prof. Code §2053.5(a)]

165. R.I. Gen. Laws § 23-74-4(2). When therapies necessarily involve healing touch, such contact may be more ambiguous than the present statutory language allows. See Cohen, *Future Medicine*, 167–211.

166. R.I. Gen. Laws § 23-74-4(6).

167. Cohen, *Legal Boundaries*.

168. Ibid., 39–40.

169. Ibid., 40–44 (citing statutes).

170. Ibid., 39.

171. Ibid., 68–69 (citing cases).

172. Ibid., 47–49 (citing Matter of Stockwell, 622 P.2d 910 [Wash. App. 1981]; *Foster v. Georgia Bd. of Chiropractic Examiners*, 359 S.E.2d 877 [Ga. 1987]).

173. The medical licensing statutes do not seem to make a distinction between the narrower notion of curing and the broader realm of healing (the latter implying a restored psychosocial and spiritual wholeness).

174. A similar issue arises in trying to conceptualize distinctions between "structure-function" claims, which are permissible for dietary supplement labels under the Dietary Supplements Health Education Act of 1994, and "disease claims," which are impermissible and bring the supplement in question within the definition of a drug. See Cohen, *Legal Boundaries*,

81 (citing sources); Cohen, *Beyond Complementary Medicine*, 114–15. Structure-function claims describe the role of a nutrient or dietary ingredient intended to affect the structure and function in human beings (e.g., "saw palmetto maintains prostate health"), whereas disease claims link the dietary supplement to the diagnosis, mitigation, cure, or treatment of a disease (e.g., "saw palmetto cures prostate cancer"). See Cohen, *Beyond Complementary Medicine*, 114.

175. Cohen, *Legal Boundaries*, 109–10.

176. Massachusetts Board of Registration in Nursing, "Holistic Nursing Practice and Complementary Therapies."

177. Cf. *Ohio State Board Chiropractic Examiners v. Fulk*, 617 N.E.2d 690 (Ohio App. 1992) (interpreting practice of chiropractic expansively—as permitting colonic irrigation even though not expressly authorized in the licensing statute).

178. Cohen, *Legal Boundaries*, 87 (citing statutes).

179. One could consider California, Minnesota, and Rhode Island as exceptions. As noted, these states have enacted statutes allowing a broad range of CAM providers to offer services without obtaining licensure but requiring them to register with a state agency that can receive consumer complaints. See, e.g., Minn. Stat. § 146A (2002). Conceptually, however, the distinction between licensure and simple registration of the unlicensed may be one of degree and not substance. See Cohen, *Legal Boundaries*, 35–37 (discussing differences between mandatory licensure, permissive certification, and registration).

180. Alaska Stat. § 08.64.32(a)(8)(A) (2002).

181. Colo. Rev. Stat. § 12-36-117 (2002).

182. See Cohen, *Legal Boundaries*, 92–95 (discussing some differences among statutes).

183. Guidelines by the Federation of State Medical Boards concerning physician use of CAM therapies provide that in considering professional discipline, the medical board should evaluate whether the physician is using a treatment that is

> effective and safe (having adequate scientific evidence of efficacy and/or safety or greater safety than other established treatment models for the same condition); effective, but with some real or potential danger (having evidence of efficacy, but also of adverse side effects); inadequately studied, but safe (having insufficient evidence of clinical efficacy, but reasonable evidence to suggest relative safety); ineffective

and dangerous (proven to be ineffective or unsafe through controlled trials or documented evidence or as measured by a risk/benefit assessment). [Federation of State Medical Boards, "Model Guidelines"]

184. See Cohen, *Beyond Complementary Medicine*, 23–26.

185. 660 N.Y.S.2d 665, 668 (N.Y. Sup. 1997).

186. Ibid. The decision was affirmed but was modified on appeal to vacate the punitive damages award, 673 N.Y.S.2d 685 (App. Div. 1998).

187. See Cohen, *Legal Boundaries*, 58–59, 62 (citing cases and discussing the potential application of these defenses to use of CAM therapies).

188. *Moore v. Baker*, 1991 U.S. Dist. LEXIS 14712, at *11 (S.D. Ga., Sept. 5, 1991), aff'd, 989 F.2d 1129 (11th Cir. 1993).

189. See Cohen, "Fixed Star," 134 (citing Stuart M. Speiser et al., *The American Law of Torts*, § 32.1, at 207 [1992]).

190. A related question is how to assess spiritual groups and determine when healthy religiosity crosses the line and becomes religious addiction. Cf. Arterburn and Felton, *Toxic Faith*, 137–59 (listing the characteristics of a toxic-faith system, including a claim that its members have special character, abilities, or knowledge; authoritarian leadership; oppositional status toward the world; a punitive nature; demands of members to give overwhelming service; lack of objective accountability; and use of labeling to discount those who oppose the beliefs of the group).

191. To some extent, all these forms of abuse overlap and intersect; they have been separated for clarification. Legal rules such as malpractice and professional discipline similarly overlap, in that an act of gross negligence, for example, can subject the perpetrator to potential malpractice liability as well as professional discipline, resulting in monetary payment to a civil plaintiff as well as loss of licensure to the state.

192. See Cohen, *Beyond Complementary Medicine*, 62–64 (discussing credentialing mechanisms to ensure provider competence). Assuming the unlicensed provider, even if within the hospital, works closely with medical staff, the hospital arguably could help immunize itself from claims of aiding and abetting unlicensed medical practice. Thus, the location of the provider offering energy healing—i.e., living room vs. community center, church basement, or hospital or clinic—could make a difference.

193. As noted earlier, though, nursing regulations in some states—such as Massachusetts—would authorize CAM practices in general, or even specific modalities such as Therapeutic Touch. Interestingly, the suggestion has been raised that distance healing (or nonlocal healing)—the applica-

tion of energy healing through intentionality at a distance, as opposed to through touch and contact—might raise regulatory issues similar to tele-medicine and/or the practice of law at a distance (i.e., via the Internet). See Kathi J. Kemper, M.D., personal correspondence (2002). From a regula-tory perspective, however, the above discussion suggests that the issues raised by energy healing have less to do with physical distance and more to do with questions of competence, professional boundaries, and standard of care.

194. Cohen, *Legal Boundaries*, 40.

195. This argument recapitulates arguments made by medical boards for therapies such as homeopathy, which similarly rely on theories historically outside biomedical convention and proof. See In re *Guess*, 393 S.E.2d 833 (N.C. 1990) (affirming conviction of a licensed physician for administering homeopathic remedies), cert. denied, *Guess v. North Carolina Bd. Med. Examin.*, 498 U.S. 1047 (1991), later proceeding, *Guess v. Bd., Med. Examin.*, 967 F.2d 998 (4th Cir. 1992).

196. See Cohen and Eisenberg, "Potential Physician Malpractice." The article offers liability management strategies for institutions offering CAM therapies or authorizing CAM providers to deliver clinical services.

197. Cohen, "Fixed Star," 135–57.

198. Cohen, *Legal Boundaries*, 112–13.

199. See Cohen, "Fixed Star," 134–57 (applying tort elements to specific scenarios involving CAM practices).

200. See Cohen, *Legal Boundaries*, 110 (suggesting that legislative scope of practice for emerging providers challenges the drafter to be specific enough to cover areas of potential ambiguity yet broad enough to support holistic practice).

201. See, e.g., *Guess*, 393 S.E.2d at 833.

202. Yet another arena of sensitivity is how to approach patients who have suffered from religious abuse, as they "may react strongly to having chaplains, ministers, nuns" (Booth, *When God*, 254) or, presumably, to medical personnel querying them as to whether they object to receiving energy healing.

203. See Cohen, *Future Medicine*, 55–57 (proposing to distinguish spiri-tual from physical notions of efficacy). One also could consider the various levels of efficacy yet another way to understand the distinction articulated between healing and curing—sometimes a patient may be cured without being healed, and sometimes the reverse may occur. From another van-tage, Eliade describes the "effectiveness" of a medicinal plant as containing

the "threefold effectiveness of the moon, the waters, and vegetation," each of which works on multiple levels (vegetation, for instance, implying "notions of death and rebirth, of light and darkness . . . of fecundity and abundance, and so on") (Eliade, "Sky, Moon, and Egg," 55–56), whereas modern pharmacology would only consider the effectiveness of the medicinal plant in terms of the effect of its identified, active ingredient. Thus, from a mythological perspective, "everything hangs together, everything is connected, and makes up a cosmic whole" (Eliade, "Sky, Moon, and Egg," 56); there is no differentiation of efficacy into separate, component parts. The drive to chronicle the world and what happens in one's own soul is, according to Eliade, a need organic to the human condition; see Eliade, "Literary Imagination," 21–22.

204. King, *Faith, Spirituality, and Medicine*, 69 (referring to prayer and spiritual ministry).

205. The hypothetical scenario comes from Cohen, *Future Medicine*, 165. Admittedly, by using the word "God," the situation suggests religion rather than the broader notion of spirituality as earlier defined; one could easily, however, substitute the notion of turning to one's innate wisdom, and the principle would be the same: "Depending on the manner in which this information (or opinion) was conveyed, it may have been helpful or hurtful, inspiring or intrusive" (ibid.).

206. Booth, *When God*, 2; see also Miller, "Moral Bankruptcy" (describing experiences with sexual abuse and its later denial by church members and officials). As suggested, this is a variation on the definition of abuse of authority offered earlier.

207. See Arterburn and Felton, *Toxic Faith*, 39–42, 49–50 (listing twenty-one typical toxic beliefs held by religious addicts, including "*If I have real faith, God will heal me or someone I know*" and "*Problems in my life result from some particular sin*").

208. Most likely, the healer would be held criminally liable for practicing medicine without a license; a physician in this situation probably would be held negligent and receive professional discipline. In the arena of parental care for children, abuse and neglect laws likely would be triggered. See Cohen et al., "Pediatric Use of Complementary Therapies."

209. Cf. Aldridge, *Spirituality, Healing, and Medicine*, 13 ("I am not arguing for idealism but a transformation of consciousness, which will demand a compassionate acceptance of the material world as it relates to an understanding of the spiritual").

210. Karpman, "Informed Consent," 939 (citing sources).

211. See, e.g., Radin, *Conscious Universe*, 159 (arguing that "the idea of field consciousness suggests a continuum of nonlocal intelligence, permeating space and time"); see also Bohm, *Wholeness*.

212. See, generally, Brennan, *Hands of Light*; Myss and Shealy, *Creation of Health*.

213. See Cohen, *Beyond Complementary Medicine*, 166.

214. See, generally, Jonas and Crawford, *Healing, Intention, and Energy Medicine*.

Epilogue

1. Cohen, *Legal Boundaries*, 15–21.

2. Ibid., 109–15.

3. Calling incremental steps "ineffective," the IOM opined that the United States must enact universal coverage for the 43 million Americans who presently lack such coverage. Rather than endorsing a specific policy approach, such as an employer mandate or government-sponsored, single-payer system, the IOM outlined five principles that should be used to evaluate the merit of various approaches: (1) Health care coverage should be universal. (2) Health care coverage should be continuous. (3) Health care coverage should be affordable to individuals and families. (4) Health insurance strategy should be affordable and sustainable for society. (5) Health insurance should enhance health and well-being by promoting access to high-quality care that is effective, efficient, safe, timely, patient centered, and equitable. The committee put forth a strong overall recommendation that by 2010 everyone in the United States should have health insurance and urged the president and Congress to act immediately to establish a firm and explicit plan to reach this goal. See Institute of Medicine, *Insuring America's Health*.

4. Flaws and Lake, *Chinese Medical Psychiatry*.

5. Institute of Medicine, *Complementary and Alternative Medicine*, devotes chapter 4 to the "need for innovative designs in research on CAM and conventional medicine." See also Ruggie, *Marginal to Mainstream*.

6. See Cohen, *Legal Boundaries*, 115–16. See also Appendix B.

7. Consortium of Academic Health Centers for Integrative Medicine. "About Us."

8. *Wilk v. American Medical Association*, 719 F.2d 207 (7th Cir. 1983), cert. denied, 467 U.S. 1210 (1984), on remand, 671 F. Supp. 1465 (N.D. Ill. 1987), aff'd, 895 F.2d 352 (7th Cir. 1990).

9. Institute of Medicine, *Complementary and Alternative Medicine*, 8.

10. Cohen, *Beyond Complementary Medicine*, 142–43.

11. Ibid., 144.

12. Shakespeare, *Hamlet*, act 1, scene 5.

13. *West Virginia State Board of Education v. Barnette*, 319 U.S. 624, 642 (1942). This introduced Cohen, "Fixed Star."

14. Cohen, *Future Medicine*, chap. 3.

15. Adams et al., "Ethical Considerations."

16. Suzuki, Fromm, and DeMartino, *Zen Buddhism*, 2.

17. Ibid., 3.

Appendix A

1. Table AP.1 is a summary of Table 5-3 in Institute of Medicine, *Complementary and Alternative Medicine*. The full table and text contain a number of qualifications that may be of interest (for example, "insufficient evidence of an effect was determined for a larger proportion of CAM therapies (56.6 percent for CAM versus 21.3 percent for conventional medicine)"; on the other hand, "CAM reviews were less likely to be classified as harmful . . . or as having no effect").

2. Institute of Medicine, *Complementary and Alternative Medicine*, 145.

All referenced Web addresses were accessed 25 October 2005.

Adams, Karen E., Michael H. Cohen, David M. Eisenberg, and Albert R. Jonsen. "Ethical Considerations of Complementary and Alternative Medical Therapies in Conventional Medical Settings." *Annals of Internal Medicine* 137, no. 8 (15 October 2002): 665–70.

Aldridge, David. *Spirituality, Healing, and Medicine: Return to the Silence.* London: Jessica Kingsley, 2000.

Alternative Medicine: Expanding Medical Horizons. A Report to the National Institutes of Health on Alternative Medical Systems and Practices in the United States. Prepared under the auspices of the Workshop on Alternative Medicine, Chantilly, Va., 14–16 September 1992. Commonly known as the *Chantilly Report.*

American Academy of Family Physicians. "Policy on Complementary Practice." 1997. Available at <www.aafp.org/x6681.xml>.

American Hospital Association (Health Forum), 2000–2001. *Complementary and Alternative Medicine Survey* (Chicago: American Hospital Association, 2002). Available at <www.hospitalconnect.com>.

American Medical Association. "Policy H-480.964." CSA Rep. 12, A-97 (1997); reaffimed: BOT Rep. 36, A-02.

American Medical Association Council on Scientific Affairs. *Alternative Medicine.* Report 10-I-96. Chicago: American Medical Association, 1996.

American Psychological Association. "Ethical Principles of Psychologists and Code of Conduct (2003)." Available at <http://www.apa.org/ethics/code2002.html>.

Angell, Marcia, and Jerome P. Kassirer. "Alternative Medicine: The Risks of Untested and Unregulated Remedies." *New England Journal of Medicine* 339, no. 12 (17 September 1998): 839–41.

Arterburn, Stephen, and Jack Felton. *Toxic Faith. Experiencing Healing from Painful Spiritual Abuse.* Colorado Springs: WaterBrook Press, 2001.

Astin, John A. "Complementary and Alternative Medicine and the Need for Evidence-Based Criticism." *Academic Medicine* 77 (2002): 864–68.

———. "Intercessory Prayer and Healing Prayer." In *Healing, Intention, and Energy Medicine*, edited by Wayne B. Jonas and Cindy C. Crawford, 13–22. New York: Churchill Livingstone, 2003.

Astin, John A., Elaine Harkness, and Edzard Ernst. "Distant Healing." *Annals of Internal Medicine* 134, no. 6 (20 March 2001): 533.

———. "The Efficacy of 'Distant Healing': A Systematic Review of Randomized Trials." *Annals of Internal Medicine* 132, no. 11 (6 June 2000): 903–10.

Aung, Steven K. H. *Medical Qi Gong*. St. Edmonton, Canada: World Natural Medicine Foundation, 1996.

Becker, Ernst. *The Denial of Death*. New York: Free Press, 1973.

Benedikt, Heinrich E. *Spirituality versus Religion: Principles of Interreligious Understanding and Self-Realization*. Verlag Lotus Publications, 1995. Available at <http://www.heinrichschwabverlag.de>.

Beyerstein, B. L. "Alternative Medicine and Common Errors of Reasoning." *Academic Medicine* 76 (2001): 230–37.

Black, D. M. "What Sort of a Thing Is a Religion? A View from Object-Relations Theory." *International Journal of Psycho-analysis* 74 (June 1993): 613–25.

Blevins, Sue A. *The Medical Monopoly: Protecting Consumers or Limiting Competition? Policy Analysis*, no. 246. Washington, D.C.: Cato Institute, 1995.

Bohm, David. *Wholeness and the Implicate Order*. Oxford: Routledge, 1993.

Booth, Leo. *When God Becomes a Drug: Breaking the Chains of Religious Addiction and Abuse*. Los Angeles: Jeremy P. Tarcher, 1991.

Brennan, Barbara A. *Hands of Light: A Guide to Healing through the Human Energy Field*. New York: Bantam, 1988.

Brody, Howard. *The Healer's Power*. New Haven: Yale University Press, 1992.

Bruyere, Roslyn L. *Wheels of Light: A Study of the Chakras*. Vol. 1. Sierra Madre, Calif.: Bon Productions, 1991.

Bryant, Barry. *The Wheel of Time Sand Mandala: Visual Scripture of Tibetan Buddhism*. San Francisco: Harper SanFrancisco, 1992.

Butler, Barry. *Butler's Lives of the Saints*. Collegeville, Minn.: Liturgical Press, 2000.

Callahan, Daniel. "Pursuing a Peaceful Death." *Hastings Center Report* 23, no. 4 (1993): 33–38.

——. *What Kind of Life: The Limits of Medical Progress*. Washington, D.C.: Georgetown University Press, 1990.

——, ed. *The Role of Complementary and Alternative Medicine: Accommodating Pluralism*. Washington, D.C.: Georgetown University Press, 1992.

Carrasco, David, and Jane Marie Law, eds. *Waiting for the Dawn: Mircea Eliade in Perspective*. Boulder: University Press of Colorado, 1991.

Cassell, Eric J. "The Sorcerer's Broom: Medicine's Rampant Technology." *Hastings Center Report* 23, no. 6 (1993): 32–39.

Chamberlain, Theodore J., and Christopher A. Hall. *Realized Religion: Research on the Relationship between Religion and Health*. Philadelphia: Templeton Foundation Press, 2000.

Chantilly Report. See *Alternative Medicine: Expanding Medical Horizons*.

Cohen, Cynthia B., Sondra E. Wheeler, David A. Scott, and the Anglican Working Group in Bioethics. "Walking a Fine Line: Physician Inquiries into Patients' Religious and Spiritual Beliefs." *Hastings Center Report* 31 (2001): 29–39.

Cohen, Jordan J. "Reckoning with Alternative Medicine." *Academic Medicine* 75 (2000): 571.

Cohen, Michael H. *Beyond Complementary Medicine: Legal and Ethical Perspectives on Health Care and Human Evolution*. Ann Arbor: University of Michigan Press, 2000.

——. *Complementary and Alternative Medicine: Legal Boundaries and Regulatory Perspectives*. Baltimore: Johns Hopkins University Press, 1998.

——. "A Fixed Star in Health Care Reform: The Emerging Paradigm of Holistic Healing." *Arizona State Law Journal* 27 (1995): 79–173.

——. *Future Medicine: Ethical Dilemmas, Regulatory Challenges, and Therapeutic Pathways to Health and Healing in Human Transformation*. Ann Arbor: University of Michigan Press, 2003.

——. "Healing at the Borderland between Medicine and Religion: Regulating Potential Abuse of Authority by Spiritual Healers." *Journal of Law and Religion* 18, no. 2 (2004): 373–426.

——. "Reconstructing Breach of the Implied Covenant of Good Faith and Fair Dealing as a Tort." *California Law Review* 73 (1985): 1291.

——. "Toward a Bioethics of Compassion." *Indiana Law Journal* 28 (1995): 667.

Cohen, Michael H., and David M. Eisenberg. "Potential Physician Malpractice Liability Associated with Complementary and Integrative Medical Therapies." *Annals of Internal Medicine* 136, no. 8 (16 April 2002): 596–603.

Cohen, Michael H., and Mary Ruggie. "Integrating Complementary and Alternative Medical Therapies in Conventional Medical Settings: Legal Quandaries and Potential Policy Models." *Cincinnati Law Review* 72, no. 2 (2004): 671.

———. "Overcoming Legal and Social Barriers to Integrative Medicine." *Medical Law International* 6 (2004): 339.

Cohen, Michael H., Kathi J. Kemper, Laura Stevens, Dean Hashimoto, and Joan Gilmour. "Pediatric Use of Complementary Therapies: Ethical and Policy Choices." *Pediatrics* 116 (2005): e568–e575 (electronic pages).

Consortium of Academic Health Centers for Integrative Medicine. "About Us." Available at <www.imconsortium.org/html/about.php>.

Crelling, Jon, and Fernando Ania. *Professionalism and Ethics in Complementary and Alternative Medicine*. New York: Haworth Integrative Healing Press, 2002.

Curlin, Farr A., Chad J. Roach, Rita Gorawara-Bhat, John D. Lantos, and Marshall H. Chin. "When Patients Choose Faith over Medicine: Physician Perspectives on Religiously Related Conflict in the Medical Encounter." *Archives of Internal Medicine* 165, no. 1 (10 January 2005): 88–91.

Danesi, M. A., and J. B. Adetunji. "Use of Alternative Medicine by Patients with Epilepsy: A Survey of 265 Epileptic Patients in a Developing Country." *Epilepsia* 35, no. 2 (1994): 344–51.

Devinsky, Orrin, Steven Schachter, and Steven Pacia, eds. *Complementary and Alternative Therapies for Epilepsy*. (New York: Demos Medical Publishing, 2005).

Dillard, James, and Terra Ziporyn. *Alternative Medicine for Dummies*. Foster City, Calif.: IDG Books, 1998.

Dossey, Larry. "The Dark Side of Consciousness and the Therapeutic Relationship." *Alternative Therapies in Health and Medicine* 8, no. 6 (2002): 12–16, 118–22.

———. *Meaning and Medicine: Lessons from a Doctor's Tales of Breakthrough and Healing*. New York: Bantam, 1992.

———. "Samueli Conference on Definitions and Standards in Healing Research: Working Definitions and Terms." *Alternative Therapies in Health and Medicine* 9, no. 3 (sup.) (2003): A10–A12.

Eck, Diana L. *A New Religious America*. San Francisco: Harper SanFrancisco, 2001.

Eisenberg, David M. "Advising Patients Who Seek Alternative Medical Therapies." *Annals of Internal Medicine* 127, no. 1 (1 July 1997): 61–69.

Eisenberg, David M., Michael H. Cohen, Andrea Hrbek, Jonathan

Grayzel, Maria van Rompay, and Richard A. Cooper. "Credentialing Complementary and Alternative Medical Providers." *Annals of Internal Medicine* 137, no. 12 (17 December 2002): 965–73.

Eisenberg, David M., Roger B. Davis, Susan L. Ettner, Scott Appel, Sonja Wilkey, Maria Van Rompay, and Ronald Kessler. "Trends in Alternative Medicine Use in the United States, 1990–1997: Results of a Follow-up National Survey." *Journal of the American Medical Association* 280, no. 18 (11 November 1998): 1569–75.

Eisenberg, David M., Ronald C. Kessler, Cindy Foster, Frances E. Norlock, David R. Calkin, and Thomas L. Delbanco. "Unconventional Medicine in the United States: Prevalence, Costs, and Patterns of Use." *New England Journal of Medicine* 328, no. 4 (28 January 1993): 246–52.

Eliade, Mircea. "A New Humanism." In *Waiting for the Dawn: Mircea Eliade in Perspective*, edited by David Carrasco and Jane Marie Law, 35–44. Boulder: University Press of Colorado, 1991.

———. "Literary Imagination and Religious Structure." In *Waiting for the Dawn: Mircea Eliade in Perspective*, edited by David Carrasco and Jane Marie Law, 17–24. Boulder: University Press of Colorado, 1991.

———. "Sky, Moon, and Egg." In *Waiting for the Dawn: Mircea Eliade in Perspective*, edited by David Carrasco and Jane Marie Law, 45–59. Boulder: University Press of Colorado, 1991.

———. "Waiting for the Dawn." In *Waiting for the Dawn: Mircea Eliade in Perspective*, edited by David Carrasco and Jane Marie Law, 11–16. Boulder: University Press of Colorado, 1991.

Ernst, Edzard E. "Harmless Herbs? A Review of the Recent Literature." *American Journal of Medicine* 104, no. 2 (February 1998): 170–78.

———, ed. *The Desktop Guide to Complementary and Alternative Medicine: An Evidence-Based Approach*. St. Louis: Mosby, 2001.

Ernst, Edzard E., and Michael H. Cohen. "Informed Consent in Complementary and Alternative Medicine." *Archives of Internal Medicine* 161, no. 19 (22 October 2001): 2288–92.

Ernst, Edzard E., Michael H. Cohen, and Julie Stone. "Ethical Problems Arising in Evidence-Based Complementary and Alternative Medicine." *Journal of Medical Ethics* 30, no. 2 (1 April 2004): 156–59.

Federal Trade Commission. *Advertising and Marketing on the Internet: Rules of the Road*. Available at <www.ftc.gov/bcp/conline/pubs/buspubs/ruleroad.htm>.

———. *Dietary Supplements: An Advertising Guide for Industry*. Available at <www.ftc.gov/bcp/conline/pubs/buspubs/dietsupp.htm>.

Federation of State Medical Boards. "Model Guidelines for the Use of

Complementary and Alternative Medical Therapies in Medical
Practice." 2002. Available at <www.fsmb.org/grpol—
policydocs.html>.

Fisher, Roger, and Elliott S. Fisher. "What Is a Good Decision?" *Effective
Clinical Practice*, July/August 1999. Available at <www.acponline.org/
journals/ecp/julaug99/essays.htm>.

Fisher, Roger, William Ury, and Bruce Patton. *Getting to Yes: Negotiating
Agreement without Giving In*. New York: Penguin, 1991.

Flaws, Robert, and James Lake. *Chinese Medical Psychiatry: A Textbook
and Clinical Manual Including Indications for Referral to Western
Medical Services*. Boulder, Colo.: Blue Poppy Press, 2002.

Fontarosa, Phil B., and George D. Lundberg. "Alternative Medicine Meets
Science." *Journal of the American Medical Association* 280, no. 18
(11 November 1998): 1618–19.

Frew, David R. *Management of Stress: Using TM at Work*. Chicago:
Nelson-Hall, 1977.

Frohock, Fred M. "Moving Lines and Variable Criteria: Differences/
Connections between Allopathic and Alternative Medicine." *Annals
of the American Academy of Political and Social Science* 583
(September 2002): 214–31.

Fulder, Stephen. *The Handbook of Alternative and Complementary
Medicine*. New York: Oxford University Press, 1996.

Gallo, Fred P. *Energy Psychology: Explorations at the Interface of Energy,
Cognition, Behavior, and Health*. London: CRC Press, 1999.

Gellhorn, Walter. "The Abuse of Occupational Licensing." *University of
Chicago Law Review* 44 (Fall 1976): 6–27.

Goleman, Daniel, ed. *Healing Emotions: Conversations with the Dalai
Lama on Mindfulness, Emotions, and Health*. Boston: Shambhala,
1997.

Goleman, Daniel, and Joel Gurin, eds. *Mind Body Medicine*. Yonkers,
N.Y.: Consumer Reports Books, 1993.

Greenberg, Lauren A. "In God We Trust: Faith Healing Subject to
Liability." *Journal of Contemporary Health Law and Policy* 14 (1998):
451–75.

Guorui, Jiao. *Qigong Essentials for Health Promotion*. Los Angeles:
Wayfarer Publications, 2002.

Harlow, Tim. "The Impact of Healing in a Clinical Setting." In *Healing,
Intention, and Energy Medicine*, edited by Wayne B. Jonas and
Cindy C. Crawford, 175–84. New York: Churchill Livingstone, 2003.

Harner, Michael. *The Way of the Shaman*. San Francisco: Harper
SanFrancisco, 1990.

Harvard Law School Program on Negotiation. "Mindfulness in the Law and ADR." Available at <www.pon.harvard.edu/news/2002/riskin—mindfulness.php3>.

Huffaker, M. Lee. "Recovery for Infliction of Emotional Distress: A Comment on the Mental Anguish Accompanying Such a Claim in Alabama." *Alabama Law Review* 52, no. 3 (Spring 2001): 1003–27.

Hufford, David. "Challenges for Healing and Intentionality Research: Social Dynamics Involved in Entering the Mainstream." In *Healing, Intention, and Energy Medicine*, edited by Wayne B. Jonas and Cindy C. Crawford, 293–303. New York: Churchill Livingstone, 2003.

Humber, James M. Review of *The Role of Complementary and Alternative Medicine: Accommodating Pluralism. Journal of the American Medical Association* 288, no. 13 (20 October 2002): 1655–56.

Humber, James M., and Robert F. Almeder, eds. *Alternative Medicine and Ethics*. Towota, N.J.: Human Press, 1998.

Institute of Medicine of the National Academy of Sciences. *Complementary and Alternative Medicine*. Washington, D.C.: National Academies Press, 2005.

———. *Crossing the Quality Chasm: A New Health System for the Twenty-first Century*. Washington, D.C.: National Academies Press, 2001.

———. *Insuring America's Health: Principles and Recommendations*. Washington, D.C.: National Academies Press, 2004.

James, William. *The Varieties of Religious Experience*. New York: Collier, 1961.

Jamison, R. "Chiropractic's Functional Integration into Conventional Health Care: Some Implications." *Journal of Manipulative Physiological Therapies* 10, no. 1 (1987): 5–10.

Janiger, Oscar, and Philip Goldberg. *A Different Kind of Healing: Doctors Speak Candidly about Their Successes with Alternative Medicine*. New York: Putnam, 1993.

Jefferson, Paul. "Strengthening Motivational Analysis under the Establishment Clause: Proposing a Burden-Shifting Standard." *Indiana Law Review* 35 (2002): 621, 644–45.

Jensen, Derrick. *A Language Older Than Words*. New York: Content Books, 2000.

Jianping, Zhu, and Ken Rose. "Chinese Medicine and Complexity." *Clinical Acupuncture and Oriental Medicine* 3 (2002): 77.

Jonas, Wayne B. "Evidence, Ethics, and the Evaluation of Global Medicine." In *The Role of Complementary and Alternative Medicine: Accommodating Pluralism*, edited by Daniel Callahan, 122–47. Washington, D.C.: Georgetown University Press, 1992.

——. "Energy Healing Research." In *Healing, Intention, and Energy Medicine*, edited by Wayne B. Jonas and Cindy C. Crawford, 83–106. New York: Churchill Livingstone, 2003.

——. "Policy, the Public, and Priorities in Alternative Medicine Research." *Annals of the American Academy of Political and Social Science* 583 (September 2002): 29–43.

Jonas, Wayne B., and Cindy C. Crawford. *Healing, Intention, and Energy Medicine*. New York: Churchill Livingstone, 2003.

——. Preface to *Healing, Intention, and Energy Medicine*, edited by Wayne B. Jonas and Cindy C. Crawford, xv–xx. New York: Churchill Livingstone, 2003.

Kaptchuk, Ted J. "The Placebo Effect in Alternative Medicine: Can the Performance of a Healing Ritual Have Clinical Significance?" *Annals of Internal Medicine* 136, no. 11 (4 June 2002): 817–25.

Kaptchuk, Ted J., and David M. Eisenberg. "The Appeal of Alternative Medicine." *Annals of Internal Medicine* 129, no. 12 (15 December 1998): 1061–65.

——. "Varieties of Healing 1: Medical Pluralism in the United States." *Annals of Internal Medicine* 135, no. 3 (7 August 2001): 189–95.

Karpman, Anna. "Informed Consent: Does the First Amendment Protect a Patient's Right to Choose Alternative Treatment?" *New York Law School Journal of Human Rights* 16 (2000): 933, 936.

Katz, Jay. *The Silent World of Doctor and Patient*. New York: Free Press, 1994.

Kemper, Kathi J., and Michael H. Cohen. "Ethics Meet Complementary and Alternative Medicine: New Light on Old Principles." *Contemporary Pediatrics* 21, no. 3 (March 2004): 61–72.

Kennedy, P. "Working with Survivors of Torture in Sarajevo with Reiki." *Complementary Therapies in Nursing and Midwifery* 7, no. 1 (February 2001): 4–7.

Kentucky Board of Medical Licensure. "Complementary and Alternative Therapies Policy Statement." Available at <www.state.ky.us/agencies/ kbml/policy/complement.pdf>.

King, C. E. "Healing Pathways through Energy Work in the Perianesthesia Care Setting." *Clinical Forum for Nurse Anesthetists* 11, no. 4 (November 2000): 180–85.

King, Dana E. *Faith, Spirituality, and Medicine: Toward the Making of the Healing Practitioner*. Binghamton: Haworth Pastoral Press, 2000.

Kisala, Robert. "The AUM Spiritual Truth Church in Japan." In *Wolves within the Fold: Religious Leadership and Abuses of Power*, edited by

Anson Shupe, 33–48. New Brunswick, N.J.: Rutgers University Press, 1998.

Klotz, Myriam. "Jewish Healing Services." *The Reconstructionist: Journal of Contemporary Jewish Thought and Practice* 63, no. 2 (Spring 1999): 26.

Koenig, Harold G. Foreword to *Faith, Spirituality, and Medicine: Toward the Making of the Healing Practitioner*, by Dana E. King, xii–xvi Binghamton: Haworth Pastoral Press, 2000.

——. *Spirituality in Patient Care: Why, How, When, and What.* Philadelphia: Templeton Foundation Press, 2002.

——, ed. *The Handbook of Religion and Mental Health*. San Diego: Academic Press, 1998.

Koenig, Harold G., and Harvey J. Cohen, eds. *The Link between Religion and Health: Psychoneuroimmunology and the Faith Factor*. Oxford: Oxford University Press, 2002.

Koenig, Harold G., Michael E. McCullough, and David B. Larson. *Handbook of Religion and Health*. Oxford: Oxford University Press, 2001.

Kohatsu, Wendy. *Complementary and Alternative Medicine Secrets: Questions and Answers about Integrating CAM Therapies into Clinical Practice*. Philadelphia: Hanley and Belfus, 2002.

Kok Sui, Choa. *Pranic Healing*. New York: Samuel Weiser, 1990.

Kopelman, Loretta M. "The Role of Science in Assessing Conventional, Complementary, and Alternative Medicines." In *The Role of Complementary and Alternative Medicine: Accommodating Pluralism*, edited by Daniel Callahan, 36–53. Washington, D.C.: Georgetown University Press, 1992.

Kory, Robert B. *The Transcendental Meditation Program for Business People*. New York: American Management Association, 1976.

Krebs, Theresa. "Church Structures That Facilitate Pedophilia among Roman Catholic Clergy." In *Wolves within the Fold: Religious Leadership and Abuses of Power*, edited by Anson Shupe, 15–32. New Brunswick, N.J.: Rutgers University Press, 1998.

Krieger, Dolores. *The Therapeutic Touch: How to Use Your Hands to Help or Heal*. Upper Saddle River, N.J.: Prentice-Hall, 1979.

——. *Therapeutic Touch as Transpersonal Healing*. New York: Lantern Books, 2002.

Lewith, George T., and David Aldridge, eds. *Clinical Research Methodology for Complementary Therapies*. London: Hodder and Stoughton, 1993.

Maslow, Abraham H. *Toward a Psychology of Being*. 2d ed. Princeton, N.J.: Van Nostrand Insight Books, 1968.

Massachusetts Board of Registration in Nursing. "Holistic Nursing Practice and Complementary Therapies." Advisory Ruling No. 9801. 2002. Available at <www.state.ma.us/reg/boards/rn/advrul/rulcomp.htm>.

McSweeney, M. "Midwifery and the Gift of Healing Touch." *Birth Gazettte* 15, no. 3 (Summer 1999): 28–29.

Michigan State University. "Doc's Work in Africa Blends Traditional Healing, Modern Medicine." Available at <www.newswise.com/articles/2002/5/EPILEPSY.MSU.html>.

Miller, Jeanne M. "The Moral Bankruptcy of Institutionalized Religion." In *Wolves within the Fold: Religious Leadership and Abuses of Power*, edited by Anson Shupe, 152–74. New Brunswick, N.J.: Rutgers University Press, 1998.

Morton, Mary, and Michael Morton. *Five Steps to Selecting the Best Alternative Medicine: A Guide to Complementary and Integrative Health Care*. Novato, Calif.: New World Library, 1996.

Myss, Caroline M., and C. Norman Shealy. *The Creation of Health: Merging Traditional Medicine with Intuitive Diagnosis*. New York: Three Rivers Press, 1993.

National Center for Complementary and Alternative Medicine (NCCAM). "Exploratory Grants for Frontier Medicine Research (2002)." Available at <http://grants1.nih.gov/grants/guide/rfa-files/RFA-AT-00-002.html>.

——. "NCCAM Research Centers Program Description." Available at <http://nccam.nih.gov/training/centers/descriptions.htm#>.

——. "What Is Complementary and Alternative Medicine?" Available at <http://nccam.nih.gov/health/whatiscam/#sup2>.

National Federation of Spiritual Healers. *Code of Conduct*. Available from the National Federation of Spiritual Healers, Sunbury on Thames, Middlesex, U.K.

Nelson, Roger, and Dean Radin. "Research on Mind-Matter Interactions (MMI): Group Attention." In *Healing, Intention, and Energy Medicine*, edited by Wayne B. Jonas and Cindy C. Crawford, 49–57. New York: Churchill Livingstone, 2003.

Nobel, Barry. "Religious Healing in the Courts: The Liberties and Liabilities of Patients, Parents, and Healers." *University of Puget Sound Law Review* 16 (1993): 599, 625–29.

O'Connor, Bonnie B. *Healing Traditions: Alternative Medicine and the*

Health Profession. Philadelphia: University of Pennsylvania Press, 1995.

O'Connor, Bonnie B., C. Calabrese, E. Cardena, et al. "Defining and Describing Complementary and Alternative Medicine." *Alternative Therapies in Health and Medicine* 3, no. 2 (1997): 49–56.

Pargament, Kenneth I. *The Psychology of Religion and Coping: Theory, Research, and Practice*. New York: Guilford Press, 1997.

Paul, Joel R. "Cultural Resistance to Global Governance." *Michigan Journal of International Law* 22, no. 1 (2000): 1–84.

Peeler, C. Lee, and Susan Cohn. "The Federal Trade Commission's Regulation of Advertising Claims for Dietary Supplements." *Food and Drug Law Journal* 50, no. 3 (1995): 349–55.

Peterson, Marilyn R. *At Personal Risk: Boundary Violations in Professional-Client Relationships*. New York: Norton, 1992.

Pfeifer, S. "Belief in Demons and Exorcism in Psychiatric Patients in Switzerland." *British Journal of Medicine Psychology* 67 (1994): 247–58.

Piscitelli, S. C., A. H. Burstein, D. Chaitt, R. M. Alfaro, and J. Falloon. "Indinavir Concentrations and St. John's Wort." *Lancet* 355 (12 February 2000): 547–48.

Radin, Dean. *The Conscious Universe: The Scientific Truth of Psychic Phenomena*. New York: HarperCollins, 1997.

Ramaratnam, S., and K. Sridharan. "Yoga for Epilepsy" (Cochrane Review). In *The Cochrane Library*, issue 1 (2003).

Rexilius, S. J., C. Mundt, M. Megel Erickson, and S. Agrawal. "Therapeutic Effects of Massage Therapy and Handling Touch on Caregivers of Patients Undergoing Autologous Hematopoietic Stem Cell Transplant." *Oncology Nursing Forum* 29 (2002): E35.

Riskin, Leonard. "Mindfulness in the Law and ADR: The Contemplative Lawyer: On the Potential Contributions of Mindfulness Meditation to Law Students, Lawyers, and their Clients." *Harvard Negotiation Law Review* 7 (June 2002): 1–66.

Roche, J. "Creative Ritual in a Hospice." *Health Progress* 75, no. 10 (1994): 45–47, 55.

Rothstein, William. *American Physicians in the Nineteenth Century: From Sects to Science*. Baltimore: Johns Hopkins University Press, 1972.

Rubik, Beverley. "Energy Medicine and the Unifying Concept of Information." *Alternative Therapies in Health and Medicine* 1, no. 1 (March 1995): 34–39.

Ruggie, Mary. *Marginal to Mainstream: Alternative Medicine in America*. Cambridge: Cambridge University Press, 2004.

Samueli Institute for Informational Biology. "Exploring the Science of
Healing." Available at <www.siib.org/vision.asp>.

Santorelli, Saki. *Heal Thy Self: Lessons on Mindfulness in Medicine*. New
York: Bell Tower, 1999.

Schaffner, Kenneth F. "Assessments of Efficacy in Biomedicine: The Turn
toward Biomedical Pluralism." In *The Role of Complementary and
Alternative Medicine: Accommodating Pluralism*, edited by Daniel
Callahan, 1–14. Washington, D.C.: Georgetown University Press,
1992.

Schmidt, Stefan. "Direct Mental Interactions with Living Systems." In
Healing, Intention, and Energy Medicine, edited by Wayne B. Jonas
and Cindy C. Crawford, 23–35. New York: Churchill Livingstone,
2003.

Schultz, Marjorie. "From Informed Consent to Patient Choice: A New
Protected Interest." *Yale Law Journal* 95 (1985): 219, 229–33.

Schwartz, Jack. *Human Energy Systems: A Way of Good Health*. New York:
Penguin, 1980.

Sered, Susan. *Women as Ritual Experts: The Religious Lives of Elderly
Jewish Women in Jerusalem*. New York: Oxford University Press, 1992.

———. *Women of the Sacred Groves: Divine Priestesses of Okinawa*. New
York: Oxford University Press, 1999.

Shafranske, Edward P., ed. *Religion and the Clinical Practice of Psychology*.
Washington, D.C.: American Psychological Association, 1996.

Shakespeare, William. *Hamlet*. New York: Penguin, 1998.

Shupe, Anson. "Economic Fraud and Christian Leaders in the United
States." In *Wolves within the Fold: Religious Leadership and Abuses of
Power*, edited by Anson Shupe, 49–64. New Brunswick, N.J.: Rutgers
University Press, 1998.

———. "Introduction: The Dynamics of Clergy Malfeasance." In *Wolves
within the Fold: Religious Leadership and Abuses of Power*, edited by
Anson Shupe, 1–14. New Brunswick, N.J.: Rutgers University Press,
1998.

———, ed. *Wolves within the Fold: Religious Leadership and Abuses of Power*.
New Brunswick, N.J.: Rutgers University Press, 1998.

Smith, Linda L. *Called into Healing: Reclaiming Our Judeo-Christian
Legacy of Healing Touch*. Arvada, Colo.: HTSM Press, 2000.

Smuts, Jan. *Holism and Evolution*. London: Macmillan, 1926. Reprint,
Westport, Conn.: Greenwood Press, 1973.

Snyderman, Ralph, and Andrew Weil. "Integrative Medicine: Bringing
Medicine Back to Its Roots." *Archives of Internal Medicine* 162, no. 4
(25 February 2002): 395–97.

Sollod, Robert N. "Integrating Spiritual Healing Approaches and Techniques into Psychotherapy." In *Comprehensive Handbook of Psychotherapy Integration*, edited by George Stricker and Jerold Gold, 237–48. New York: Plenum Press, 1993.

Sparber, Andrew G., Cindy C. Crawford, and Wayne B. Jonas. "Laboratory Research on Bioenergy Healing." In *Healing, Intention, and Energy Medicine*, edited by Wayne B. Jonas and Cindy C. Crawford, 139–50. New York: Churchill Livingstone, 2003.

Spencer, John W., and Joseph J. Jacobs. *Complementary and Alternative Medicine: An Evidence-Based Approach*. St. Louis: Mosby, 2003.

Stone, Douglas, Bruce Patton, and Sheila Heen. *Difficult Conversations: How to Discuss What Matters Most*. New York: Penguin, 1999.

Straus, Stephen E. "Complementary and Alternative Medicine: Challenges and Opportunities for American Medicine." *Academic Medicine* 75 (2000): 572–73.

Stricker, George, and Jerold Gold, eds. *Comprehensive Handbook of Psychotherapy Integration*. New York: Plenum Press, 1993.

Studdert, David M., David M. Eisenberg, Frances H. Miller, Daniel A. Curto, Ted J. Kaptchuk, and Troyen A. Brennan. "Medical Malpractice Implications of Alternative Medicine." *Journal of the American Medical Association* 280, no. 18 (11 November 1998): 1610–15.

Suzuki, D. T., Erich Fromm, and Richard DeMartino. *Zen Buddhism and Psychoanalysis*. New York: Grove Press, 1960.

Talbot, Michael. *The Holographic Universe*. New York: HarperCollins, 1992.

Tart, Charles. *Waking Up: Overcoming the Obstacles to Human Potential*. Boston: New Science Library, 1986.

Umbreit, A. W. "Healing Touch: Applications in the Acute Care Setting." *American Association of Clinical-Care Nurses Clinical Issues* 11, no. 1 (2000): 105–19.

United Kingdom House of Lords. *Sixth Report of the Committee on Science and Technology, Complementary and Alternative Medicine*. 2000. Available at <http://www.parliament.the-stationery-office.co.uk/pa/ld199900/ldselect/ldsctech/123/12301.htm>.

Utts, Jessica, and Edwin May. "Non-sensory Access to Information: Remote Viewing." In *Healing, Intention, and Energy Medicine*, edited by Wayne B. Jonas and Cindy C. Crawford, 59–73. New York: Churchill Livingstone, 2003.

Vaysee, Jean. *Toward Awakening: An Approach to the Teaching by Gurdjieff*. New York: Arkana, 1980.

Venkatesananda, Swami. *The Concise Yoga Vasistha*. Albany: State University of New York Press, 1994.

Villaire, M. "Healing Touch Therapy Makes a Difference in Surgery Unit." *Critical Care Nurse* 19 (1999): 104.

Vincent, Charles, and Adrian Furnham, eds. *Complementary Medicine: A Research Perspective*. New York: John Wiley and Sons, 1997.

Walker, P. C. "Evolution of a Policy Disallowing the Use of Alternative Therapies in a Health System." *American Journal of Health-System Pharmacy* 57, no. 21 (2000): 1984–90.

Weaver, D. F. "Nurses' Views on the Meaning of Touch in Obstetrical Nursing Practice." *Journal of Obstetric, Gynecological, and Neonatal Nursing* 19 (1990): 157–61.

Weiger, Wendy A., Michael Smith, Heather Boon, Mary Anne Richardson, Ted J. Kaptchuk, and David M. Eisenberg. "Advising Patients Who Seek Complementary and Alternative Medical Therapies for Cancer." *Annals of Internal Medicine* 137, no. 11 (3 December 2002): 889–903.

Weintraub, M. I. "Legal Implications of Practicing Alternative Medicine." *Journal of the American Medical Association* 281, no. 18 (12 May 1999): 1698.

West, Robin. "Law, Rights, and Other Totemic Illusions: Legal Liberalism and Freud's Theory of the Rule of Law." *University of Pennsylvania Law Review* 134 (1986): 817, 846–47.

White House Commission on Complementary and Alternative Medicine Policy. *Final Report*. 2002. Available at <www.whccamp.hhs.gov/finalreport.html>.

Wilkinson, D. S., P. L. Knox, J. E. Chatman, T. L. Johnson, N. Barbour, Y. Myles, and A. Reel. "The Clinical Effectiveness of Healing Touch." *Journal of Alternative and Complementary Medicine* 8, no. 1 (February 2002): 33–47.

Williams, Martin H. "Boundary Violations: Do Some Contended Standards of Care Fail to Encompass Commonplace Procedures of Humanistic, Behavioral and Eclectic Psychotherapies?" *Psychotherapy* 34, no. 3 (1997): 238–49.

Wolpe, Paul Root. "The Maintenance of Professional Authority: Acupuncture and the American Physician." *Social Problems* 32 (June 1985): 409.

Wytias, Charlotte A. "Therapeutic Touch in Primary Care." *Nurse Practitioner Forum* 5, no. 2 (June 1994): 91–96.

INDEX

Death and dying, 5–6, 11, 20, 45, 103, 106, 115
Defense Department, 74
Descartes, René (Cartesian), 10, 20–21, 84–85, 105
Detroit, 158
Dietary supplements, 12, 15, 31, 34, 164–67. *See also* Dietary Supplements Health Education Act; Food and drug law; Herb; Nutrition
Dietary Supplements Health Education Act, 12, 166. *See also* Dietary supplements; Food and drug law; Herb; Nutrition
Diet for a Small Planet, 89

Ecclesiastes, 102
Ecology, 14; and healing, 73–97 passim, 108. *See also* Environment
Eddy, Mary Baker, 99
Eliade, Mircea, 116
Emerson, 86
Energy healing (energy medicine), 15, 23, 74, 92, 94, 167; compared to spiritual healing, 120–24; and the environment, 79–97 passim. *See also* Spiritual energy; Vital energy
Enlightenment, 6, 9, 59, 104
Environment (environmental), 8–14, 21; and healing, 73–97 passim, 99, 108. *See also* Ecology
Epilepsy (epileptic), 14, 65–72, 78
Epistemology (epistemological), 2, 6, 57, 76, 99, 155–56
Ethics (ethical), 5, 8, 13, 15, 20–22, 25, 30–31, 54, 58, 60–62, 65, 72, 103, 132–33, 147, 154, 156, 158–60, 167; application of to clinical decision making, 37–39, 44–47; unresolved dilemmas in, 25–27
Evidence (evidence-based), 7, 11, 13, 22, 24, 31, 41–42, 50, 57, 61, 67–69, 74, 91–92, 97, 159–60; critical assessment of, 52–53; and spiritual healing, 116–

19; state of (with respect to CAM therapies), 163–64; use of in clinical decision-making concerning CAM therapies, 34–39, 46

Faith, 57, 69, 71, 114, 117, 119, 128, 143, 150
Federation of State Medical Boards, 166
Feminism, 73
Fisher, Roger, 27–29, 43
Flexner Report, 57
Food and Drug Administration (FDA), 12, 34
Food and drug law, 15, 31, 33, 70, 166. *See also* Dietary supplements; Dietary Supplements Health Education Act; Herb; Nutrition
Fraud (fraudulent), 15, 31–32, 34, 55, 58–60, 63, 91, 101, 107–8, 128, 131, 145–36, 140, 142–44, 149, 154, 159
Freud, 157
Fromm, Erich, 9
Fromm-Reich, Frieda, 99

Getting to Yes, 27–29
Ginkgo, 35–36, 167
God, 80, 114, 117, 123, 126, 132, 136, 148
Guided imagery, 62, 74, 125, 139
Gurdjieff, 101

Hamlet, 94, 181
Harvard, 7, 157
Hastings Institute, The, 50
Healing, Intention, and Energy Medicine, 77–97 passim
Heisenberg's Uncertainty Principle, 56
Herb (herbal medicine), 19, 23, 26, 36, 107, 125, 137, 154. *See also* Dietary supplements; Dietary Supplements Health Education Act; Food and drug law; Nutrition
Hinduism, 101
Holism (holistic), 10, 21, 73, 132, 139

Holy Spirit, 113
Homeopaths (homeopathic, homeopathy), 19, 23, 57, 124, 147, 155, 166
Hospice, 62, 77
Hospitals (institutions), 7–8, 11, 15–16, 22–25, 32, 34, 48, 51, 65, 68, 77, 83, 114, 116, 120, 141, 147, 154–55
Hufford, David, 82–83

India (Indian), 1, 17, 102
Informed consent, 42, 46, 62, 77, 108, 129, 140, 142–43
Institute of Medicine (IOM) at the National Academy of Sciences, 12–13; and *Crossing the Quality Chasm*, 74; and *Report on Complementary and Alternative Medicine*, 61–62, 74, 99–100, 156–59, 163
Institutions (institutional). *See* Hospitals
Insurance (third-party reimbursement), 15–16, 33, 70, 83, 107, 154
Integrative medicine (integrative care), 7–8, 24, 33, 37, 45, 47, 63, 65, 68, 71, 73–74, 101, 104, 106, 108–9, 147, 153–54, 158, 160; definition of, 8
Intention (intentionality). *See* Consciousness
Interspecies communication, 78, 87–92, 109
Intuition (intuitive), 8, 10–12, 41, 69–70, 107, 112, 134, 148, 150, 159

Jacobson v. Massachusetts, 125
James, William, 2, 68
Japan, 17
Jensen, Derrick, 78–97, 99–100, 102–3, 158–59
Jesus, 69, 96, 113
Jonas, Wayne (and Cindy Crawford), 17, 54, 56–57, 77, 79, 81–83, 87, 91–97, 99, 102
Journal of the American Medical Association, 22–23, 50

Kabala, 101
Kentucky, 76
Kipling, Rudyard. *See* "Ballad of East and West"

Laetrile, 2
Language Older Than Words, A, 78–97 passim
Latin American folk medicine, 17
Leonard P. Zakim Center for Complementary and Alternative Medical Therapies at the Dana Farber Cancer Institute, 157
Liability. *See* Malpractice
Licensure (and credentialing), 5, 15–16, 22, 32–34, 70, 77, 87, 91, 107–9, 122, 127–30, 135–40, 144–49, 153–55, 166–67

Maharishi University of Management, 120
Malpractice (liability), 5, 15, 25–27, 30, 33–34, 61, 70–72, 108, 135, 138, 141–43, 146, 149–50, 153, 167; application to clinical decision making, 34–37, 42, 44–47
Maslow, Abraham, 15, 99, 102, 105, 108–9; and the hierarchy of needs, 15, 59, 63, 66, 160
Massage therapy (massage therapist), 5, 19, 22–23, 36, 51, 66, 112, 121, 135, 138–39, 145, 147, 149, 153–54, 164
Matrix, The, 95, 100–105
Medical doctors (physicians), 3, 6, 8, 16, 20–21, 25–26, 28–34, 37–39, 42–43, 47, 57, 60, 80, 91, 100, 107, 111, 121, 127, 130–31, 138, 144–50, 153–54, 166; and M.D. degree, 55; and patient's religious preferences, 71–72
Medical schools, 7, 23, 50, 116
Meditation, 4, 28, 673–74, 104, 106, 120–22, 127, 166. *See also* Mindfulness
Mental health care. *See* Psychotherapy

Studies in Social Medicine

Nancy M. P. King, Gail E. Henderson, and Jane Stein, eds., *Beyond Regulations: Ethics in Human Subjects Research* (1999).

Laurie Zoloth, *Health Care and the Ethics of Encounter: A Jewish Discussion of Social Justice* (1999).

Susan M. Reverby, ed., *Tuskegee's Truths: Rethinking the Tuskegee Syphilis Study* (2000).

Beatrix Hoffman, *The Wages of Sickness: The Politics of Health Insurance in Progressive America* (2000).

Margarete Sandelowski, *Devices and Desires: Gender, Technology, and American Nursing* (2000).

Keith Wailoo, *Dying in the City of the Blues: Sickle Cell Anemia and the Politics of Race and Health* (2001).

Judith Andre, *Bioethics as Practice* (2002).

Chris Feudtner, *Bittersweet: Diabetes, Insulin, and the Transformation of Illness* (2003).

Ann Folwell Stanford, *Bodies in a Broken World: Women Novelists of Color and the Politics of Medicine* (2003).

Lawrence O. Gostin, *The* AIDS *Pandemic*: Complacency, Injustice, and Unfulfilled Expectations (2004).

Arthur A. Daemmrich, *Pharmacopolitics: Drug Regulation in the United States and Germany* (2004).

Carl Elliott and Tod Chambers, eds., *Prozac as a Way of Life* (2004).

Steven M. Stowe, *Doctoring the South: Southern Physicians and Everyday Medicine in the Mid-Nineteenth Century* (2004).

Arleen Marcia Tuchman, *Science Has No Sex: The Life of Marie Zakrzewska, M.D.* (2006).

Michael H. Cohen, *Healing at the Borderland of Medicine and Religion* (2006)